SPEAKING

OF

GEORGE

GILDER

CONCEIVED AND EDITED BY

FRANK GREGORSKY

PUBLISHED BY DISCOVERY INSTITUTE PRESS

Speaking of George Gilder
conceived and edited
by Frank Gregorsky

Copyright 1998 by Discovery Institute

ISBN 0-9638654-4-7

Published in the United States
by Discovery Institute, Seattle, Washington

Printed by Consolidated Press
Cover design by Robert L. Crowther, II
Photo: Glenn Davis

Books by Discovery fellows, and books published by Discovery Institute Press are available in quantity for promo-
tional and premium use. For information on prices, terms
and ordering books contact: Director of Publishing, Discovery Institute, 1402 Third Ave. Suite 400, Seattle, WA 98101
or visit the Discovery website at: www.discovery.org.

Speaking of George Gilder

Topical Index

A conventional alphabetical index appears at the end of the book. This <u>topical</u> index is simply for readers who want a quick grasp of the substance of each of the "all-quotes" chapters, which comprise well over half the book.

Rules And Tools for the Business of Life 44-101

People, Companies and Strategy   130-185

Money, Morals and the Merger   112-129

Gilderism On Demand   198-241

Glad Tidings   316-327

Each Source And Its Code

At the end of each quotation in this book you will find a code. Those codes reference the following array of sources.

1981 RATHER — Dan Rather meets George Gilder, and so does the nation, in this interview for *Sixty Minutes*, filmed in Tyringham, sometime during the Spring of 1981.

1981 EAGLE — Speech to Phyllis Schlaffly's Eagle Forum, inferentially titled "The Wages And Work Patterns of Women" (month unknown).

1981 RV-CHRON — Story by Cima Star and Marlin Pritzer: "George Gilder, The Compassionate Conservative," in the December 1981 *River Valley Chronicle* (volume 5, issue 10, Berkshire Edition).

1984 KING — Gilder discusses *The Spirit Of Enterprise* with Larry King on December 10, 1984. Broadcast by Mutual Radio.

1985 LENOX — An unprecedented fusion of early and modern Gilder entitled "God's Way Of Business," delivered at The Bible Speaks church in Lenox (MA) sometime during the Spring of 1985. This talk appears whole as Chapter 5 and the editor regards it as the single most important "find" in the researching of this book.

1986 BOSTON — "The Age Of Intelligent Machines," a Gilder address to the Boston Computer Society (appearing with Ed Feigenbaum). Month and date are unknown.

1987 CALTECH — Gilder's tribute to Carver Mead at Caltech's "IRC Executive Forum": January 26, 1987.

1988 E-FORUM — "The Doomsayers, The Supply-Siders And The Entrepreneurial Future," not an interview of Gilder, but a special issue written by him, for the Spring 1988 *Entrepreneurship Forum,* published by the Center for Entrepreneurial Studies (NYU Schools of Business).

1988 SUCCESS — Five columns from that magazine: "The Spearhead: Don't Solve Problems, Pursue Opportunities" (January/February), "The Secrets Of Failure" (April), "High-Wire Acts: Men Take Risks Because Women Are Superior" (May), "World Champions" (June), and "The Myth Of The Balanced Life" (July/August).

1988 HILLSDALE — Speech to Hillsdale College students on "Why The Trade Gap Is Good News," Summer 1988. NOTE: Most of this text appears as Chapter 7.

1989 DREXEL — Formal presentation, originally titled "The Enduring Spirit Of Enterprise," to the 11th annual institutional research conference of Drexel Burnham Lambert, in Beverly Hills (CA) April 5, 1989. All of this text appears as Chapter 2.

1989 MONITOR — Special edition of the syndicated TV program *Monitor Forum*, for which John Parrot interviews Gilder: October 14, 1989. This is a superb exchange, in tune with the just-released *Microcosm*.

1990 HILLSDALE — Gilder is back at Hillsdale, giving a speech that is later misleadingly titled "Colleges As Seedbeds Of Innovation": February 8, 1990.

1990 LONGBOAT — Four-day Northern Telecom conference held in early April 1990, Longboat Key (FL). Gilder appeared on Thursday, April 5. See pp. 41-52 of "Longboat Key Symposium 1990."

1990 UPSIDE — Two-part interview of Gilder by then-editor Rich Karlgaard, appearing in the October and November issues.

1991 AMERITECH — Q-and-A from the Fall 1991 issue of *Signals*, "the magazine for business from Ameritech."

1992 HILLIS — "Hillis vs. The Law Of The Microcosm," article by Gilder in *Upside*: January 1992.

1992 DEM-GOV — "The Dawn Of Digital Dominance," transcribed highlights of Gilder addressing the Democratic Governors' Association in Aspen (CO), June 1992.

1992 NIGHTLINE — In the wake of Congress's override of President Bush's veto of the cable-reregulation bill, Gilder and another technologist are interviewed by Ted Koppel on the October 5, 1992, ABC *Nightline*.

1992 GREGORSKY — A November 10, 1992, interview in Tyringham by the editor, which was published in two segments the following winter by *We The People,* then-magazine of The Congressional Institute Inc.

1993 DUDLEY — Post-mortem on the 1992 elections titled "The Future Of Conservatism" held for Dudley Hull Alumni on March 26-27, 1993.

1993 UPSIDE — "Face-Off: Which Way For IBM?," an *Upside* Symposium, April 1993, see p. 42.

1993 ACTUARIES — Before the Society Of Actuaries sometime in 1993, Gilder takes the insurance and accounting sectors into the microcosm. This transcript is later titled "Revolution In Technology."

1993 KMB-VID — From a 1993 *KMB Video Journal* exploring "The Wireless World And Its Relationship To The Wireline Infrastructure." (Appearing with Gilder and addressing the same issues is Dr. Alfred Kahn.)

1993 LEHRER — Interview with Robin MacNeil on the *MacNeil-Lehrer News Hour,* the news hook being AT&T's completion of the McCaw Cellular buyout. PBS-TV: August 18, 1993.

1993 CON-SUM — Gilder's remarks of August 28, 1993, at a San Diego "Conservative Summit," organized by *National Review* magazine.

1993 ECONOMIST — Essay entitled "The Death Of Telephony" in their 150th anniversary issue (dated September 11-17). NOTE: Along with the 1996-97 "NEWSLETTER" quotes, *Success* passages, HILLIS and E-FORUM, this is a rare source of <u>non</u>-spoken Gilder material for this book.

1993 BIONOMICS — Keynote address to the first annual conference of the Bionomics Institute. Title: "Into The Telecosm." San Francisco: October 9, 1993.

1993 DISCOVERY — Portland (OR) conference on technology and the schools held on October 19, 1993, organized by Discovery Institute and sponsored by GTE.

1994 REPORTER — Q-and-A with Jeffrey Young in *The Hollywood Reporter*'s "International Interactive Special Issue": January 11, 1994. One of the most extensive Gilder exchanges with a entertainment-sector pro so far recorded.

1994 MARSHALL — Long exchange with a great deal of

give-and-take, later titled "From Microcosm To Telecosm: The New Age Of Networks," at the Marshall Institute (Washington Roundtable on Science and Public Policy): January 11, 1994.

1994 PUBLIC — "Technological Change and America's Future," a concise yet wide-ranging three-page Q-and-A in *The Public Perspective*: January/February 1994, pp. 25-27.

1994 RECAP — Formal presentation by Gilder on February 24, 1994, to the Independent Institute at San Francisco's Sheraton-Palace Hotel. Title: "Recapturing The Spirit Of Enterprise." This speech nearly became its own book chapter, but contained too many dated asides. (It is available via www.discovery.org, the Discovery web-site's Gilder Archives.)

1994 ACTON — "Freedom From Welfare Dependency," an 1,800-word interview in the Acton Institute newsletter *Religion & Liberty*: March/April 1994.

1994 USWEST — Interview on pp. 4-7 of the company's 20-page technology tour-book *Window To The Future*.

1994 TECHNOPOL — Gilder discusses the changing role of newspapers on *TechnoPolitics*, a syndicated PBS TV-show: April 22, 1994.

1994 UPSIDE — Two-part interview, conducted by then-editor Eric Nee, appearing in the May and June issues.

1994 E-LEARN — Fairly short Q-and-A in the May/June issue of *Electronic Learning*, pp. 30-31.

1994 EDUCOM — George Gilder in *Educom Review*, July/August 1994.

1994 MICROTIMES — "Scoping Out The Data Highway," interview in Tyringham by Mary Eisenhart for *MicroTimes* of July 25, 1994 (beginning p. 90).

1994 BERKSHIRE — A story by Hans Fantel, with extensive quotes, beginning on page C1 of the June 24, 1994, *Berkshire Record*.

1994 CIO — Interview conducted by Lew McCreary and Thomas Kiely, titled "The Gildered Age" but really dwelling on dumb networks, in *CIO* magazine for October 1, 1994.

1995 EDUCOM — Gilder's slice of a set of responses to "Universal Access: Should We Get In Line?," in *Educom*

Review: March/April 1995.

1996 LIMBAUGH — A 4,100-word interview in *The Limbaugh Letter* for January 1996.

1996 HERRING — Interview by editor Anthony B. Perkins in *The Red Herring*: February 1996 pp. 43-47.

1996 SENATE — "Testimony prepared" for the Senate Committee on Commerce, Science and Transportation: April 18, 1996 (differs slightly from actual remarks).

1996 HARPERS — Forum entitled "Does America Still Work?" Gilder plus Ron Blackwell, Albert Dunlap, Edward Luttwak and Robert Reich, moderated by Paul Tough. See *Harper's* May 1996 pp. 36-47.

1996 INT-ENG — Speech plus extensive Q-and-A at a Chicago meeting of the International Engineering Consortium: November 16, 1996.

1996 DISCOVERY — Opening remarks by Gilder at a dinner hosted by Microsoft veterans and organized by Discovery Institute in Seattle: December 3, 1996.

1996 NEWSLETTER — Extracts from the first five issues of the *Gilder Technology Report*, July thru November.

1997 NEWSLETTER — Extracts from *GTR* Volume Two, specifically "The Dark-Fiber Paradigm" (February), "The Tetherless Telecosm" (March), "The Low-Pressure Paradigm" (April), "Beyond The TV Temptation" (May), "Will Java Break Windows?" (June), and "Out Of The Conference" (October).

1997 RETREAT — Quotes from a high-level off-the-record gathering about which no more can properly be said.

1997 FRAGMENTS — This category covers two comments, one on intellectual property, the other on cable/telco collaboration, from the GTG offices in Housatonic (MA) during the editor's early January 1997 *Telecosm*-rework visit.

1997 CATO — Dinner speech to guests and supporters of the CATO Institute in Washington (DC): April 17, 1997.

1997 VATICAN — Late-April address in Rome to an assembly of Cardinals as part of a delegation organized by the Acton Institute. An edited version appears in this book as Chapter 9.

1997 IEEE — Interview by Charles Petrie for the preview issue of *Internet Computing* (May 1997), although the actual taping took place on December 9, 1996.

1997 TURNPIKE — A 12,200-word discussion with the editor, recorded June 6 and 8. The transcript, which appears whole as Chapter 8, also brings together his perspectives on much of the tech world as it stood mid-year.

1997 LIMBAUGH — An unusual appearance by Gilder, 48 hours after the Microsoft/Apple alliance, on Limbaugh's radio show: August 8, 1997.

1997 TCSM-CONF — Excerpts from the first annual Telecosm Conference, presented by *Forbes* magazine and George Gilder in Palm Springs (CA): September 14-16, 1997.

1997 NC-ONLINE — Interview by Christine Hudgins-Bonafield for *Network Computing Online* (http://techweb.cmp.com/nc/online/gilder97.html) first posted on October 23, 1997.

Notes & Acknowledgments

This is the only George Gilder book for those with short attention-spans — in short, a Gilder assembly for the stressed-out majority. Read only what interests you, in whatever order you choose.

Speaking Of George Gilder is designed around two innovations: First, it consists overwhelmingly of his spoken words — from magazine interviews, radio and TV appearances, and remarks to corporate and academic groups. Second, except for some more or less complete speeches, and the marathon June 1997 interview he and I did while Bruce Chapman drove the rental car, the text-blocks are not long.

The book's mission is to take "Gilderism" well beyond the op-ed, newsletter, *Forbes ASAP* and serious-book realms that now define George's universe — by bringing over 16 years of buried treasures to light in a format that conveys the full measure of Gilder insights to people who have yet to spend time with him.

We at Discovery Institute in Seattle thank the sole sponsor, Bell Atlantic Corp., which provided not only funding but also vital technical support (in the form of great scanners).

A second vital supporter is Dr. Robert Cihak of Aberdeen, Washington; his donation made possible this book's final production, and he personally organized its index.

Also helping out: Karen Howard, Chad Marshall, Marshall Sana, Dr. John West and — the Gen-Xer who did 100% of the typesetting and designed the cover — Rob Crowther.

Style Notes: Except for the June 1997 Q-and-A (which runs 12,200 words and has some lengthy questions), all the text in the chapters that isn't spoken by George Gilder appears in boldface type. Also, the last names of his favorite interviewers — Rich Karlgaard, Rush Limbaugh, Eric Nee, John Parrot, Anthony Perkins and this editor — are included whenever they enter the dialogue.

For investment advisors interested in George's monthly newsletter, which focuses on the companies producing the technology (and is definitely not a quick read), contact the Gilder Technology Group at 1-888-484-2727 or by using gtg@gilder.com.

For those who wish to support the philosophical and public-policy components of George's work, the back of this book shows how to become a member of Discovery Institute. You can see the full range of Discovery offerings using www.discovery.org, as well as download from the official Gilder Digital Archive.

Finally, since this volume is experimental, and since the population of Gilderites is ever more diverse and international, we encourage you to tell Discovery exactly what this book meant — pro or con — to you, your Board, your clients and friends. Overall reactions can go to Bruce Chapman, Discovery's President, at (206) 292-0401, ext. 102. Specific requests and research angles can go to me as gilderite@millennials.com.

— Frank Gregorsky, February 1998

George's Journey

by Bruce Chapman

As you read this, George is probably in the air, flying from Albany, near his home in the Berkshire mountains of western Massachusetts, to a speech in Birmingham, Alabama, or Birmingham, England. Or is he on his way out to the Forbes *ASAP* offices in Silicon Valley to edit an article, or down to Washington, D.C., to testify? In any case he may stop in New York to appease his publisher or visit a relative; and he could decide to do either at the last minute, perhaps without telling anyone ahead of time.

Some conservative group, wondering why he doesn't write more about social issues these days, nonetheless is filling his e-mail box with pleas to appear at their anniversary dinner in Florida. A tech company on whose board he sits is leaving anxious voice-mail messages asking if he'll make the next meeting. And his colleagues at Gilder Technology Group back in the Berkshires — their office inside the old mill above the Housatonic River — are fretting that he might not get back in time to finish the next *Gilder Technology Report* newsletter.

All the while, George's think-tank colleagues here at Discovery Institute in Seattle are a bit more serene. We know that the journey and George go together. We like to think George can best be understood Long-Term.

As for the boisterous family back in The Red House along the Main Road in tiny Tyringham, they are truly serene, protected by the benisons of domestic grace and the sure knowledge of a hidden order to Chaos Theory. With or without George in the house, the family is able to find that order, comfortably protected by walls of books in nearly every room, many sports, their home-schooling and church routines and a no-TV rule.

The Gilder Repertoire

George professes to dislike "going places" and is indifferent to the plush lodgings and lush locations that secure his presence around the globe. In his tumultuous youth, he paid for an air ticket to Italy, where he had never been, to see a girlfriend. He landed, only to be told that she had lost interest in him; so he turned right around and flew home. He still has little desire to experience the foreign in person.

He says he travels to put four children through college and to meet an entrepreneurial challenge. But he also does it because of the stimulation he gets from the people he meets. This apostle of cyber-communications, this artist of sequential thought, this constant reader (who may lug a stack of political and technical journals to his bath and stay there until, presumably, the water gets cold or the magazines sink) still gets some of his best information and ideas from conversation with live human beings. He finds that a scientist who really knows what is going on will talk more in the lab than on the phone; the entrepreneur often makes more sense in his living room than in *Fortune.*

As for technology's public-relations operatives, George, in a kind of wise innocence, does not manipulate or threaten them, he simply goes past them to where the real information lies. His manners are tutored, but his insouciant charm is natural. People tell him things. He learns.

Then, too, like the hectored executive, he finds space for mental concentration in a thrumming airplane cabin and the reliable anonymity of a hotel room. He runs each day to reconnect to earth and time. Time, George says, has become the most precious commodity in the world; this is certainly so in his world.

It is also the case that George likes to think while speaking, and sometimes only a live audience will do. However, the flying bits and bytes from the planetary net in his head make his facial muscles gyrate in a way distracting to an audience; and, within that face, the gyrating tongue can distract the speaker himself. Unlike the cautious and

scripted lecture-circuit performers, George Gilder occasionally will depart from his notes and chase a new thought
down a dark alley with hardly anyone able to follow behind. Experience has mostly cured him of an old habit of
rolling his tie up and down like a window shade. That had
the result of entrancing the audience like a cigar whose ash
just keeps getting longer: *How long can he keep this going?*
(At least on the west coast, George has dealt with his neck-
tie tick by foregoing neckties, a sensible decision anyway in
the casual culture of computerland.)

In fairness, the new Gilder is a far more disciplined
speaker. His hands may still chop in some awkward Yankee
imitation of Italian passion, but nowadays he really can
depart from the text and carry listeners with him. When
George's thinking-out-loud connects with the brains of an
alert audience, the result is excitement.

The scope of the Gilder Repertoire is impressive, for his
journey has been extensive. Two years ago, he was asked by
impresario Jose Salibi to come to Brazil to speak for 16
hours over two days to a conference of business executives.
Instead of ducking this invitation to mental and physical
excess, he put outlines of a veritable Gilder-on-Everything
course on a PowerBook and did the job. He's never been the
same since. At his now-annual Gilder Technology Group/
Forbes *Telecosm* conference, a three day intellectual marathon, he manages to participate in all phases and yet remain
totally focused, spirited and provocative.

More relevant to the readers of this book: When Gilder
speaks, he is not the only one thinking hard. He challenges
people to move into new territory, even those who have
heard him often. Watching George toil over a speech out-
line, I have asked him why he didn't just use an old one.
"Bruce," he says, with weary tolerance, "people pay me a
lot of money for these speeches. Each one has to be at least
partly an original." The results, therefore, read even better
than they sound.

Gilder's travels are narrative encounters, but the intellectual journey is the substance. That's why George almost
never has written for money alone. I was with him 15 years
ago when he was offered $250,000 to write the biography of
a businessman who was interesting, but not especially

novel. George could've used the money, but he turned it down. Instead he finished *Microcosm,* one more work that answered questions in his head and gave him answers to share.

His adult life has been the raising of such questions, and the answering of them, in a long dialectical path. If the rest of us will come along, so much the better, but he still does what he feels he has to do.

Of Lineage And Landscapes

The journey has its origins in the uprooting of his early life. George's father, Richard Gilder, was a confident young writer who saw the Second World War coming and the crucial role airpower would play in winning it. He had visited Hitler's Germany as a student and, horrified, began civilian flight-training shortly after college. He put his life on the line to fly for the early Army Air Force and died on the way to the warfront. For George, a certain amount of hardship lay ahead, even though his father's roommate, David Rockefeller, helped secure George's education at Exeter Academy and Harvard College.

Behind lay the unfunded legacy of an old and distin-guished New York and New England family. It shone with the entrepreneurial accomplishments of Tiffanys and Alsops, and with the reputation of George's great grandfa-ther, Richard Watson Gilder, a public intellectual and writer who edited *Century* magazine and was a friend of Theodore Roosevelt.

Another friend, the celebrated portraitist Cecilia Beaux, painted most of that Gilder generation, while still another, Augustus Saint Gaudens, sculpted them in *bas relief.* A pious great aunt left much of her fortune to endow the Gideon Bible Society, which seemed to a young George like a droll waste, but must strike him as much nobler now as he en-counters her largesse in hundreds of hotel nightstands each year.

Gilder principles derived from America's high WASP culture; but, by the time they were taught to George, the money that once gave the ancient standards their worldly glitter was gone. There were Persian carpets on the floor, but they were threadbare. George grew up in "the shabby gentry." This gave him an incentive to revive the family fortunes as well as the family fame — though for a long, frustrating time, he lacked confidence in his ability to affect either.

The rustic Berkshires are one of the fairest districts of the land, where Americana is suffused with music and art, where mighty names like Herman Melville and Samuel Clemons once resided during the summer, and where many a notable name of our own time find respite. There are original Currier & Ives landscapes and Norman Rockwell townscapes. George's wife, Nini, grew up in neighboring Lenox, and their four children today enjoy the human scale of a valley with such modern rarities as a village pond for swimming, country lanes and wide fields and woods for running or cross-country skiing, and visual and historic touchstones like the former Shaker community up the hill.

It is no wonder that Nini became a trained historic preservationist.

George's childhood in those precincts was less charming. Like a New England stone wall, it had some sharp edges to it, but they were softened and rounded mainly by the culture his mother handed down and the educational opportunities that allowed him to leave. After a dismal stint in the U.S. Marines, and the peregrinations of a free-lance writer, he would eventually come back in style.

Two Extreme Moderates

I first met George in 1959. He was newly released from the Marines, in whose company he had spent some time after dropping out of Harvard. Actually, he was "severed" from Harvard, as they say, and had to reapply for admission after his military six months, plus a stint of summer school.

George was so quick that he helped other fellows write papers in their courses and earn As. But he was so blocked by his own inhibitions that he could not turn in papers of his own. The future author of *Wealth And Poverty* flunked several freshman general-education courses and scarcely passed Economics One. For funds, he helped run a business selling sandwiches in the corridors of the law school at night and sold programs at football games in the autumn.

His solace was his running — he was a fervent trackman

during seasons when he escaped academic probation — and the acknowledgment of his friends that, whatever grades he got in class, he was very smart and a master of writing. Grounded in Latin, Greek and the Great Books back when Exeter prized such things, his amusement was building a Buckley-like vocabulary.

The two of us as roommates helped found a Republican magazine, *Advance,* which eventually went national for a couple of years. As editor, George solicited other young writers, assorted politicians and leading professors of the early '60s, among them New York Sen. Jacob Javits and one of George's professors, Henry Kissinger (commonly mimicked: "I don haf time for schtudents!").

Ideologically, this was still a preparatory time for George. He probably would not today own up to all the views he held then, though they certainly were respectable "progressive Republican" fare. In contrast to classmates who were founding the radical Students for a Democratic Society and campaigning for nuclear disarmament, George was an admirer of Herman Kahn and "thinking about the unthinkable," fully at home with the intellectual arabesques of nuclear strategy in the Cold War.

But his views on economics, though broadly conservative, were poorly formed and undermined by the calculated politics of moderation. We both had promoted Nelson Rockefeller for President in 1959 and early '60 (though neither of us was voting-age yet). Five years later, disheartened by the Goldwater "takeover" of the GOP, we wrote a book to be called *The Party That Lost Its Head.* I wrote one half, George the other; then George lost his handwritten chapters in the trunk of a rented car stolen from where he had pushed it outside a Radcliffe dormitory. With the delay, the book didn't come out until 1966. Meanwhile, just as we were helping some political friends start a ginger group, the Ripon Society, to develop "progressive Republican" research, *Advance* folded.

George and I differed from the political right in ways that would cease to matter in another decade. We backed the civil-rights laws of the mid-'60s (as did most Republicans in Congress). We were scornful of the zany fringe that thought Dwight Eisenhower was a communist and some

Establishment conspiracy was selling out the country. At every opportunity, we asserted that "Republicans should use conservative principles to design programs of their own rather than simply opposing the liberal programs of the Democrats." We lamented that the party organization had lost the war of ideas, indeed had abandoned the field, leaving the GOP marooned as "the Stupid Party," a term of George's that echoed John Stuart Mill's characterization of the British Tories.

When people ask how George changed, part of my answer is that he didn't, the country did. After the early 1960s, any "moderate" who did not keep redefining his views in response to changing fashions (which, unfortunately, is what some people think moderation means) necessarily found himself further and further to the right.

The grotesque economic and social dislocations described years later by George in *Sexual Suicide, Visible Man* and *Wealth And Poverty* — from the explosion of government spending and taxation to New Class permissiveness and family breakup that were the chief legacies of the Great Society and the New Left — occurred after the days when George and I wore buttons proclaiming, "I Am an Extreme Moderate." So did the appalling erosion of America's military strength and international purpose.

But conservatives changed, too. George and I once rather stridently rebuked two policy influences on Barry Goldwater: Karl Hess, who came up with the famous line "Extremism in the defense of liberty is no vice," and William J. Baroody Jr., founder of the American Enterprise Association (now the American Enterprise Institute), whose works we found "simplistic." Hess justified our critique by flipping out and over to the New Left. But Baroody and his AEI — and later the Heritage Foundation, the Hoover Institution, Hudson Institute and eventually a parade of think tanks at both the national and state levels — over time raised the intellectual power of the American right to heights it perhaps had not attained since the American Founding.

By the '70s, too, few conservatives would defend segregation or oppose equal opportunity, as many had done earlier. And the George Gilders — who earlier focused on voting and educational and employment opportunities for blacks, based on the special constitutional responsibility to remedy the ravages of slavery — were quite able to distinguish between that kind of equal-opportunity law and the liberals' job and education quotas for 70% of the population (including wealthy white women). In this atmosphere, a Thomas Sowell and other black intellectuals could become leading conservative spokesmen.

One conservative who helped heal the breach was Bill Buckley. The founder/editor of *National Review* had aided the rivals to *Advance* and the Ripon Society. But he also was a writer who could appreciate George Gilder, who did a profile of Buckley for *Playboy* magazine. Gilder had always admired Buckley's writing and in time came to admire his views. Buckley took Gilder to the mountaintop, as it were. He even took him to Phoenix to visit Senator Goldwater, who graciously gave George an exhilarating airplane ride through the Grand Canyon. George had written hard words, personal words, about Goldwater in the past. But old wounds on this visit were not probed, merely allowed to close.

Slowly, George was changing too. But only slowly, for his late twenties and early thirties were years of gypsy roaming, in both his occupation as writer-intellectual and in his personal life.

Peripatetic And Nocturnal

He would look back upon this time as the life he finally rebelled against. If he was not the male "naked nomad" of whom he eventually would write, he was close enough to acquire insight into the real thing.

His disorganization and absent-mindedness were rampant. A group of friends bought George a Brooks Brothers suit, since he had left so many garments in an unmarked trail behind him as he moved about that he no longer had anything to wear to a business meeting. George took the suit, unworn, to New York in a rental car, parked just for a moment to run an errand at a friend's house and returned, some time later, to find the suit and the car both gone.

Another time, he drove from Boston to Philadelphia to attend the Penn Relays, then caught a plane back — and wandered around Watertown, Massachusetts, wondering where he'd parked his car. In Rockefeller Center, David Rockefeller once received an unsolicited visit from a pair of Michigan policemen with a warrant and a huge wad of unpaid parking tickets credited to a car he owned — a car that a daughter, it turned out, had lent to George while he was writing speeches in Lansing for George Romney.

Well into his marriage, George was known to have appeared at a speech without socks. Even today, in the midst of a long trip, he will show up with lime green sneakers at the base of a business suit, carrying at his side a small duffel bag for other belongings and a couple of big cloth shopping bags overflowing with books and papers. Clothes and other possessions interest George Gilder about as much as foreign climes.

Deeper in his personal life, George caught romance where he could find it, but somehow was attracted to a string of smart young women who were only intermittently attracted to him.

His work in those years, the late 1960s and early '70s, was less bizarre, and often brilliant, but lacked direction. George wrote the odd article and worked as an editor for a while in New York at the Council on Foreign Relations, then headed by his godfather and namesake, George Franklin. He learned his trade as an all-purpose editor, writer, courier and copy-reader at the conservative laborite *New Leader* magazine, which later had to hire three people to replace him.

Because he read constantly and intelligently, he followed the ideas in vogue in domestic policy as well as foreign affairs. He thus was prepared for a series of notable if temporary speechwriting jobs over a decade's time, counting among them the campaigns of such Republicans as Rockefeller, Nixon and Robert Dole, as well as Romney.

He was peripatetic and nocturnal. At the office of Senator "Mac" Mathias of Maryland, George was considered a ghost; no one ever saw him. Some of the staff doubted his existence, but others noted that they would leave in the evening and come back the next morning to find that someone — George, as it happens — had been working all night and had left a speech draft for the Senator. Bob Dole, in his angry but still funny period, strewed a Gilder-drafted speech across the floor of a hotel room like some mess a dog had made and, pointing successively to each errant page, scolded George: "Bad! Bad! Bad!"

Up in Cambridge, Gilder got into Harvard's Kennedy Institute of Politics for a spell as a fellow and served for over a year as editor of the Ripon Society *Forum*. In that capacity he wrote a defense of President Nixon's veto of the Mondale day-care bill. This was the Fall of 1971, the dawning of the age of feminism, and Ripon Republican women, at least in the Northeast, were not about to let such a view go unpunished: George, who, as mentioned, had helped assemble the group that founded the Ripon Society, was forced out.

But George had taken up a new subject — the signifi-cance of sex and gender to the ordering of society — and it started his journey down a whole new road.

Those First Two Books

Through several turbu-lent personal relationships, George had been pondering the literature on human sexuality and, in 1973, the

Growth, Japan, TV — Gilder Was Right

Speaking to an alumni group in February 1993, Gilder parted company with Republicans on the panel who feared some superliberal agenda would unravel the U.S. economy. They pro-jected another Carter, but he knew what was really in store. The danger was politi-cal rather than economic, he insisted — although, being George, he had to dramatize the point: "[President Clinton will be] the beneficiary of just the most explosive advance in technology in the history of the human race. It's the one thing that could com-pletely save Clinton — it could engulf his Administra-tion with prosperity in a way that would render many of his adverse policies almost irrel-evant. That's their big hope, and they are trying to asso-ciate themselves with tech-nology on all sides, although all their policies are hostile to technological progress. A boom is most likely."

Continued page 32

result of his ruminations on the excesses of feminism was
Sexual Suicide. It quickly earned him the National Organization for Women and *Time* magazine designation of Male
Chauvinist Pig of the Year. He wasn't clear what the bat-
tered previous recipient, Norman Mailer, meant when he
told him, "George, you're welcome to it!"

But he found out. It meant that the supposed free marketplace of ideas was not open to anyone at that time who
questioned the assumptions of feminism, and that the
feminists — in shrill full throat — literally would shout
down and physically beset (as happened to George on the
Dick Cavett talk show) the rare male critic who raised his
head.

Moreover, you would be hard-pressed to think of a more
militant kind of feminist than those found at publishing
houses in those days: Young bright graduates of Vassar and
Smith, their ideological consciousness raised high, they
were frustrated by low-paying jobs as researchers and
editors, and they threatened to strike at several houses if
George Gilder was taken on as an author.

At both Yale and Dartmouth, invitations to George were
withdrawn under feminist pressure, though at Dartmouth a
rump group denounced the officially-sanctioned censorship
and staged a triumphant event so Gilder could be heard.
Even opponents of his views were impressed by his conge-
niality and openness, and one former political colleague of
like age grasped the real story.

In *National Review* for July 4, 1975, Jeffrey Hart reported:
"[N]othing had prepared me for the appearance of George
Gilder as an electrifying and controversial presence on
campus. I had not seen him since 1968 when we were both
speechwriters in the Nixon presidential campaign [and] he
was a liberal Republican... But during the interval in which
I had not seen him, something marvelous and strange had
transpired. George Gilder experienced what can only be
called a revelation, had an enormous insight, a genuine
insight. It changed him profoundly, and in many ways..."

George had toyed with a parody of the feminist argument that women are especially mistreated in society, as
witness social disabilities that they suffer disproportion-
ately. Why, he thought, the data show that single men suffer

even worse disabilities, so they must deserve even higher "victim" status!

Then it occurred to him that the parody actually bore an important truth: Not that single men deserve some special treatment, but their condition — statistically speaking — reveals that men need women to "tame" them, to channel their drives and ambitions in reliable, productive directions.

The result was *Naked Nomads,* less successful than *Sexual Suicide,* and even more strongly sabotaged at publishing houses and ignored by book review columns. *Nomads* was newly released as Jeffrey Hart watched George defend his ground: "As Gilder said at Dartmouth, single men over 25 years old have a mortality rate three times that of married men and four times that of women. Single men are three times more likely to die of a heart attack, four times more likely to commit suicide, seven times more likely to commit a crime than married men. By virtually every index, notably, single men are more vulnerable than single women. Sexism in

Continued from page 30

Four years (and one election) later, we heard Alan Murray declare in the *Wall Street Journal*: "Pinch me. That could have been the opening line of President Clinton's address to the nation last week... Economists remain mystified why, after six years of an expanding economy, inflation remains dormant. Friday's employment report provides further stunning evidence of noninflationary growth... [I]n the past year alone...better-than-expected growth, slower-than-expected health-cost inflation, and an inexplicable surge in federal tax revenues...have shaved $100 billion off deficit estimates for the next five years."

Inexplicable? From across the Atlantic, in the *Financial Times*, Gerard Baker provided the context: "Productivity-driven improvements in information technology have transformed the cost-equation for many U.S. companies. Each year computers with much higher levels of performance are available, at the same or lower prices, a process that is extending its benefits throughout the economy."

Continued page 34

American society? Gilder: Single men and single women of the same age and qualifications earn the same amount of money. Heresy. But Gilder has the figures. He really is threatening the established ideology."

And, for they next decade, the ideologues responded in force. Until the term "PC" came along, there was little ground for fighting back against their tactics.

But, while *Naked Nomads* did not sell well, it led by 1986 to a synthesis of it and *Sexual Suicide* called *Men And Marriage.* That manuscript again was boycotted at self-righteous publishing houses and finally forced to Pelican, a small press in Louisiana. Most bookstores often won't order it or stock it — yet it has been selling thousands of copies every year. It is one of those books that change lives, the way Gilder transformed his own.

In 1975, Jeff Hart found it "notable that no attempt was made to heckle him or shout him down," although his new campus sponsors "were fully prepared for disturbances should any occur, whether by students or faculty." In 1998, with one daughter at Dartmouth and another soon entering, Gilder has been welcomed back on an official basis. This is progress.

Visible Breakthroughs

Even today, some people who admire Gilder the technology guru, and others who recall his books on economics with affection, are aghast at the social theories expounded in *Sexual Suicide* and the two related Gilder volumes.

One who took them with relative stride was Nini Brooke, native of the Berkshires, and as close to home and hearth as George's other girlfriends had been distant and aloof. It was a year or so after the success of *Sexual Suicide* (which did succeed, despite and because of feminist outrage) that George finally slowed down long enough to court someone who was manifestly right for him — and who, to his amazement, fancied him in return.

There was, however, a slow period in their romance, which had followed a wonderful holiday time together in the winter countryside around Lenox. Trying to find something suitable to send to Nini as a remembrance, he walked into a bookstore in Salisbury, Connecticut, turned his back to the poetry section, walked backwards to it, reached over his head and pulled out a volume. Then, without looking, he opened the book and plunked his finger down on two poems by Sara Teasdale about walking through the snow of Lenox, Massachusetts at Christmastime and falling in love. Eureka! The perfect poem, found by sublime serendipity. Surely Nini would see that they were meant for each other.

And, in her way and time, she did.

I once asked Nini how she handled queries about her male-chauvinist husband. At that very moment, she noted, he was changing the baby; that he did the dishes and any other chore and errand; that he was unfailingly thoughtful and supportive, and faithful; that he was cheerful and complimentary and didn't complain. George lived, and lives, the male role he sees as desirable, even necessary, for the progress of civilization. And he cherishes the role his wife plays. Argue if you must against George's prescription for civilization, but give him credit for taking his own medicine, and gaining the benefits the

Continued from page 32

Another way in which Gilder the Contrarian is shown triumphant is his April 1989 speech (appearing here as Chapter 2) dismantling the arguments favoring Japan at the expense of the American system of individual entrepreneurship. Nearly eight years later, Randall E. Stross could write: "The prowess of American programmexrs is partly the triumph of a cowboy type of approach to software-development" (*U.S. News & World Report* 6/2/97). And a February 1997 *Financial Times* editorial entitled "America Forever" observed: "Japan had a clear lead in the relevant technologies, those of manufacturing. Second, its monolithic social and economic structures were ideally suited to pushing the products of those technologies into world markets. All that has now been reversed. U.S. industry has learnt to copy Japanese techniques of manufacturing. Meanwhile, the information-technologies which the U.S. has pioneered are in a state of explosive and unpredictable growth."

One month earlier, Paul Gigot recalled how "Writers who purported to understand

Continued page 36

cure predicts — for himself, his wife and their four children.

Before their marriage and well into it, Nini continued
her work in the historic-preservation office of the State of
New York, over the border in Albany. (Her interest persists
today; she's currently researching a book on historic houses
in Lenox.) George visited her at the office and got to know
many of her co-workers. Among them was "Sam," a young
black mail-room clerk who seemed to get in trouble often.
One case involved a rape charge. Steeped in the research for
Sexual Suicide and *Naked Nomads* and influenced by the
"non-fiction fiction" of Mailer, among others, Gilder sought
to make Sam the center of a true account of the inner city
and the modern origins of poverty.

The title, *Visible Man,* was a tribute to Ralph Ellison's
classic *Invisible Man,* but the protagonist of the Gilder tale
was a victim not of racism, but of a "welfare state [that]
attacks the problem of the absence of husbands by rendering husbands entirely superfluous." Here was the personifi-
cation of many of his gender theories. "The key problem of
the underclass — the crucible of crime, the source of vio-
lence, the root of poverty — is the utter failure of socialization of young men through marriage. The problem resides
in the nexus of men and marriage. Yet nearly all the atten-
tions, subsidies, training opportunities, and therapies of the
welfare state focus on helping women function without
marriage." Sam — predatory, guilty, useless — was the
human face behind the statistical profile.

Here, in the late 1970s, was another strange transition in
George's career, laden with the kind of irony he cherishes.
He had two books in mind, the first an account of welfare's
usurpation of the black male and the second a text on the
revival of supply-side economics, a highly contrarian claim
of altruism for the capitalist system. He offered publishers
this matched pair, a study of poverty and a paean to
entrepreneurialism. One publisher, Crown, was eager to get
Visible Man, although they wanted to recast it as a "thriller"
— but they spurned *Wealth And Poverty.* Basic Books then
bid $500 more — a total of $8,000 — for a "lordly two-book
deal," as George puts it, that promised to publish *Wealth
And Poverty* as well as *Visible Man.*

Once again, George the social critic was stiffed by the critics. *Visible Man,* a drama worthy of Hollywood treatment (where is Spike Lee for Sam's kind of truth?), and this time "unhampered by protesters, zoomed out of the stores at a pace of some 800 copies the first year," George recalls. In contrast, a couple of years later, in 1981, *Wealth And Poverty,* the publishers' idea of an afterthought, hit the best-seller list and sold over 500,000 copies.

Visible Man was ahead of its time (which would have been the welfare-reform atmosphere of the '90s), while *Wealth And Poverty* was perfectly, if accidentally, timed to arrive with the Republican era of limited government and lower taxes. Newly elected President Ronald Reagan, who had read several chapters of the book in manuscript, brought the finished product as a gift on a highly publicized hospital visit to an ailing Senate Finance Chairman Dole. It was hailed as the "Bible" of the new Administration's supply-siders. Like most of George's books now, it has been republished and is still selling.

Continued from page 34

Japan's government genius became policy-wonk superstars: James Fallows, Pat Choate, Chalmers Johnson, John Judis and even Laura Tyson... Talk about bad timing. These gurus flourished just as Japan was beginning what has now become five straight years of economic trouble."

And what about TV? When the first edition (financed by Federal Express) of George's *Life After Television* came out in 1990, people of varying ideological stripes took it for granted that young America was abandoning text for videos and other visuals, in an ever-contracting national attention span. Seven years later, in the March 5, 1997, *Financial Times,* we were told by Paul Taylor: "Young adults in the U.S. between the ages of 18 and 35, who previously spent an average of four hours a night watching television, are now devoting one of those hours to the Internet." In the *WSJ* of May 22, 1997, Kyle Pope added: "Viewership of broadcast television continued to slide in the season that ended last night, with 1.7 million fewer homes watching the big

Continued page 38

Altruism and Accidents

George backed into economics through the door of sociology, but he turned around to find a field of study far richer than he had expected — or could have imagined in his sad time-serving at Harvard. Far from "the dismal science," economics properly displayed man trying to make a better world, giving of himself in necessary service to others. And, just as poverty was bred in a culture of broken families, the entrepreneur is he who satisfies his creative urges in both home and occupation, the one giving support and purpose to the other.

Following Thomas Sowell and Jude Wanniski, George helped rediscover the French economist Jean-Baptiste Say, especially his theorem that "the sum of the wages, profits, and rents paid in manufacturing a good is sufficient to buy it," and that there "always will be enough wealth in an economy to buy its products." Hence, supply does create its own demand.

Further, George showed, mankind knows this by intuition, even if planners try to drive the wisdom from our heads. We make something on faith that someone will want it. We invest in the good sense of our customers. In a broad sense, we give to them before we get from them. We give on faith, in fact.

Gilder's insights contributed to the flowering of a group of supply-siders who had found a home on the op-ed pages of *The Wall Street Journal* in the late '70s. Some of their work had developed in the dinner-table conversations of the Lehrman Institute, founded by entrepreneur/politician Lewis Lehrman at a New York townhouse. (It was a precursor to today's Manhattan Institute.)

Most importantly, *Wealth And Poverty* helped knock the props of self-righteous moralizing out from under the left and recruited a generation of young conservatives (among them the editor of this volume, Frank Gregorsky) who could now see the idealism, as well as the practicality, of capitalism.

I had the pleasure and inspiration of reading the book in manuscript form. My wife and I had offered George, Nini and baby Louisa respite from the phones back east in our small apartment in Seattle's Pike Place Market, and then at my in-laws' farm on Vashon Island in Puget Sound — the two sites where the writing took place. George said he hoped the book would not "embarrass me," because I was still a "progressive Republican." Far from it, the experience of reading and critiquing — arguing and struggling with George — educated me to new political possibilities and pulled me right.

Fifteen years earlier we both had called for a politics that made conservatism a voice of hope. Here was my friend offering just that, giving conservatism at last a human face — one smiling, moreover, and looking eagerly ahead. No wonder Reagan liked the book.

As its adversary, *Wealth And Poverty* targeted liberalism's growing pessimism, dwelling on "the resource crisis, the thermal threat, the nuclear peril, the 'graying' of technology, the population advance, the famine factor, and whatever else is new in the perennial jeremiad of the rational budgeter and actuary of our fate." Where

Continued from page 36

four networks than a year earlier... [S]ome in the industry were startled at the magnitude of the decline."

Reporter Pope then served up this delightful reaction from Jonathan Sims of the Cable Television Advertising Bureau: "It's shocking what has happened... If anybody had been standing in 1994 and said there would be this decline, they would have been laughed out of the industry." Well, George Gilder did predict it, and well before 1994. But he wasn't laughed out of the industry because — fortunately — he was never part of it.

I must agree with Gigot: "[T]he fall of Japan as an economic role model does have the clarifying effect of showing who was right and wrong, and who we should heed in the future" ("Potomac Watch," *WSJ* 1/13/97). Not just Japan, but many other issues reinforce the point here: If you haven't paid heed to George Gilder during the past 25 years, you have a second chance — and we have a second 25 years — beginning with this book.

Bruce Chapman

these preoccupations constipated liberal governance, Gilder saw in them "the mandate for capitalism."

Capitalism required freedom, as all conservatives knew, and it required self-confident entrepreneurs willing to take risks. But it also required, George said, confidence in the goodwill of others, in the future, and, most often, in God. These last elements were, and are, controversial, even in some conservative circles. But I found them to be true, and was proud to be the first to rally to George's banner.

Yet that banner wasn't flying to Washington. In 1981, George Gilder could have taken a federal job, formed a consulting group, and coasted for a decade. But his journey had new intellectual questions to answer. Let others write policy memos and attend meetings.

The Spirit Of *Microcosm*

Gilder had studied the moral conditions that give rise to wealth or to poverty, and he had personalized the latter in Sam. What began to grab his attention now were the inner-workings of the individuals who make capitalism work. He wanted to understand the entrepreneur in person.

The result was another pair of books. They started out, actually, as one, to be called "The Spirit Of Enterprise." George interviewed some of the emerging figures of the new American economy and discovered again the importance of family, not only for instilling values, but for providing incentives to excel. He found that capitalism does not care much where you come from; it rewards the humbly born and foreign-born along with the children of the rich.

He discovered something else. Many of the most intriguing fortunes were being made in high-technology, whether the spectacular Simplot family of one-time pioneers in Idaho or a Japanese electronics rebel named Honda. As he wrote about them, he had to understand their contributions — their gifts. This entailed research into physics and other sciences, just as George's social studies had drawn him into economics. The book got longer and longer, until it split.

The Spirit Of Enterprise came out in 1984. Among the contributions it made to policy thought was the fresh demonstration that freedom is the oxygen of capitalism and that entrepreneurs, however driven, cannot work their magic in an atmosphere of heavy government involvement. It was an antidote to the persistent belief of the left in those days (and on most days) that American "competitiveness" had to be managed — by government, of course.

George showed, indeed, that the leading edge of American competitiveness was the relatively unregulated computer and software industry, which permitted dynamic competition and low barriers to new entrants. Giantism did not guarantee monopoly in an environment where new technologies could overthrow old and established business structures. This analysis brought cheer to the Reagan White House, of course, since it vindicated its economic policies. (Gilder, one historian discovered when that Administration was over, was the living author President Reagan quoted in his speeches more than any other.)

What George needed to do in his next book — *Microcosm*, which had been cleaved off of *Spirit* — was to expand on the theme of the entrepreneurs in this one field, technology. Mixing his tales of men like Gordon Moore (whose Moore's Law predicts a doubling of the transistors on a single silicon chip every 18 months) or Andy Grove of Intel, another immigrant success (from Hungary), and their achievements allowed the reader to learn a lot of heavy physics within a narrative stream of human interest. George's mastery of the physics was at least equal to his grasp of the human beings advancing the technology as scientists, inventors and businessmen.

Microcosm came out in 1989, exploring the "expanding universe of economic, social and technological possibilities within the world of the silicon chip." It was the kind of book that explains a new industry and a new economy so well that both insiders and outsiders find them suddenly illuminated.

Quantum physics had been embodied in the microchip and led to the transforming new technology of the computer. Gilder followed the trail. Accepting Cal Tech professor Carver Mead's advice to "Listen to the technology and find out what it is telling you," George declared that it was telling him that "the centrality of machines and things" was being overthrown by "the primacy of human thought and creativity." And he ended the book with a philosophical rumination on the meaning of all this, which he (in contrast to many other writers) sees as the triumph of mind over matter — and over the "superstition" of scientific materialism. He had put down a marker for a later philosophical and scientific debate.

Then, just as *Microcosm* had been cleaved from *The Spirit Of Enterprise,* an insight that claimed one chapter in *Microcosm* grew into a little book with a big message. In *Life After Television* (1990, '92 and '94) George described the coming convergence of computers and software with telephony and fiber optics, in a way that would make the entire industry of broadcasting — and its hunger for "lowest common denominator" programming — ever more obsolete. The TV would give way to the "teleputer," a single instrument, for home and office, combining the functions of business, entertainment, education and social communication.

TV's obituary will not be written this year or next, but year by year the "teleputer" is emerging in the form of the Internet and "world wide web," the latter a phrase Gilder used first in *Microcosm.*

The Author Acquires A Few Subsidiaries

George helped me found Discovery Institute in Seattle in 1990, while we both were associated with Hudson Institute, located in Indianapolis, and waiting for *Life After Television* to appear. He became the first Senior Fellow and head of Discovery's technology and public-policy program, helping to obtain leading support from the M.J. Murdock Charitable Trust of Vancouver, Washington.

Two years later, he and Rich Karlgaard launched a technology magazine — *Forbes ASAP* — for subscribers of the parent publication.

In 1996, further complicating his life, George teamed up with friends in Massachusetts to start a high-tech newsletter, *The Gilder Technology Report,* which attracted capital from the *Forbes* empire and grew quickly into a great success — a digital compass for investors and others who need George's latest take on this era's most exciting people and products.

In 1997, the first annual "Telecosm" conference was organized by GTG and the Forbes Conference Management Group in Palm Springs, demonstrating that business leaders, investors and others will pay remarkable sums ($3,900 for this inaugural conference) to join Gilder and his favored speakers in three days of solid tech talk along with networking of the human kind. ("Chapman's Law": At the Gilder Telecosm Conference, George and other speakers can be crowded together without limit and the number of business insights doubles every 18 minutes.)

Unlike many in the new technology and the new economy, Gilder (despite his conservative critics) has not lost track of the purpose and the promise of these changes. Which is also to say that he has not lost interest in the issues that concerned him earlier in his journey, from the state of the world and the defense of the United States, to the condition of the family, the nature of poverty, and the path to wealth for individuals and societies.

The 20th-century utopian scheme to engineer new people and a new society, Gilder believes, is a byproduct of 19th-century industrial era science and philosophy. In an address prepared as a Discovery Institute Fellow and presented at a conference organized by the Acton Institute and held in the Vatican in 1997, George asked, "Where Is The 'Soul' Of Silicon?"

It is a question both pertinent and impertinent. And that inquiry, appearing here as Chapter 9, is a treatise as well as a speech, casting light on the next leg of George's journey. Along with the short, and still shorter, pieces in this conjurious chrestomathy of Gilderism going back 17 years, it offers good companionship for the trip, whether one has read the Gilder books yet or not.

A trip to the library, meanwhile, reveals that George now shows up in a half-dozen books of popular quotations, though one doubts that their selections are comparable to the rare gems — not one of which, the editor insisted I point out, is from the books or from *Forbes* — that were unearthed for this volume.

Bruce Chapman is President of the Seattle-based Discovery Institute. To learn more about Discovery Institute, and George Gilder's role in it, see the back pages of this book. Note especially the Discovery program on Technology and Public Policy and the Center for the Renewal of Science and Culture.

Rules And Tools
For The Business Of Life

Advertising

Current ads are just incredibly inefficient. Broadcast ads, for example, support less and less real programming as time passes. You need more and more ads for less and less substance. Broadcast advertising focuses on capturing people's eyeballs for a few seconds and minutes, with no guarantee [of] or even clear means to a sale in most cases. So what we think of as advertising is mostly a tremendously inefficient broadcast commercializing, and it will be blown away by new transaction-oriented commercial processes on the Net.

1994 MICROTIMES

Narrowcasting is much more effective than broadcasting if you're actually thinking about selling something — which, after all, is the goal of advertising. The best advertising will be two-way: You will advertise what you want to buy and the vendors will advertise what they have to sell, and the computers can reconcile those two advertisements.

When people [predict] less free service in a narrowcasting world or a teleputing world, I say there'll be more free service. Less advertising will be able to support more substantive programming. In recent years there has been a contrary trend — more advertising to support declining amounts of substantive programming on television. That trend will be reversed and it'll take less and less advertising to support more and more programming.

The "infomercial" is an important precursor. It's crude

in its current form, but ultimately advertisers producing programming that people watch is desirable... When they get more refined and they're delivering more specialized products, they're going to have to change. They will be a positive force, in general.

1994 UPSIDE

[The journal] I read most faithfully and regularly is *EE Times*. A lot of the copy in *EE Times* is written by people in the various computer and communications companies — actually describing products and technologies which they also are selling. But, in doing this, they have to explain the technology, and mention that there are competitors [also] producing it, and make some sort of honest effort to describe some of the competitive products.

These are really written infomercials in a sense.

I think there will be a lot more of those, but they are chosen by the editors. A lot of these articles are better than the articles that reporters might write who had much less time to explore and really master the technologies at hand. So they don't reduce the value of *EE Times*, they enhance the value of *EE Times*. You gladly read them and pay for them...

It's the value-subtractive model of advertising which currently dominates. And I think that's the wrong way to look at it. Advertising has to be value-added in a broadband world. If you had to think of buying an issue of *MicroTimes* or *PC Magazine*, or *ASAP* for that matter, with advertising or without, you'd choose the one with the advertising. The advertising contributes to the value rendered.

You would actually, in all likelihood, be willing to pay substantially more for the edition with ads. This implies that they are adds rather than minuses — [but] I think that broadcast advertising mostly consists of minuses, and what we're going to have is real advertisements that are value-added information products...

So I think advertising will be much more effective, but it will have to change a lot. You won't be able to trick people into watching your ad. You'll have to choose advertising copy or whatever that people deliberately choose to read.

Kind of what the catalog guys are doing now.

Yeah, what the catalog guys are trying to do. So I think this new technology will radically change the entire advertising business. All this constant bombardment by irrelevant and distracting and mostly ineffectual images will expire. Advertising will be much more effectively targeted, and people will get it when they want it.

So it will essentially be pull rather than push.

That's right.

1994 MICROTIMES

Specialized ads are much more effective and powerful than the sort of broadcast ads pumped over the air on television. The key is in making video as friendly as audio is today, so you can dial up any program, movie, database, special interest that you have on your TV — your telecomputer — as easily as you can dial up your telephone. This is the key promise of the new era: That we can have specialized, personalized video.

1990 LONGBOAT

Broadband Economy

Economists are always trying to translate the technology trends you describe into the future industry structure. Where's the industry structure going to end up on the conduit side of this business?

I think that the movement toward a broadband economy will be spearheaded by hundreds of companies and, in a dynamic era of creative destruction, there will be many different choices. I don't see the whole system consolidating into one type of centralized network pattern at one point in time. There will be constant bypass technologies, new inventions, and new ways of delivering information. It takes constant innovation, rigorous discipline, and entrepreneurial risk-taking to deliver these new technologies, which doesn't lead to centralization.

The broadband network we are moving toward transcends the old models of centralized versus decentralized systems. The network, collectively — that is, the Internet — is one system. You could call it a centralized system. But, at the same time, it <u>distributes</u> processing (such as the new Java engines) to the optimal places throughout the Net. It's not a return to "dumb terminals"; these are <u>smart</u> terminals: Rather than being restricted to their own hard drives, these terminals have access to hard drives throughout the Internet.

So the power of the distributed terminal becomes vastly greater. Instead of the network freezing into one corporate conduit, it will consist of a variety of different wireless, wireline and fiber systems.

1996 INT-ENG

Centrifugal

[T]he microchip is not a neutral force. It's a centrifuge. It flings intelligence from the centers to the fringes of all organizations, and all industrial structures, and all information systems.

1993 ACTUARIES

Inevitably, all the power in all systems will migrate to the periphery. People will have supercomputers in their pockets. And all technologies that are based on retaining the intelligence in the center of the network will necessarily fail.

1993 DISCOVERY

Code Division Multiple Access

You've been following the war between CDMA and TDMA for dominance of the digital cellular and PCS markets. Tell me what's happening in this arena.

CDMA was launched in 1989 by Qualcomm, led by Andrew Viterbi and Irwin Jacobs. It represents one of the many technologies — Java is another — that baffle the backers of its rivals by prevailing against all odds because it fits with the dynamics of the Internet.

CDMA is a direct-sequence spread-spectrum solution that attracted me because of its elegance for data bandwidth on demand and its use of information theory — the concept of broadband noise as the highest density source of information. I've been pushing it since 1989. It accords with Claude Shannon's thesis that digital bandwidth can serve as a replacement for both power and switching. This trade-off will become more and more attractive as battery-powered mobile computers move up spectrum where bandwidth is plentiful.

But it's a war out there! With 25 million phones globally, GSM is the only successful industrial policy of the European Economic Community, period. The EEC contrived GSM in response to the proliferation of analog standards in Europe, which prevented roaming. There was a different analog standard in each country.

By contrast, we had AMPS (analog mobile phone service) and a coherent analog mobile phone system. So the EEC mandated GSM, a very conservative standard with 200-KHz channels that achieved only a threefold advantage over analog. Nonetheless, it allowed Europe to jump ahead to digital before we did. When Qualcomm introduced CDMA, it precipitated one of the most dramatic standards battles ever.

Why is it so intense?

Even though it would seem today that, with 25 million phones, GSM pretty much prevails, in fact the potential for wireless local loops, wireless Internet access — and all the other applications of PCS — is so immense that 25 million represents only the beginning of the game. And, although GSM certainly is a viable technology, it looks like it will not prevail as the dominant global standard. Suddenly CDMA is taking off like a rocket.

For some reason, people were unusually intense in opposition to CDMA technology. Bruce Lusignan, a brilliant professor of electrical engineering at Stanford, said that CDMA, as Qualcomm described it, violates the laws of physics — and this was quoted over and over again. So that laws of physics — laws of God, if you will — were involved in this debate! And because it was said to violate the laws of physics, lots of people jumped to the conclusion that Irwin Jacobs and Andrew Viterbi (of the Viterbi algorithm fame) were pushing a technology scam!

So this was the cold fusion of telephony.

Yes, to old analog hands CDMA seemed too good to be true. It exploits the special advantages of digital, which unlike analog improves by the square of the bandwidth, and requires signal-to-noise ratios 40 decibels lower. The same codes that spread out the signal are inverted and used to despread it at the receiver. The signal pops out above the background-noise level, and the real noise spikes and ingress are spread, and sink below the background noise level.

It's magic if you don't get it.

I spent a fascinating day with Lusignan, and while he started by trying to persuade me that theoretically no gains are realized by moving from frequencies or time slots to codes, he ended up by arguing quite earnestly that there was no reason to go to digital. He saw analog as elegant, efficient, convenient, robust, and just great, and as incorporating a whole array of his patents.

When I discovered that the most sophisticated opponent of CDMA was really opposing the whole digital revolution, it seemed to me that the case was collapsing.

I then went to Thomas Cover, the leading information-theorist at Stanford. Cover likes CDMA...but confirmed that, in theory, a time-division [i.e. the "TD" in TDMA] system would have just as much bandwidth as a code-division system.

So does CDMA give real gains?

Yes — it works in practice but not in theory. Lusignan of course is right that, in Shannon's terms, it does not matter how you slice up the bandwidth — the limit will remain the same. But CDMA's advantages derive from the efficiencies of digital, the exponential advance of microchips, and the decline of time-division multiplexing for all data applications.

Whether in wires or the air, TDM is failing for data because it does not correspond to the bursty flows of bits — some time-slots are empty and others are flooded... If TDM didn't work efficiently for data in wires, how was it going to work in wireless? When I saw that, I knew CDMA would prevail, because obviously Internet data would be an absolutely essential application of any new-generation wireless technology.

The key advantage of CDMA is it uses all the spectrum all the time, so that it can accommodate bursts and it can accommodate bandwidth on demand.

Also, the people who said it wouldn't work said it was too complex. But, in digital semiconductors, the complexity sinks into the chip and becomes simple. And so the fact that it was too complex in 1989 or 1990 was not relevant to 1995 or 1996, when you could put the whole thing on a single ASIC, as Qualcomm is now doing.

So is CDMA working?

It had its problems in the beginning. Managing all the codes and power levels is very complex with CDMA. All signals have to be received at about the same power or the system doesn't work. Power was going to be a critical issue anyway because, with any wireless application, battery issues are central. The CDMA people had to solve the power-control issue, and they did. Lo and behold, it turns out that power is a lot simpler to control than time-slots and frequency channels. As a result, CDMA uses between one-tenth and one-thousandth the average transmit power of ordinary AMPS or GSM. This is radically more efficient, and it's another huge win for CDMA.

1997 IEEE

Computers: And Kids

According to the Census Bureau, about 46% of kids between three and 17 use computers, either at home or at school. The new generations are more receptive to this technology than the old ones are. My kids are better at computers than I am — even though I spend all my time consulting on computers. They just have a natural aptitude for using 'em. And an appetite too.

1993 KMB-VID

Consumption — Void

[We supply-siders] banish the concept of consumption, because that is an after-effect of production, and production is what matters. All of us are producers. Our incomes cannot exceed our output. The driving force of the economy is not dollars in people's pockets, it is the ideas in their heads — what they plan to do now. The dollars in their pockets reflect what they did before. What matters about the future is people's current projects and ideas.

1981 RV-CHRON

Economic Measurements

In 1982 or '83, Charles Schultze, head of Brookings and previous head of Carter's Council of Economic Advisors, debated me on *MacNeil-Lehrer*. He said all my stress on computers was a mistake, because computers constituted well under 1% of GNP, and they couldn't have any basic impact on the future development of the economy.

Five years later, we learned that fully 60% of all the productivity gains in the U.S. economy in manufacturing during the mid-1980s (and this was the period of the fastest productivity gains in manufacturing of the entire postwar era) came from the computer industry alone. So computers have been absolutely central to the evolution of the economy and are the driving force.

It was a great commitment that the United States made. It's why the 1980s were not lost. During the 1980s, every year compounded, there were 28% more software engineers than the year before, and 43% more computer scientists than the year before. The U.S. ended the 1980s with three times the computer power, per capita, than the Japanese or Europeans commanded. That's MIPS per capita, number of millions of instructions per second per capita.

1993 ACTUARIES

Computers seem to rise relatively slowly because the mainframe business is combined with the personal-computer business. But, if you redefine the industry as distributed computer processing, then you find that the personal computer is the fastest rising technology in history. It rose from virtually nothing in the early 1980s to nearly 96 million personal computers today, still well over half of them in the United States.

1990 LONGBOAT

When I talk to phone companies, they always say to me: "Well, if bandwidth is going to be nearly free, how can we make money?" But, of course, what happened to the computer industry is that the transistor became nearly free. (It's 400-millionths of a cent now, more or less.)

As a result, the computer industry is the dominant world industry — [yet] its force is obscured by plummeting prices. If, beginning in 1965 or so, they measured the computer industry the way they measure the automobile industry, the computer industry would be measured to be thousands of times bigger than the entire economy!

Now I know that kind of index is not really right; but it [demonstrates starkly why] the way economists measure value-added systems is very deceptive and fallacious.

1994 CIO

Database Systems

Among the technologies that everybody imagines to be dominant and modernistic are these centralized database systems. They're one of the great frustrations in my life, because I love to use them — [but doing so] is just maddening. These places are almost exclusively for rich corporations with money to waste. It's really a scandal...

[Y]ou also see it with Dow Jones. They at least have a massively parallel computer running that system. They have one of Danny Hillis's Thinking Machines, and they still aren't making money with it, according to reports. It's yet another top-down system in a distributed world. It's just idiotic that you are supposed to call into Dow Jones and tap into some kind of time-sharing system just like in the olden days. It is one of those hierarchies that is going to fall.

UPSIDE 1990

A year-and-a-half ago, Knight-Ridder bought Dialog from Lockheed. Dialog is a big online database composed of 320 huge data-libraries. They paid 180 times earnings and three times revenues for Dialog, which is essentially a big mainframe computer with a lot of disk drives attached to it by wires. Anyone who tries to access this database discovers very quickly how cumbersome and difficult it is. It costs thousands of dollars to do any substantial search for information in the Dialog database. As a matter of fact, if you want to get any substantial amount of business information, it can cost as much money as an entire personal computer with a CD-ROM plus an optical scanner on your desk.

Soon it will be possible to put by your desk a package of encrypted CD-ROMs. Each one of the new generation of CD-ROMs will be about two gigabytes, so you'll get 2,000 big books on each CD-ROM. So you could have a huge library on your desk of the information you need. And it can be upgraded, updated over telephone lines, or possibly over sideband FM. Your optical scanner will scan the information that you want and integrate it with the encrypted volumes already on your desk.

Now, you need it encrypted because you couldn't afford to have a whole library on your desk if you had to pay for all the information. But that's the problem with these big online databases: Even when you just want a glass of water you gotta pay for the reservoir (as Peter Sprague, chairman of a new firm called Cryptologics, puts it).

The online database system concentrates the intelligence in one place and then runs wires to and from it. It's really a top-down system in a bottom-up world. I don't think it is going to survive the convergence of these two new technologies of sand and glass.

1990 LONGBOAT

Editing: And Jobs

I think there will be a lot of work for people who structure information and who package it, and who make it available in dependable forms, and who reconcile conflicts. The editorial function will not disappear. Newspaper won't disappear, contrary to what people think.

1993 ACTUARIES

Editorial Guidance

Bill Gates sort of dismissed my [October 1993 *ASAP*] article on this subject, because he said that the reporters and the columnists and everybody else will be able to contract directly with the reader. But the newspaper is more than a group of autonomous writers. It's an editorial organization that defines stories, decides who will cover what and how much time they will spend, and supports their efforts. It's not simply the spontaneous contributions of a bunch of entrepreneurial writers.

Now, the big entrepreneurial writers of today already syndicate themselves, and in the future they'll be able to make much more money than they do today, because they'll be able to charge for each use thru new encryption technologies.

NEE: Newsletters are like that as well.

The Computer Letter is an excellent newsletter, and you get a real sense of editorial leadership. It's no longer Dick Shaffer writing the thing. It's a whole staff that covers the field. And they are assigned to different beats, and you really get a sense of an ongoing enterprise that is covering the computer and communications realm with a guiding intelligence behind it. I don't think these people could scatter to the winds and all do their own separate newsletters and be as effective as they are now.

1994 UPSIDE

Electromagnetic Spectrum

I think it may yield a simpler kind of metaphor for the

overthrow of matter than the quantum theory did. The electromagnetic spectrum [is where] everything goes at the speed of light — matter evanesces, time and space collapse. The electromagnetic spectrum is a perfect epitome of tele-communications, and it is the critical resource of telecom-munications. Exploring that science will yield valuable insights into the future of telecommunications and comput-ers [and] also give a vision of the future of microelectronics.

1990 UPSIDE

The key breakthru in semiconductors was the recogni-tion in the late 1960s that as transistors became smaller they did not become hotter, slower, more fragile and more costly, as previously thought, but [instead became] cooler, faster, cheaper and better.

The key breakthru in spectronics is the recent discovery that, as information systems move up spectrum, they do not necessarily become more expensive, power-hungry and immobile, as previously thought. Rather, higher frequencies with shorter wavelengths can use smaller, cheaper anten-nas, at lower power, and offer more bandwidth. Bandwidth, as Claude Shannon [of Bell Labs] showed [50 years ago], can serve as a replacement for power and for switches.

1996 NEWSLETTER

Entrepreneurial Pressure

The universal marketing of personal computers ap-peared irresistible to Stephen Jobs of Apple in his Cupertino garage. But it seemed altogether too risky or costly to au-thorities at Hewlett-Packard. The immense treasure of natural-gas reserves that loomed in the mind of John Mas-ters as he pondered oil-company log books in western Alberta seemed a ridiculous exaggeration to the experts of Exxon or the Department of Energy. The early prediction of engineering workstations — today a $3 billion market — struck Scott McNealy and William Joy at Sun Microsystems as the birth of a new industrial era. But it seemed a far-fetched and low-priority idea for several years to the corpo-rate leaders at IBM, Hewlett-Packard and Digital Equip-ment Corporation...

Entrepreneurs do not succeed thru marginal increments. They succeed by shooting for the Moon and hitting natural gas under the blastoff site.

1988 E-FORUM

Failure

Failure is the hidden strength of capitalism. The value of failure is its role in the learning process. Unless failure is possible, no learning is possible. In other words, every company is really almost a laboratory test of an entrepreneurial idea — and, in the realm of ideas, unless falsification [of a thesis] is possible, learning isn't possible.

As a matter of fact, in information theory, no information is transmitted unless negation is possible, and so the tolerance of failure is absolutely critical to the success of Silicon Valley. If you don't tolerate failure, you can't permit success. The successful people have a lot more failures than failures do.

1990 UPSIDE

Federal Communications Commission

[I]f I was the FCC, I wouldn't be eager, in the face of these new technologies, to assign exclusive rights to frequencies. CDMA allows lots of different people to use the same frequencies in the same cell. You differentiate the calls by their codes, not by their frequencies. So you have a situation where the assignment of these specific frequency channels just no longer makes sense.

NEE: But you can bet that the FCC is not going to write itself out of a job.

I did have a role for the FCC — sometimes I forget it, but there is one [laughter]. Among other things, you don't want people using big interfering technologies like TDMA violating the rules. The transition is going to be quite awkward, with all kinds of incumbent users, so I'm sure the regulators will find something to do.

The government finally figured out a way to make some money off these frequencies by auctioning them. And

now you're saying that they are not pieces of property that can be exclusively owned.

Right. The Steinbrecher radio can treat UHF as dark fiber and stick it in packets without interfering at all with the users of those frequencies. This is the future. It's not exclusive domination of specific frequency bands. It's not beachfront property, it's the ocean...

You said the FCC is going to have a diminished role in the future. What about things like ensuring reliability and availability of 911 services? Or can that be left to the market?

I don't think the government has much of a role there. If you are doing kiddie porn or really vicious stuff, lots of laws allow you to be prosecuted, and you <u>should</u> be. Otherwise, all this regulation assumes scarce spectrum and, if we are really moving into an era of bandwidth-abundance, the rationale for regulating the use of the air becomes <u>tenuous</u>.

1994 UPSIDE

Fiber Optics

Using the current fiber technology, installed between the east and Chicago by AT&T, you could send the entire Library of Congress over one fiber the width of a human hair, in 24 hours. Using our current <u>telephone</u> wire technology to the house, at 9,600-baud modem — the most advanced modem — it would take 500 <u>years</u> to transmit the Library of Congress. As a matter of fact, you could never do it, because it'd be growing faster than you <u>could send it</u>.

1990 HILLSDALE

I think the phone companies actually could run fiber-optic cable to the home, rather cheaply, within their current budget of some $20 billion a year of annual investment. The phone companies could bring fiber to every home in the United States without any new investment, no new capital needs. This whole idea that it'll cost some immense new amount of money is false. Fiber-optic will be enormously cheaper than current phone-company technology as time passes.

1992 NIGHTLINE

Today, these silica threads lay between Chicago and the East Coast and transmit about 2.6 gigabits a second... Even this underestimates the power of fiber optics, because the true transforming impact this technology is going to have is not yet well understood.

Every time you amplify light waves for transmission, you have to convert them to electronics and then convert them back to photons again. Essentially, the light has to pass thru an electronic bottleneck — yet transistors can't switch much more than two or three billion times a second, and probably never will switch much faster than that. So there's this obstacle to using the tremendous "true" bandwidth of fiber optics: [I]f you really could tap the full capacity of these fiber threads as thin as a human hair, you could run all the communications of the country thru one thread on Mother's Day, which is the peak.

Fiber will not be a replacement for copper, as is often [claimed]. It will be a replacement for air. Indeed, a one-fiber thread can accommodate a thousand times the bandwidth of all the radio frequencies currently used in the air, from AM radio to KU-band satellites. One fiber can hold all that capacity.

Of course, there is the electronic bottleneck, the terrible limitations afflicting these electronic microchips. Until recently, far less than 1% of this capacity has ever been tapped. Now, in the last two years, IBM, Bell Labs and NTT in Japan have invented all-optical networks. All-optical networks mean that the electronic bottleneck is eliminated. They [use] erbium-built amplifiers, which means that messages can pass thru the entire network on wings of light and never have any conversion. You tune into the messages like radios. You treat [the medium] as if it's air. Your terminals tune in to the signal you want, rather than having to process all the signals and find your own message.

1993 ACTUARIES

I see the all-optical network as comparable to the original integrated circuit. The integrated circuit made it possible to put an entire computer system on a single sliver of silicon. An all-optical network makes it possible to put an entire communications system on a seamless web of silica and send messages from origin to destination entirely on wings of light. This is made possible by a whole series of breakthrus in optical amplifiers.

So, you have another million-fold rise in the cost-effectiveness of communications compounded by the million-fold rise in the cost-effectiveness of computing hardware. Just as the growth of the world economy has been driven over the last 20 years or so by the plummeting price of transistors, so I think this impulse of growth will continue, but it will be compounded by a similarly plummeting cost of bandwidth. We will move to an age of bandwidth abundance in fiber optics.

1994 MARSHALL

[E]nvisage a fibersphere emerging in which you tune in to your own messages. Everyone has their own frequency, and you tune into it, just as radio does today, and this will transform communications, just as the microchip put all industry thru a wringer because it made transistors essentially free.

Today, a transistor on a memory chip costs about two or three hundred-millionths of a cent. This is down from about $7 30 years ago. So, essentially, transistors are free.

The prime rule of thrift in business is to waste transistors, and we all do it. We waste transistors on playing solitaire — we do, don't we? We are correcting our spelling. These days, nothing is too humble to waste transistors on. Essentially, businesses thrive by wasting the cheapest resource, and the cheapest resource [over the past decade] is mips and bits, resulting from free transistors...

The effect of fiber-optics is to render communications power essentially free. So, all of a sudden, you prevail by exploiting communications power. Bandwidth becomes free. When bandwidth is virtually unlimited, you don't need switches anymore, because you can tune in — you don't have to switch.

Phone companies that regard their crucial expertise or core competence as switching — as they all do — will discover they face a technology that doesn't use switches, but that uses passive optical systems, which are incomparably cheaper. Already today the cheapest bandwidth on the face of the earth is a prototype all-optical network at IBM. It connects all the various laboratories of IBM around Westchester County. It's a 9.6-gigabit network and it costs $16,000 per terminal to build, and this is crafted out of prototype equipment...

The air is not scarce, either. We have to face a world where the key resources are the cheapest resources — which, in part, are always the best products. They're essentially centrifugal in their architecture, because all these technologies are technologies of wires and switches. In the computer industry, the wires and switches are laid out across the silicon substrate of microchips. In the telecommunications industry, the wires and switches are laid out across the mostly silicon substrates of continents and seabeds.

But they are all one essential technology, and it's a centrifugal technology.

1993 ACTUARIES

What's the difference between the approach to fiber technology in the United States and in Japan?

The United States holds a lot of the patents. We command a lot of the most significant technology.

But we treat fiber optics as a special business technology to be applied to a few high-tech applications. They treat it as a potential technology for every home and office in Japan. That means we have a potential market of a few thousand expensive devices, while they have a potential market of millions. Of course, when you are producing in those volumes, your costs go down rapidly and quality improves.

The Japanese are behind, but they are targeting fiber to every home and office in Japan in the next 20 years. So, if

we imagine we can make big industrial optical switches —
like the big industrial VCRs we were making in the 1970s —
and have any kind of play in the world economy, we are
kidding ourselves.

**How will the nation pay for a [similarly ambitious] fiber
network?**

Entertainment video is going to pay for fiber: Movies,
entertainment, news, the whole array of programming
that's currently delivered to your TV set. We really won't
get breakthrus until we link the television set to a global
network — that will drive the installation of fiber everywhere. If that doesn't happen, I don't think fiber is going to
come to the home...

**What are the key regulatory issues in fostering the
installation of fiber to the home?**

There is only one important issue, and all the rest is a
distraction. The key point is that cable TV should be delivered over telephone lines.

1991 AMERITECH

Fiber Optics: In *Life After Television*

**NEE: Thinking back on what you wrote in that book,
what has turned out to be right, and what has turned out
differently?**

I think it was right in its general thrust. It was wrong in
saying that fiber would reach homes sooner rather than
later. I mean, it did have a vision of faster deployment of
fiber than actually occurred. Fiber <u>has</u> moved steadily
closer to more and more of the top 10% of households.
When I wrote that book, the average top-10% household
was a thousand homes away from a fiber node. Today, it's
well under a <u>hundred</u> homes from a fiber node... But I
focused more on fiber as an access medium than I would
today. Today I'd focus more on a wide variety of wireless
and DSL and cable modem [and] satellites.

1997 TCSM-CONF

Fiber Optics: Plus WDM

In 1996, the new fiber paradigm emerged in full force. Parallel communications in all-optical networks, long depicted as a broadband pipe dream, crushed all competitors and became the dominant source of new bandwidth in the world telecom network.

The year began with a trifold explosion at the Fiber-Optic Conference in San Jose when three companies — Lucent, NTT and Fujitsu — all announced terabit-per-second WDM [wavelength division multiplexing] transmissions down a single fiber. Sprint Corporation confirmed the significance of the laboratory breakthrus by announcing deployment of Ciena's MultiWave 1600 WDM system, so called because it can increase the capacity of a single fiber thread by 1,600%. It passes 16 data streams per second down a single fiber thread for 120 kilometers (compared with 35 kilometers and a single data-stream for TDM).

The revolution continues in 1997. At the beginning of January, NEC declared that, by increasing the number of bits per hertz from one to three, it had raised the laboratory WDM record to three terabits per second... The implications of the WDM paradigm go beyond simple data pipes. The greatest impact of all-optical technology will likely come in consumer markets.

A portent is Artel Video Systems of Marlborough (MA), which recently introduced a fiber-based WDM system that can transmit 48 digital video channels, 288 CD-quality audio bitstreams, and 64 data channels on one fiber line. Aggregating contributions from a variety of constant sources — each on different fiber wavelengths — and delivering them to consumers who can tune into favored frequencies on conventional cable, the Artel system represents a key step into the fibersphere. It can be used for new services by either cable TV companies or telcos.

1997 NEWSLETTER

Geography: Delete

Jeane Kirkpatrick recently gave a speech saying that you cannot understand the world without understanding geography. This is no longer true. We are no longer in geo-

graphic time and space. We're in <u>real</u> time and space, and
territory no longer matters very much any more. We're in a
world in which Israel — desert-bound Israel — can provide
80% of the cut flowers in Europe. And we're in a world
where Japan actually could export lumber by sawing it on
its massive transport ships: They buy the logs and saw them
on the boat...

Discussing with the Pentagon, you hear people talking
about landmasses and sea-lanes and chokepoints, where
strategic minerals might be blockaded. The Pentagon is still
fighting the last war, as there's a great inclination to do on
the victorious side. But the real threats [are now] terrorism
[by] small groups of people who can wreak tremendous
damage. And the real response to that threat has to be
various forms of information technology.

1987 CALTECH

Immigration: Add

Andrew Grove is President of Intel Corp. and I devoted
several chapters of *[Microcosm]* to exploring his life,
thoughts and career. But Grove apparently now is opposed
to immigration and upholds industrial policy. And I
thought this was pretty peculiar, since Intel itself was [built
by] immigrants [and] could not exist without immigrants.

I mean, his microprocessor was created by an Italian
immigrant and a Japanese immigrant. The memory technology was created by an Egyptian immigrant, his basic process by a Belgian immigrant, his EPROM technology by an
Israeli immigrant — and Grove himself, of course, is a
Hungarian immigrant.

This is something we have to come to terms with in
developing immigration policy: The fact that America's
high technology is utterly dependent on immigration. It
wouldn't exist without immigration, and it's worth understanding that. I go from one company to another, back and
forth across the land, and there are virtually none where —
when you go back to the engineering department — the
actual work [is] not dominated by immigrants.

1993 CON-SUM

Insurance: And Moral Hazard

The insurance business has been kind of a last bastion of the mainframe computer and the big centralized computer system with the dumb terminals attached. It's changing, but it has been peculiarly resistant to the kind of centrifugal effects of the technologies to date. I think that's because these technologies still have remained expensive. Memory and storage technologies have been particularly expensive. It's been harder to distribute large quantities of information than in the past.

But memory technology is on just a fabulous learning curve today. Today, people are figuring out how to have a centralized movie database, from which you can tap into 15,000 movies from anywhere in the country. It will blow away Blockbuster, which gets half its profits, incidentally, from late charges. That's true — that's how the business works: It tries to trick you into not returning your movies.

For a movie central, probably the cheapest thing to do is to have 15,000 two-gigabyte hard drives that cost a couple of thousand bucks or less. The big centralized DASD systems are no longer going to be cost-effective. RAID drives and all these other systems will essentially function with workstations. This is going to affect all industries, with special impact on insurance.

The big insurance companies are really now suffering a kind of socialization by regulation — regulatory socialization — because the government has increasingly gone into the insurance business. As far as I can tell, when the government goes into the insurance business, it doesn't appear to consult actuaries. It seems to me the government defies the principles of actuarial soundness in any insurance venture it launches, including moral hazard. [To clarify the principle of moral hazard], I like the example of the building: Chemical changes occur in buildings when the payoff rises above the value of the structure, and spontaneous combustion often results.

Almost all government insurance programs have defied the principle of moral hazards. For example, we have disability insurance programs that essentially promote disability, encouraging people to cultivate their disabilities into completely crippling conditions. The program Aid to Families with Dependent Children is another example. It was designed as insurance against orphans, against the death of the spouse, or some other catastrophe. Now people in the inner city, which I used to spend most of my life writing about, often orient their whole lives around this so-called insurance system.

Deposit insurance has the same kind of moral-hazard problem. If you insure deposits, you effectively insure the loans and the assets as well, and so you defy the principle of moral hazard again. The S&L crisis resulted from this error: Socializing insurance in defiance of moral hazard. What's now happening is that the government is increasingly imposing on you the same kind of principles that govern its own business at the government level...

I [foresee] a new environment of decentralization in insurance. In the next decade, companies that transform themselves...from master/slave organizations into peer networks of largely autonomous entities will prevail...

Insurance is already sold in considerable intimacy with customers, and that's good — [but] this effect will increase and apply to more and more products. You'll be able to adjust the product to the unique conditions of individual consumers, and to a much greater extent than even before.

1993 ACTUARIES

Intellectual Property

What entrepreneurs do is establish defensible intellectual property. And to say, as [John Perry] Barlow does, that because the technology changes, intellectual property rather evaporates and has to be re-embodied in varying forms, I think is [going overboard].

But he brilliantly evoked and described the problem — really, I just love that article ["Selling Wine Without Bottles," 1993 on]; I've given it to lots of people. I love it. I think it's really original and brilliant.

At the same time, the fact is, what entrepreneurs have to do is create defensible forms of property. If it's not defensible — if it's not readily defensible — then it isn't property! You know, [when it comes to] something that's really just ubiquitous and available, government can't establish property rights effectively — [because] it involves <u>constant</u> policing of people who believe that they're honest.

The problem of software is not that "thieves" steal it. Thieves steal all kinds of things. The problem is that <u>honest</u> people steal it.

GREGORSKY: [And they] outnumber the thieves by huge amounts.

Right. And if honest people steal it, then government is in a hopeless position. So it's because honest people steal it that [this entire area is so] difficult. And the reason honest people steal it is because the software industry has yet to figure out a formula that allows people to pay for the value received. The process of booting up a software package, and getting it working and debugging it and learning it, is so onerous that the idea you can't then give it to your mother is just preposterous. You've invested so much in it yourself —

Beyond laying out the money.

Yeah — that it's your own property, in a sense. You've mixed your own labor with it, to an extent, that renders it, in a sense, your property. It's "common law" (or whatever it is).

So really, what the software people describe as an intellectual-property problem is, I believe, fundamentally a pricing and delivery problem. You gotta learn how to price it. You gotta make it deliverable more readily. You need to eliminate some of the bugs and obstacles that mean that at least half of the programs that get distributed are never really used very fully. If you really talk about all the programs that get distributed, including all these AOL disks, you know, most of 'em don't.

It's really a pricing and delivery problem, and that's what the web is doing — solving that problem. And thus solving web-encryption, crytolopes, new forms of transactions of very small amounts on the Net for small rentals, temporary functions — you know, all this is solving that problem.

By decentralizing "software" into a series of —

Components. And allowing very cheap transactions, with a cost low enough so you can sell something for five cents, if you want. Currently, the transaction costs of web commerce are too high to accommodate software sales — but that is changing. And Microsoft is gonna figure this out.

It's a pricing problem — pricing and packaging, rather than a fundamental problem of intellectual property. I don't know what the analogies are. If I groped around, I might come up with one.

1997 FRAGMENTS

Internet: Cracking Windows

Today, communications technologies are unleashing the Internet as the definitive force of a new industrial era, rendering the CPU peripheral, and the net central. This shift is even more fundamental than the rise of the PC [and] the new paradigm will not roll over the LAN and the client-server model without gaining the momentum to roll over the desktop as well.

In the new paradigm, the installed base is your enemy. You cannot see the future thru Windows.

Over the next two years, the Wintel model will scale its highest peaks of sales and earnings. Fifty to 75% lower prices for Pentiums, DRAMs and portable displays will unleash a new boom before the transition. But the transition is inexorable. By early 1998, the new paradigm will blow away the current Wintel grip and open up a far more diverse and prosperous information economy...

With the prevailing computer architecture approaching a point of diminishing returns, an increasing share of these new PCs will be network machines, optimized for the coming invasion of Internet bandwidth, on land and sea and in the air. Huge operating systems and related applications, linked awkwardly to communications protocols, impose a rising burden on the memory-processor bus and fail to take advantage of the rise in network bandwidth. This problem offers a beckoning opportunity to launch new PC or teleputer architectures that are entirely optimized for the Net.

1996 NEWSLETTER

Internet: Profitability

PERKINS: If you can download programs free over the Internet, then who makes money?

You will essentially rent software components for a limited period of time and pay for it on a transaction-by-transaction basis. It allows people to use software they might not normally be able to afford.

If you think about it, this new approach really helps overcome the piracy issue, which is the software industry's biggest problem today. Software theft does not result from the evil and corrupt nature of all software-users; it is just that, until now, there has been no reasonable way for users to acquire the use of software for a limited purpose or limited period of time.

1996 HERRING

Japan: Manufacturing, Yes

Japan is strong in manufacturing precisely because they have a tremendous proliferation of small firms. They have seven times as many small manufacturing firms as the United States. That is the reason why Japan is tremendous at manufacturing, not that they have these Goliath fabs.

America had the model of three big centralized auto companies. Japan has the model of 12 bitterly competing automobile companies associated with a huge range of reasonably autonomous suppliers; they were independent businesses that functioned independently. I think for us to try to imitate a model that Japan never pursued in the name of "competing with the Japanese" is a mistake.

1990 UPSIDE

Japan: Semiconductors, No

Remember the semiconductor crisis? Supposedly we weren't going to have any semiconductor industry in a few years unless the government intervened and launched some massive effort in favor of semiconductor competitiveness. At that time I said we were solving this alleged problem and that shortly the United States would regain dominance in semiconductors. I said this in 1985 and 1986, when it appeared that the Japanese were surging ahead.

But, sure enough, this year the United States, including all our production, is about 10% ahead of Japan in semiconductors and microchips. We're massively ahead in computers and we're massively ahead in the essential dimensions of telecommunications.

During all these years when crises were being announced, the United States was pulling decisively ahead in the most critical areas of the information economy. This will assure [America's] dominance for decades to come.

1994 RECAP

Japan, Trading With

There will always be businesses suffering in competition that want to blame their problems on foreigners. All these forces can be very destructive to this intricate global fabric of relationships and commitment that represent the information industry...

The Japanese are good at what they do. That is a great asset for the United States. The U.S. would not be as vibrant and creative in the computer industry without the kind of competition the Japanese have offered, and without the very cheap memory chips they have provided, which is crucial in the expansion of opportunities for software. Whenever you make memory more expensive, you make computers more expensive. You restrict the market for software, which is the biggest American strength. You hurt America.

1990 UPSIDE

They [the Administration] go over to Japan and think that the big heroic job they can do for the U.S. is to close the trade gap with Japan. It would be a catastrophe if they closed the trade gap with Japan! The trade gap...consists of largely a lot of wonderful memory chips that are indispensable for our world-leading computer industry... Meanwhile, we've sold them all sorts of ideas and services and just a tremendous flow of value back to Japan in ways that are not measured in the Third World metrics they use. It's a very healthy relationship — couldn't be better...

1994 CIO

So what if we have a trade deficit in commodity products that is measured in the trade balance? We have a surplus in <u>services</u> all around the world. If you really combine the service trade with goods, we probably have a rough balance.

The trade gap is a good thing. It represents both a stream of very valuable components for all sorts of crucial American industries that are globally dominant — such a computers, telecommunications and networking — and also a flow of capital to the United States, which we need because we save less than a lot of other countries.

NEE: Why is a trade deficit positive?

Because the inverse of the trade deficit is a capital surplus. The Japanese earn dollars. And they can do two things with them: They can either purchase our manufactured products or they can purchase assets — make investments. Or they can exchange their dollars for other currencies with people who want to use their dollars to either buy American goods or American assets.

There's this illusion that, somehow, if they buy an asset, like a hotel or a technology license, it's bad — while, if they buy a good, that's positive, because that contributes to our balance of trade. The real difference is that they buy the orange or the side of beef, they eat it, and we don't have it anymore. But when they buy the hotel or the technology license, we still retain the technology and the hotel.

The idea that someday we are going to have to buy them back — which is the implicit assumption of [those who say] our trade gap is putting us into debt with the foreigners — is just nonsense. There are no reasons for us to ever buy them back.

If you were to total up all the money the Japanese invested in the 1980s in the U.S., we made out like bandits. They overpaid for most things.

They did overpay for a lot of stuff. As a practical matter, some of the stuff they allegedly overpaid for turned out to be a good deal. MCA and Columbia, regarded to be big disasters by some people, may have been good deals. Judging from the valuations of Paramount, Sony has about a $2 billion capital gain on Columbia. And MCA actually also has a big capital gain.

The gyration of attitudes toward Japan is not very sound. One moment they can do no wrong, they're going to drive us into the sea, and we're all going to be flipping hamburgers for them. The next moment their economy is crashing and all their companies are hopeless failures. The omnipotent image was always false, and I always said it was false. The [more recent] idea that the Japanese have had it is also wrong. They have just got tremendous resources — tremendously smart, capable people; tremendous manufacturing skills unique in the world (although they are spreading thru Asia recently) — and I think they are going to do well, as long as they spurn all of America's advice.

1994 UPSIDE

Jungles To Highways

If you encountered an automobile in the middle of the jungle, you might regard it [as] quite an impressive technology, particularly if you'd never seen an automobile before: Heat, light, air-conditioning, radio communications, big back seat, even a loud horn to frighten off fierce animals. You might never imagine — in contemplating this car in the jungle — that the real magic of automobiles comes in conjunction with roads. Indeed, for the past 30 years or so, we've mostly used our computers like cars in the jungle — [for] desktop-oriented applications — without ever imagining that the real magic of computers comes in conjunction with networks.

1997 CATO

Knife-Edge, Universal

Everywhere the key issue in the world economy is whether to permit the innovation and change that is essen-

tial to growth. Failure of growth will inevitably lead to
wars, strikes, famines and xenophobia. For example, if
China cannot grow, as the environmentalists believe, then it
will have to fight. If the world is zero-sum, the best fighters
rather than the best producers will prevail.

1997 NEWSLETTER

Knowledge Plus Money

Adam Smith said that the key law of capitalism is incentives, which really misses the point. The reason that capitalism succeeds at the entrepreneurial level (beyond the level
of fighting for the next meal) is that capitalism lets people
get rich so that they can reinvest their riches. Capitalism
grants to those people who have already demonstrated their
ability to create wealth the right to reinvest it, and that's
what entrepreneurs do with their returns — overwhelmingly they reinvest it... That means the wealth is constantly
flowing into the hands of the people who are best able to
magnify it. That's the secret of capitalist growth... The very
process by which they generate the wealth taught them how
to reinvest it.

1990 UPSIDE

The source of earning is <u>learning</u> — that is the real basis
of capitalist growth. And the crucial point is that the people
who <u>create</u> wealth <u>control</u> it... Every business generates a
dual yield — a financial yield, and a yield of knowledge
and learning. And if you divorce the financial yield from
the yield of learning, you have economic stagnation and
failure. Because it's the process of <u>creating</u> wealth that's the
best learning process for <u>reinvesting</u> it.

1993 BIONOMICS

Property rights link the giving of enterprise to the rise
of the capitalist economy. The key principle of economic
policy is to assure that the same people who create wealth
also invest it — because the best conceivable education for
the further creation of wealth is the demonstration of past
creation of wealth. The entrepreneurial experience allows

the entrepreneur to invest effectively because it joins the two principle yields of enterprise. One yield is the financial profit, and the other yield is the profit of learning, of knowledge. A capitalist economy is a knowledge system and the reason it prevails is because the same people who create wealth also reinvest it. The knowledge profit is joined with the financial profit and this link generates new wealth and opportunities for everyone.

1994 RECAP

Knowledge In Networks

Adam Smith maintained that the creative power of capitalism derives from the division of labor, the increase in specialization that drives and expands the market. Well, this is what computer networks are: They're engines of the division of labor. Computer networks make it possible for the best people in the world to solve particular problems together, regardless of the constraints of geography. The spread of computer networks will spur a huge expansion of economic growth around the world.

1994 RECAP

Layoffs To Grow

The fact is that layoffs are a good thing. I remember back in the early '70s, in Seattle, Boeing laid off about half of its workforce. It was widely prophesied that this was the end of the line for Seattle [and] Seattle was going to be a basket case in the future. Since then, Seattle has become the richest and most prosperous city in the country.

Pittsburgh was, at the time of the collapse of Big Steel, regarded as a hopeless case. What was the result in Pittsburgh? Pittsburgh became America's most livable city. Thousands of new machine shops and small businesses emerged. In North Carolina, tobacco companies laid off scores of thousands of people. It was supposed to be a catastrophe. The people there have prospered.

The fact is, layoffs are crucial to growth. The more layoffs in a particular area, the more business starts and the more long-term economic growth. An economy with layoffs is an economy that can create jobs and opportunities.

So, whatever changes you may propose, [Labor Secretary] Bob [Reich], the last one you should do is to make it more difficult to lay people off. Because, if you can't lay people off, then you can't hire people so readily. Systems of credentialism get entrenched, and opportunities close. And I think an open economy with less credentialism and more opportunities is desirable. It takes courage, guts, to lay people off, but it unleashes new powers.

1996 HARPERS

The deep depression suffered by the auto and steel industries will be seen — in the course of time — as easing the shift of resources into the energy, service and high-technology companies that are leading us into an era of productive possibilities unprecedented in human history.

1988 E-FORUM

"Level Playing Field"

You can't have a level playing field — never. Anybody talks about a "level playing field," laugh 'em out of the room. It can't happen in capitalism. Only socialism can have a level playing field, with everybody equally poor, and a few bureaucrats in charge. Competition means somebody wins, and somebody makes money, so they can move with the tremendous dynamic thrust of the technology...

The RBOCs have advantages, they should exploit those advantages, see how far it takes them. The long-distance people have advantages, the computer companies have advantages, satellites — all these companies have advantages. Let 'em compete.

What "competition" means in Washington is essentially allocation of markets at the hands of regulators... Whenever a politician says they're "promoting competition," that's what they're doing: Giving more power to regulators to allocate markets.

1997 CATO

Macrocosm and Microcosm

PARROT: George, I'm turning to you, sort of like a hesitant hang-glider, waiting to leap off into things I can't see or understand. What does "quantum theory" really mean? Can you help in a simple explanation?

The key to quantum theory was expounded by Max Planck, the inventor of quantum theory, when he defined it as a fundamentally different domain.

He [described] the macrocosm, where entities obeyed the usual laws — of gravity, friction, entropy — all the key laws of Newtonian physics that we see in billiard balls, pots and pans, and whatever.

Basically things we can see ourselves [and] can get our hands on — they have a logic to them.

That's right. And then [there's] the quantum domain, which Planck called the microcosm...of <u>invisible</u> entities that obey completely different laws. The microcosm does observe completely different laws and, because of it, as we move our technology from the macrocosm to the micro-cosm, everything in society is transformed...

In the macrocosm — in the world at large — the more "things" you get to organize, the more complicated everything becomes. When you have a bunch of kids in the room, and one leaves, the noise level drops decisively — much more than the departure of one out of eight kids would suggest. And that is because, in the macrocosm — in the world of kids — complexity interactions grow by the <u>square</u> of the number of entities to be organized.

In other words, noise, racket, interplay, increases by the square of the number of kids. Whatever it is — kids, soft-ware, modules — complexity increases, exponentially, with the number of units. In the microcosm, on the microchip, <u>efficiency</u> grows by the square of the number of entities (or nodes, or transistors, or switches) to be organized.

So you have the outside world — where you run into constant "complexity explosions" as the number of entities increase — [versus] inside the microcosm, where things get better and faster and cooler and more powerful, and more efficient, by the square of the number of nodes. ("Nodes" are transistors or switches or whatever — logical elements.)

And so this is a tremendous centrifugal force in the midst of the world — this marvelous technology that overcomes the law of complexity...with the law of the microcosm, where everything grows better and faster as the individual electrons move toward their "mean free path," which is the distance they can travel without colliding with the very structure of the matter in which they reside.

What's this mean? To you and me as individuals? What I'm hearing is that simplicity is leading to a faster and faster interaction of ideas...

The chip grows in efficiency — it's a processor, and it grows with tremendous efficiency in processing. Exponentially, doubles every year. But — the number of wires <u>from</u> the chip is very limited — chiefly limited by the circumference of the chip. And so it hardly increases at all — it just increases slowly as chip-sizes expand.

So you have this exponential increase of processing power, on it, and very little [enhancement of] communications power — just like us. We have the most powerful processor in the world.

Our capacity to think.

Our brains — they are hugely powerful. As a matter of fact, the human eye can perform more visual processing than all the supercomputers in the world put together... And yet our <u>communications</u> powers are terrible. The mouth is one bottleneck, plus body language [laughter]. This is why an economy works to the extent that it emancipates individuals — because it is tapping this tremendous processing power, and it can short-circuit the communications problem which individuals have.

Polanyi calls it "tacit knowledge" — most of our knowledge we can't express.

1989 MONITOR

Mainframes: As Trains

This is a moment like the transition from trains to auto-

mobiles earlier this century. You get in a train. You have to
go to the station on the schedule prescribed by the train
management. You have to ride to a few destinations that are
specified by the train system. It's all controlled from above
and you adapt to the railroad system. Well, the automobile
changed all that. It empowered individuals to get in a car
and go where they want to go with the persons they want to
go with. That's essentially the change from the top-down
broadcast system to the computer.

1993 ACTUARIES

Maslow Hierarchy

[A]s you move up the Maslow hierarchy, you first satisfy your needs for food and lodging. When you get to the
end point, all of your gratifications are — broadly considered — information products. Economies will tend to move
up that escalator to increasing preoccupation with information products and increasing dominance of information
products in the economy. That's why people who build
information conduits, like phone companies — even if they
can charge less per circuit connection — will still have a
very profitable, successful business. The whole economy
will be moving toward them.

1994 UPSIDE

Materialism

Materialism has been the dominant superstition of this
century. But materialism collapsed at the heart of matter
itself: When it became clear that the atom is an empty in
proportion to the size of is nucleus as the solar system is in
proportion to the size of the sun, and that a particular
electron didn't have a specific location [but is instead] a
probability amplitude (which is more like a thought than a
thing), materialism itself collapsed at the heart of matter. It
was the breakthrus of quantum theory that allowed the
manipulation of matter from the inside.

1993 BIONOMICS

Math and Science

Math and science alone are impotent to fuel innovation. If math and science alone could do it, the Russians would be the world's leading innovators.

1990 HILLSDALE

Microcosm, Origins of

I became interested in semiconductors from some friends, including Peter Sprague, who is chairman of National Semiconductor, and from Nick Kelley, who is head of a local company called Berkshire Corporation which makes products used in clean rooms. I remember Peter and Nick both talking about what this technology entailed, and it seemed to me vastly more important than any of the economic analyses I was doing...

The transistor on one of these transistor chips — or 20 million transistor chips — occupies no discernible space and operates beyond human comprehension. That led me to study how this was possible and took me to a study of quantum theory, which was a real diversion for me [and] very hard. I probably read more than a hundred books about physics, and spent a lot of time at Caltech...

I went thru [Richard] Feynman's three volumes very carefully, page by page. That was my fundamental training and my first real exposure to rigorous physical writing...

KARLGAARD: But tell us why you decided quantum physics was the route to understanding the electronics industry.

The critical dynamic seemed to me to be physics, not business. I mean, business enterprise was critical to its success, but it was immediately evident to me — when I read all the books [and] articles about the history of this industry — that something very essential was missing.

Everybody started with Babbage [Charles Babbage, British designer/builder of mechanical computing machines that, 160 years ago, anticipated the principles underlying the modern electronic computer]. It just seemed to me that ability to create some big mechanical device that could add, subtract and calculate had nothing to do with Silicon Valley. Even the creation of software — although ultimately indispensable and maybe even paramount to many forms of electronics — wasn't it.

Rather, the key breakthru was solid-state physics and the ability to manipulate the inner structure of matter, the ability to understand matter from the inside out, and thus put scores of transistors on the point of a pin. This was the breakthru, not creating an analytical engine or developing Boolean logic. All these achievements were of some significance, but the semiconductor industry was something radically new in the world. Its novelty came in applying quantum theory to solid-state phenomena and allowing the creation of powerful machines — that's the foundation of the computer revolution...

The key to the chip is that the switches on the chip are cheap. The logical functions on the chip are cheap. But, if you move off the chip, then everything becomes expensive and complicated and difficult to sustain. That is why, in the end, all computers are going to be about equal: They are all going to be supercomputers; you won't have the hierarchy of different computer capabilities. There will be lots of applications — specific applications in places — but all computers will be supercomputers, and they will enhance the capabilities of the individual.

1990 UPSIDE

Microcosm Plus Telecosm

Industry is being driven by two exponentials. The first is the Law of the Microcosm, which states that computer processing power and value double every 18 months. This law has really been the driving force behind world economic growth over the last 20 years.

The huge new opportunity that is emerging [now] derives from the Law of the Telecosm, which declares that when you take any N [i.e. number of] computers and connect them on networks, you get N-<u>squared</u> performance and value. It's not just an increase in the <u>number</u> of computers, but also an increase in the <u>power</u> of each computer.

So the steady increase in the power of the computer is imparted by Law of the Microcosm and compounded by Law of the Telecosm. These two compounding exponentials explain the explosive role of the Internet and all the technologies associated with it. Now things will really start popping.

1996 HERRING

Middlemen

The key thing computer networking does to any business is change vertical systems into horizontal systems. It eliminates middlemen — middle executives — of all descriptions. And the heart of Hollywood today is intermediation. About 70% of the cost of making a movie is in areas such as distribution and advertising, and about 30% goes to the people involved in making the movie.

Most of that 70% will be collapsed by a truly pervasive fiber-optic network system. It will collapse when you can make it available to the entire world, and you don't need to attract some miscellaneous audience to theaters in Des Moines, San Jose, Seattle and Pittsfield [MA] at once. The 70% cost of the film drops to 5%, or even less for some.

Meanwhile, the remaining 30% of the cost of a film is getting these people whose star properties come from their lowest-common-denominator appeal and from their monopoly position of being able to finance those 70% costs. Those costs can be drastically reduced.

1994 UPSIDE

Mind Over Matter

PARROT: You make the point that the nations that, in the coming decades, will survive and succeed will be the nations with ideas. Can you expound on that a bit?

Well, when you can put whole words on grains of sand — which is what a silicon chip is: A world inscribed on a tiny sliver of silicon (which is made of sand) — specific territories lose their significance.

Today, people still behave as if land makes a difference

[and assume] it's really vital to control land. Yet the countries which have increased their power most dramatically over the last decades have been little barren islands, mostly, in the Pacific — Singapore, Hong Kong, Japan, Korea (which is a peninsula). Asian countries with <u>less</u> natural resources than virtually any other nations on the face of the Earth have increased their power [much] more rapidly than huge "resource-rich" lands like Argentina — which before the Second World War was one of the world's richest countries, and now is deep in the Third World...

These islands substituted mind for matter. They didn't have matter, so they were forced to stress mind — which is infinitely more powerful than matter... And those parts of the United States that committed themselves most fully to the promise of the microcosm also led our economic growth.

1989 MONITOR

Monopoly: Withering

It is often said that, if the Baby Bells are granted the power to create this [universal digital-optical] network, somehow they will restrict communications. It's really an amazing idea that somehow this will resolve into some menacing monopoly. I think it's like all the other great infrastructure projects. Did the national highway system inhibit transportation? Did it reduce the power of individuals to travel and control their own travel plans? No.

What the system did was greatly empower individuals. They could get in their cars and go wherever they wanted, faster than before. Similarly, the fiber network will empower communicators and individuals who want to transmit information. The increase in bandwidth of the fiber network over the copper network is millions-fold greater than the increase in bandwidth of the paved highway systems over the dirt roads and railroads that preceded.

1990 LONGBOAT

What this agreement [AT&T buying McCaw] does is <u>demolish</u> all the assumptions of the regulatory apparatus [premised on] a "natural monopoly," somehow, in telecommunications... There [will] never be any kind of monopoly in communications again. What's really happening is that the entire industry is becoming part of the computer industry, which itself consists of thousands and thousands of companies... This situation is moving too fast for any company to dominate [and] to talk about laws promulgated in 1983-84 is looking back into the Dark Ages. It just is going to be a completely different arena... "Telephones" will be as archaic a word as "picture radios" or "iceboxes."

1993 LEHRER

PERKINS: What do you think about the consolidation going on in the entertainment business, such as the merger of Disney and Capital Cities/ABC?

I take a certain prurient interest in them — you know, dinosaur couplings are kind of exciting. But I don't think these mergers are really where it's at.

The fear that big companies such as Disney are going to control all content is really kind of ridiculous. Content is going to proliferate and become more decentralized. So, while I think the film studios will continue to prosper because of better distribution, they will also have much more competition.

The TV business, for example, is already suffering from the competition of the Internet and the Web, and this competition will become increasingly acute as Java animations and programming become more available.

1996 HERRING

Moron's Law

The essential conflict is between Moore's Law, which governs the technology, and government regulation — ruled by what venture capitalist Roger McNamee calls Moron's Law. And this is the essential conflict, because Moron's Law is inexorably hostile to this flood of creativity.

1997 CATO

Nation-State, National Strength

I believe that the nation-state is becoming increasingly irrelevant as an economic entity. It is crucial as a cultural entity and as an historical entity, but it is increasingly irrelevant as an economic entity.

1990 UPSIDE

In the past, to offer a chip, you essentially had to own $100,000,000 semiconductor fab. And, indeed, almost all the chips were authored by the owners of the fabs. It's as if books were all authored by printers. But, as the diffusion of computer-aided engineering [proceeds], the number of chips designed will probably increase from 10,000 last year to some hundred thousand in the next three or four years. And more and more of these chips will be designed by individuals and companies across the country, rather than by engineers in semiconductor firms.

Similarly, most of the new software products are productions of individuals or small teams. It's no longer necessary to have a huge capital plant in order to generate the critical products of the new era. So the key lesson of the age of intelligent machines is that knowledge is power.

But today that's true in a new sense. It means that other things are not power. And the things that no longer confer power are all the dreams and goals of tyrants and despots over centuries: The control of territory, the control of natural resources, the control of military manpower, and the control of national economic planning. This is an age when entrepreneurs can flash their capital down fiber-optic cables and bounce it off satellites, send it around the world in microseconds, and the entrepreneur can follow it in hours on a 747, and he can move his company in weeks.

Against this new power of individuals and entrepreneurs, the state is increasingly impotent and at bay. The good news for entrepreneurs is deadly news for the Socialist Dream. The only way the state can enhance its wealth and power today is to emancipate individuals to create new knowledge.

1986 BOSTON

The balance of trade is no longer really a very significant index of anything important. What will matter in the
new global economy is not a surplus in the current account,
but a surplus in the accounts of Liberty. The entrepreneurs
will be coming, and I hope you are ready for them.

1987 CALTECH

Negroponte Switch

Voice traffic and video traffic...are exchanging places.
Voice traffic will be mobile and wireless. And video traffic
will increasingly travel thru the broadband pipes of the
fiber-optic network. Ironically, I think the actual connections to the homes, in many cases may indeed be wireless.
Recent advances up the spectrum to 28 gigahertz by a
company in New Jersey called Cellular Vision show the
possibility of delivering video — broadband video,
two-way — directly to home. So it won't be a completely
neat switch — where all video traffic goes by glass, and all
voice traffic by the air. A lot of voice will use the
fibersphere, as I call it... But in general this does indicate
the directions of the change: Increasingly, voice will be
wireless and, increasingly, video will go thru the fiber-optic
network.

1993 KMB-VID

"Network Is The Computer"

Just as teenagers rebel against Dad and Mom, leave
home, and launch a new life, in the late 1990s, your computer is doing the same thing, rebelling against Pa Intel and
Ma Microsoft. No hard feelings. The change in the industry
has little or nothing to do with hostility to the 16-year-old
Wintel [Windows plus Intel] structure that still fuels industry growth. People still love their PCs.

The change derives from a fundamental shift in computer architecture as the network becomes central and the
CPU becomes peripheral. The result will be a new computer
architecture, hardware and software — a Java-based network computer or teleputer that focuses not on displacing
Dad and Mom but in functioning successfully in the

world...

Java is prevailing because, in a multiplex world of proprietary systems optimized for various desktop processors, Java is shrewdly and resourcefully optimized for the Net and for the network teleputers about to burst on the scene. Based on a generic Java interpreter, built into every new browser and operating system, Java is truly and uniquely platform-independent. With programmers writing for the generic machine rather than the proprietary OS, Java offers a compelling promise of component software rented and downloaded just-in-time from the Net.

In a period when typical computer-users spend more time accessing remote memories than local memories, it fits the new paradigm. It can save as much as $9,500 of the $11,900 that the Gartner Group estimates as the annual cost of an office PC. Together with Java teleputers, Java promises to save a representative Forbes 500 company, with 15,000 available seats, as much as $100 million a year in hardware- and software-maintenance costs.

Java systems render most PCs optimized for the desktop — however fast and fully-featured — quite abruptly obsolete.

1996 NEWSLETTER

Network Computer (NC)

Describe for me what a Network Computer's gonna be, when it becomes available. If I understand you right, basically the Internet will serve as the CPU, and the CPU or the chip in your computer [becomes] basically a peripheral.

Right. That's a good way of thinking about it.

Essentially, all the personal computers in use today are optimized for the desktop. They're optimized for a world in which you spend more time in your own hard drive than you do accessing remote information.

But, with this 200-fold rise in Internet traffic, most users today spend more time tapping remote memories than they do their own local memory. And this means it no longer makes sense to design your computer for the desktop, it makes more sense to redesign the computer to operate robustly and easily on the Net.

That's what the NC does. It is not "inferior" to a PC, it will actually be <u>superior</u>, because its facility in accessing remote Internet sites will be critical — and that's <u>millions</u> of possible sites rather than just the one in your computer. So it actually increases the power of your computer by a factor of millions.

1997 LIMBAUGH

Newspapers: The Next

I think newspapers will be the big winner from the information superhighway, and the advances in display technology that will make computer displays competitive with paper.

The problem of computer display today is that it slows your reading down by about 25%. But when computer displays — which are currently equivalent to 72 dots per inch — rise up to the level of a computer <u>printer</u>, a laser printer, 300 to 600 dots per inch, then you will read your computer screen or your news panel — as readily as you can read paper today. When that happens, newspapers will move onto newspanels [and] be like notebook computers: They'll go anywhere, and contain a whole year's worth of newspapers.

1994 TECHNOPOL

It will be a much more effective way to deliver a readership than a current newspaper is, so you'll be able to charge more for advertising. The advertisers will get so much greater yield that you'll be able to share in the yield that the ads generate.

Small newspapers will be able to gain from this. Local newspapers do have a specialty and a virtual monopoly on news that effects their particular locality... That's a real niche [and makes for] a defensible business proposition — to deliver that local readership, with its local ties and connections and interests. And deliver advertising to them.

And actually allow those local people to transact business with both local and remote businesses.

The newspaper will succeed because we already control the newspaper. It's more like a computer than the TV. When you buy a newspaper, you read what you want when you want it. It's not like TV... The television set is very much like the railroad model, and the newspaper is very much like the automobile. The newspaper will prevail, because the only thing it lacks is digital magic. Its delivery system is archaic [when you consider how] its delivery system depends on the Teamsters Union, plus a 10-year-old kid on a bike. It's just terrible distribution. And that's what the computer and networks can supply: A much better distribution system...

The computer will offer all the visual rewards of a news program, plus the timeliness and as much depth as you want. You can call up archives that relate to the story that interests you. The newspaper is not going to die. The newspaper fits perfectly in the computer-form factor and will succeed as a supplier to computer networks.

1994 UPSIDE

What will a digital newspaper look like?

It will look a <u>lot</u> like your current newspaper. You'll have a front page, with headlines; you can click on a headline and the story will fill up the page. Then you can click on a picture, and the picture'll fill up the page. Click on a chart, and it'll fill up the page. Click on an advertisement, and <u>it</u> will fill up the page.

Then click on "further information" about the advertisement — on thru to a final transaction. So this newspaper will be able to deliver specific products. Sound will be a later development [and perhaps] the newspaper could be <u>read</u> to you: If you want an audio newspaper, you can get that, or you can get video.

What it's gonna do is blow away <u>TV</u> news. It's not that TV is gonna usurp the newspaper, it's that newspapers are gonna usurp TV...

You will have 10,000 newspapers, but still, in a digital

highway with just <u>floods</u> of information, floods of bits, people will want to go to a familiar place to organize their entries into the digital highway. It seems to me that branded newspapers will retain an advantage as a comfortable place to go in this great info-sphere, or whatever you want to call it... But more newspapers and magazines will be out there, so there'll be more choice. And you'll be able to read your hometown newspaper just as well if you go to London as when you're at home. You'll be able to <u>access</u> your newspaper more readily. You'll also be able to access archives... The newspaper becomes a much richer environment than it is today.

1994 TECHNOPOL

Personal Communications Services

I think PCS will be the central phone service. So to exclude the phone companies from PCS is to kick 'em out of the business, essentially, in the long run. You really do have to allow everybody to come in, because the phone companies themselves are incapable of <u>supplying</u> all these services without collaboration from hundreds of other companies and scores of other industries around the world. It'll be a kind of collaborative effort.

You can use all the spectrum, all across the country, with very high-powered machines and only a few people using 'em. Or you can have lots of little cells, where the entire spectrum is available, and...millions and millions of people using 'em — and that's where we're moving. We started with just a few hundred subscribers per city with city-wide high-powered radio services. Now we have 10 million subscribers [for cellular] and we'll have a hundred million in the next decade. That 100 million will be accommodated with broader-band services, by far, than those first few hundred a city, using the entire spectrum, could command — because the technology will use spectrum much more efficiently. Reuse it much more effectively.

1993 KMB-VID

[S]mart radios can radically simplify the cellular land-

scape. Freed of most wires, poles, backhoes, trucks, workers, engineers and rights of way, cellular should be far
cheaper than wireline.

For example, the conventional analog base-station that
receives your cellular calls and connects them to the telephone network requires a million-dollar facility of a thousand square feet. This structure may contain a central-
office-style switch to link calls to the public switched telephone network; huge backup power supplies and batteries
to handle utility breakdowns; and racks of radios covering
every communications channel and modulation scheme
used in the cell. This can add up to 416 radios, together
with all the maintenance and expertise that multiple standards entail.

In the near future, one wideband radio will suffice.
Digital signal processors ultimately costing a few dollars
apiece and draining [only] milliwatts of power will sort out
all the channels, codes, modulation schemes, multipath
channels and filtering needs. Gone will be the large buildings, the racks of radios, the arrays of antennas, the specialized hardware processors, the virtual honeycombs towering
in the air in time and space with exclusive spectrum assign-
ments and time-slots...possibly [taking with them] even the
battalions of lawyers in the communications bar.

All can be replaced by a programmable silicon base-
station in a briefcase, installed on any lamp-post, elevator
shaft, office closet, shopping-mall ceiling, rooftop, or even
household. The result, estimated Don Cox of Stanford, the
father of American PCS at Bell Laboratories, could be a
reduction of the capital costs of a wireless customer from an
average of some $5,555 in 1994 to perhaps $14 after the turn
of the century.

1997 NEWSLETTER

Pictures Versus Text

I think the people who imagine they can supplant text
with pictures alone are gonna be deeply disappointed, and
that's the problem with the current interlaced television
system: It's terrible at delivering text. And if you wanna sell
a product, an expensive product, you're gonna need text,

you're gonna need detail, you're gonna need specs. And so it seems to me that newspapers are gonna be better at selling products than are ordinary television presentations.

1994 TECHNOPOL

In *Forbes* a while ago you said a word is worth a thousand pictures. Could you explain this?

A picture may be worth a thousand words, but it takes millions of computer "words" to transmit. A really high-resolution color picture could take a gigabyte. But you don't need gigabytes, you need many megabytes to project a high-resolution picture and a megabyte is actually a 400-page book.

You also said if you strip the pictures away from an encyclopedia, you still have an encyclopedia. Take the words away and you have nothing.

That's right. And that's one of the problems with the current encyclopedias. The CD-ROM has now taken over the encyclopedia business. But these electronic encyclopedias are all done by "techies" who are eager to display their full-motion video and their animations, their cute little atoms with the electrons whirling around them, and their maps. The bulk of the megabytes that a CD-ROM can hold are devoted to these pictures and relatively little is devoted to the words.

1994 MARSHALL

R&D: Government

NEE: Where do you draw the line on government involvement? There is a role for government in the funding of basic research and military R&D, thru agencies like the National Institutes of Health and the Advanced Research Projects Agency. But the problem arises when the government stays in too long and begins supporting specific companies after they should be standing on their own, like it did with Thinking

Machines.

That's right. A lot of the leading critics of industrial policy have been from the Brookings Institute, which is generally a liberal think tank in Washington. But the argument they've made is that when you move into that arena, you inevitably politicize it.

Where has government blocked innovation?

If government is too deeply involved in economic activity, it will ally with the existing installed base and create a major obstacle to technological progress and human progress. You see the worst examples of that in places in Latin America. They may not be explicitly socialist, but they established companies so closely allied with the government that they are virtually arms of the government. The government channels all capital in the country to these institutions — and change is agonizingly slow.

This is really the predicament of Brazil. (I have a brother-in-law who is *The New York Times* correspondent in Brazil, so I read his stuff.) The structure, at a certain point, of the government and major institutions becomes so deeply intertwined they can no longer differentiate the two. It becomes impossible to dismantle the establishment.

In Brazil, they decided to have an autonomous, indigenous computer industry and they excluded foreign computers — [which] merely meant that companies in Brazil used obsolete equipment. It meant that companies become less and less competitive in the world. Meanwhile, Chile completely dismantled all of its tariffs, accompanied by all sorts of predictions (from the same kinds of people now waging a trade war against Japan) that opening up Chile's economy would be a catastrophe for the poor; all the small businesses would be destroyed.

Instead, Chile became the fastest-growing economy in the Western Hemisphere, and has been for the past six or seven years. It's just amazingly prosperous, and a perfect counterpoint to Brazil. Brazil had more resources and everything else, but they pursued a doggedly protectionist policy. Chile opened up completely to the world and underwent a couple years of quite agonizing adjustment, but emerged with a truly competitive, world-class economy.

Each step of industrial policy creates a constituency for that policy. It becomes very hard to change, even if the technology radically changes.

1994 UPSIDE

Do you know of any example in which government industrial or technology policy was successful, or even useful?

No. But half of our R&D is financed by government, so I think that our universities probably wouldn't support science-and-technology training and research nearly [at the levels] they do if it were not for DARPA [the Defense Advanced Research Projects Agency], the Naval Institute, and other government sources.

A lot of this is an optical illusion. Whenever the advocates of industrial policy want to make their case, they go back to the 1950s. All R&D and all industrial research was devoted to military purposes coming out of the Second World War, and continuing thru the Korean War and into the Cold War — this included even truck and automotive technology. Except for some telephone technology — Bell Labs and some others were mutually productive — the fact is that almost everything was impacted by government at that point.

So, if you follow the pedigree of any technology back into time, you'll always find a place where it was dominated by government. Advocates of industrial policy use that to maintain that government was indispensable...

In examining World War One, World War Two and after, it seems that the military effort has had a great deal of influence in bringing forth new technology. Do we not owe a lot of progress to the military, scientific and governmental efforts of World War One and World War Two?

Yes. But I don't think progress was faster during that period than it has been for the last 20 years. I don't think progress was a lot faster during that period than it was in Japan over the last 30 years with virtually no, or negligible, defense spending.

Japan, incidentally, is an example of a country where the vast bulk of R&D is private. People claim that somehow Japan is more government-run, and MITI is more powerful. But we have a much higher proportion of our total R&D financed by government than Japan does.

1994 MARSHALL

Government is 35 to 40% of the economy. It's 50% of R&D monies. It's a huge customer for every business. The government necessarily has to develop an array of policies that directly impinge on information technology — and can't avoid it... The government has to set policies and defend structures and enforce laws. But it should not enter the fray and become a direct participant in picking winners and losers.

1994 CIO

What the federal government should do for the Information Superhighway is be an intelligent consumer of the technologies. The government represents a third of the U.S. economy, and what it buys, and the kind of procurement decisions it makes, can have a big influence on how the Information Highway gets built... Let the marketplace of users build the network, as it already has done. Networks are driven by public demand, shared by human needs, and rooted in a moral universe of growth thru sharing. Experience creates the expertise to maintain and use it. No government interference is needed.

1994 USWEST

In the context of the Internet, you frequently portray the government as the villain. To quote *Life After Television*, "A federal program of fiber-optic freeways will end like the great concrete freeways built in the Third World, running from nowhere to nowhere and used chiefly as shelters for the homeless."

I really do think that networks will be best maintained

thru some market structure, and I would prefer to improve the market. The government does not have a lot of additional resources available to lavish on creating vast new communications networks. And I don't think this is bad. I think ultimately the most robust Internet will emerge from a market process, from market signals. The problem with the market signals today is they're distorted. You know, your T-1 lines that cost the phone company $100 to deploy cost $500 to $1,600 a month to lease.

Tom Kalil, a senior director to the White House National Economic Council, doesn't believe government needs to lavish money on maintaining the Internet. He said they should instead feed the research that spawns successful technologies using relatively small amounts of money.

In the U.S., most research and development is financed by the government. I don't think this is a necessary, permanent condition, but it is the existing system that we have installed.

Isn't this good?

You know, it depends. It's not necessarily good. It's bad to the extent that it means that political lobbying becomes the chief governor of rewards in research in America. And some of this is already happening, particularly on environmental issues.

Let's talk about computer science, which has been funded by DARPA for the last 30 years. DARPA has said more or less that they're planning to get out of that game. What will this do to computer science in this country?

Maybe DARPA says it's not going to be financing as much computer science, but this illusion that there are no defense problems anymore is not going to survive the next big catastrophe. You get one nuclear explosion anywhere and there's going to be great amounts of money thrown at universities to push whatever technologies are emerging. And certainly computer technology is such a core capability for meeting any of these threats that any federal money will yield benefits for computer-science departments.

But you don't agree that the government should seed technology-development other than thru defense spending? For example, the October 1996 initiative by the Clinton Administration to fund development of network technology — you and your friend Newt Gingrich aren't going to support this?

The reason the government can present a list of successfully sponsored technologies is that, during the period when the R&D for these technologies occurred, government dominated all research and development. We came out of the Second World War with radar and a myriad of new technologies. We moved into the Korean War and the Cold War and, it doesn't matter what technology you talk about, it was financed by government.

So of course if you follow the pedigree of any technology you can name, you can always find a government dollar in there.

Now if you want to imagine that government dollars have some magical property that renders them especially crucial as seed dollars, then you can show that government financing is indispensable to any technology.

There is another model to look at, and it's worked very well, although perhaps not as well in some respects as the U.S. model. In Japan, rather than 50% of R&D financed by government, the figure is less than 5%, which is contrary to what people imagine. You have the Hitachi University, and so on, and they've developed all sorts of other means of seeding and financing technology. But in the U.S. where the government does it for nothing, U.S. companies don't have the same incentive that Hitachi does to create a Hitachi University.

So you believe if the government gets out of the research business that we'll start getting GM Universities?

Yes, we'll get GM Universities [and] all sorts of private ventures that perform long-range research on contract. And we'll have a variety of universities funded by different forms of endowment. That is imagining this wonderful libertarian disquisition where government cuts back substantially on the proportion of total national income that it captures.

However, I think under existing circumstances I would vote for most of those programs that you're talking about, and I would tell Newt Gingrich, if he asked me, to vote for them.

One of the disputes I have with the organized libertarians is that they assume we have a perfect world and they don't understand the significance of the installed base. The installed base today — the legacy system — is overwhelmingly oriented toward government financing of R&D at the university complex in America. I agree it would ultimately improve the quality of R&D if most of this were wiped clear.

Of course there would be a transitional phase which would be quite catastrophic for hundreds of thousands of people in universities and government labs. Thus it would be nearly impossible politically to cut it back, which means, as a practical matter, we have to optimize the current system.

1997 IEEE

Software Breakout

During the period of the most fabulous growth in this industry [of information technology], all the leading U.S. companies lost market-share — and yet the U.S. retained complete dominance in the global computer industry. Very impressive. How did it happen?

The key to it was the emergence — completely unexpected — of some 14,000 new software firms. During the 1980s, the number of software engineers increased about 28% a year, year after year, throughout the 1980s... They transformed the computer from a cult instrument guarded by information-processing gurus — a kind of priesthood of information-processing in air-conditioned central computing units — into a general appliance on everybody's desktop.

1990 HILLSDALE

The American system works remarkably well when you consider that we still have close to 67% of the global supercomputer market, 48% of the semiconductor capital-equipment market, 40% of the global semiconductor market, and actually still dominate many of the leading-edge markets in the semiconductors.

KARLGAARD: Not to mention 75% of the world's software market.

Effectively, we dominate the world's market-share in software, at a time when software is becoming an increasing portion of value added in information technology. Xerox has continued to dominate the high end of the copier market, not thru its manufacturing technology but thru the two million lines of software code in the high-end copier.

1990 UPSIDE

Speed Of Light: Bottom Line

The speed of light has previously been regarded to be in abundance — it's the ultimate velocity. But, in information technology, of course, the speed of life has become the critical limit — which does shape and constrain the future evolution of information technologies.

I believe that the ultimate impact of the speed of light — measured electromagnetic waves move nine inches a nanosecond, approximately — at a time when microprocessor cycle-times are moving down to the nanosecond range, dictates that the smallest computers will be the fastest computers, and that they will be widely distributed throughout the world economy.

The speed of light also dictates that it takes 30 milliseconds or so for a signal to cross the country [and] 250 milliseconds to reach a geosynchronous satellite. Although these milliseconds seem short in the "real world," in the world of information technology they represent eons. So they dictate that these compressed supercomputers — "pocket supercomputers" — will be interconnected in essentially a cellular structure: You won't have centralized networks, you'll have distributed networks. This really is dictated by the speed of light.

And so I conclude that the most common personal computer of the next era is likely to be a digital cellular phone. It will be as portable as a watch, as personal as a wallet; it'll recognize speech, it'll navigate streets; it'll collect your mail, it'll make transactions. It'll have an Internet address, it'll probably have a Java run-time engine. And it'll be interconnected in a cellular mesh.

So that's the speed of light, and what you can conclude [for information technology] from the speed of light.

1996 DISCOVERY

Student Protesters

Twenty-five years ago [i.e. 1965], protests against computers were quite common. Students in Berkeley carried placards that said: "I am a human being. Do not fold, spindle or mutilate." The students were somewhat justified. Centralized computers were hostile to human life, because human beings are distributed in intelligence. What's happening now is our information systems are acknowledging the distributed nature of individual intelligence.

1990 UPSIDE

Technical Journals

What about technical journals? Is the hard copy pretty much on the way out, and how long do you see this taking?

I'm on the Board of a company called Wave Systems, which creates an encryption/decryption metering tool, so that you can pay the authors of articles for every time they are used. One of the first areas where this tool was employed was in various scientific journals. The chief effect of it was the discovery that the 80:20 rule does not apply to academic journals. Instead it's about a 98:2 rule — about 2% of the articles get all the attention. This result was so scan-

dalous [it seems to have] retarded the p
technology thru the world of academic
the Internet probably distributes as mai
articles as do the journals themselves.

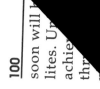

NEE: What about Universal Access: ᴵᵗ ˢ ᵃ ᵖ······ᵖ··
that's governed telephone service.

TV didn't have any universal-access constraints and
within 40 years it managed to get about 98% penetration.
Telephones with their universal-access constraints have
taken 100 years to get 94% penetration. There's a real question about whether the universal-access requirements were
needed, or did much good.

Universal-access constraints today would probably
reduce the penetration of digital video because you will
inhibit the natural development of the industry, the initial
adoption by the aggressive technology adopters in markets.
They're the ones who take the original risks and subsidize
the further development.

I think the market will provide universal access faster
than the FCC. The French did universal access with Minitel,
and they now have about a quarter the amount of computer
power we do and they have no important computer or
semiconductor companies. But they have Minitel, and
everyone has these little dumb terminals in their homes and
every place, and they are very proud of that.

But it really is not comparable to the spread of computers to a third of American homes.

1994 UPSIDE

Universal access is not a legislative right (it took 50
years to achieve this, more or less, in the phone business).
Universal access is a technological and entrepreneurial
achievement. As such, it will occur far sooner without
obtrusive government intervention.

For example, universal access to cable has just been
enacted thru direct-broadcast satellite and universal access

...be achieved globally thru low-earth-orbit satel-
...iversal access to broadband networks will be
...ved most rapidly not thru any new tax or mandate but
...u permitting and encouraging collaboration between
phone companies and cable companies in their own districts
— the very breakthru that is most doggedly opposed by the
incumbent proponents of what they call universal access,
but what in fact is merely a pretext for universal meddling
by the government.

1995 EDUCOM

Uniqueness

Most people make a big mistake in their search for
success: They look for a job. Yet, in a free-enterprise society,
the truly successful are those who <u>create</u> their jobs and
become world champions — whether they work for themselves or for someone else... The same principle applies to
company-owners and employees in the ranks. A successful
worker is constantly searching for ways to improve, to be
unique. That means being a nuisance, asking probing questions, and finding areas ripe for innovation. It means con-
vincing the boss to rewrite the boundaries of your job.

1988 SUCCESS

Workaholics

People who accomplish a lot are driven. One of the
things that really makes me laugh is when I hear about the
"workaholic." Workaholics are what make the world go.
This idea that it's somehow sick to work hard is itself sick...
Entrepreneurs, particularly during the period when they're
launching their companies, have to be somewhat obsessive.
They have to be focusing very intensely on the goal of
making their company serve the interests of the public, and
that does take a certain degree of obsessiveness. And to try
to eliminate that by laughing [at] or attacking workaholics
is, I think, a mistake.

1984 KING

Show me a success in any field, and I'll show you an

obsessive. If your life is "balanced" by languid afternoons at the museum, you cannot develop a new business, break an important story, or make a contribution to the world. The meaning of life does not come from skimming its surface, but from plunging into the depths of a project — from knowing deeply and achieving greatly...

It is the jet-setters with inherited wealth who lack meaning in their lives. Without the discipline of hard work, they fall victim to cocaine, large psychiatric bills, and unscrupulous art-dealers... The ultimate meanings of life come from religious faith. But our task on earth — laboring in service to others — can only be satisfied thru hard and unbalanced work.

1988 SUCCESS

Psychic Epidemic
(by Iggy and the Blue Chips)

Drexel Burnham Lambert's 11th Annual Institutional Research Conference — April 5, 1989; Beverly Hills (CA)

You have often heard the story:

The U.S. is living beyond its means. During the 1980s, we borrowed a trillion dollars from Japan and threw a party. Some people called it an orgy of greed, some a binge of consumption. In the process, we transformed ourselves from the world's largest creditor into the world's largest debtor.

Now the nation faces an appalling Day of Reckoning. One way or another, economists grimly declare, we will have to pay it back — either by a long era of austerity and privation, or by an equally catastrophic inflation. The eventual outcome, say many pundits, is the Coming Great Depression. It's coming any day now. You can tell from the ominous signs of increasing unemployment and economic growth. Get ready, folks, for The Morning After.

According to the experts, one thing is clear: The U.S. is not an investment-grade credit. Both the U.S. Treasury and U.S. importers are issuing "junk" bonds, bearing what by world standards are premium interest rates. The money markets seem to concur with the dismal visions of the economists. Since 1985, for example, the dollar has plunged between 20 and 50% against the currencies of Britain, France, West Germany and Japan. The collapse of the dollar, it is clear to most observers, signals a global recognition of the collapse of American competitiveness.

The sad thing is that most Americans agree: Polls suggest a broad public consensus that the U.S. has lost economic leadership to Japan and Europe. Even our acknowledged achievements in high technology are now said to be in grave jeopardy, unless we begin major government campaigns to catch up to the Japanese in computer memory chips and in high-definition television.

Carl Jung once said that physical ailments can be remedied, but diseases of the mind — psychic epidemics — are beyond all antidotes of doctors or statesmen. Our problem here is a psychic epidemic. The fact is, there is nothing wrong with the U.S. economy that couldn't be solved by turning a few thousand lawyers into engineers, or a few score congressmen into potted plants. But U.S. economists seem to have contracted a dire mental illness — a psychic epidemic — that threatens the prosperity of the world.

The best term for the epidemic is economic hypochondria, or *hypoconomy* for short. The trouble with hypochondria is that it can prompt its victims to summon the doctor. Unnecessary medicine administered to a healthy patient can then produce what is called iatrogenic illness — illness caused by the physician. The problem of the U.S. economy is hypochondria, followed by appeals to the Doctors of Economics and Political Science, Business and Law. The Doctors rush forward and inflict real damage on the economy.

The kind of damage I have in mind is a 50% devaluation of the dollar, to a point far below any reasonable measure of purchasing-power parity. It was achieved by a massive campaign by the U.S. government, supported by the entire establishment of what I call investment-grade Americans.

Investment-grade Americans believed that a cheap dollar would strengthen America. Apparently they did not understand that a cheap dollar not only lowers the price of U.S. goods, it also raises the price of imported commodities and capital goods. It promotes inflation. And it lowers the price of U.S. assets, lowers the value of U.S. profits, and weakens U.S. entrepreneurs competing in the world.

The only firms that are helped are investment-grade firms with huge capacity already in place in the U.S. and around the world. Let's call these firms the Iggies, for

Investment-Grade Institutional Establishment Securities.

Over the past decade, Iggies have created virtually no jobs in the U.S. Totally dominated by Iggies, the European economies have created no jobs in <u>decades</u>. They have been reducing investment as a share of GNP. And all their growth has derived from exports to the U.S. and from government consumption. Only Great Britain, with fewer investment-grade companies than the rest of Europe, has achieved real domestic economic growth. Yet the hypoconomists declare that we are losing ground even to Europe.

The bizarre beliefs of the debt-boom economists would not be especially significant, of course, if they were not highly infectious. Epidemiologists point out, however, that infected hypoconomists are concentrated at the commanding heights of the economy. Iggies are concentrated on Wall Street, in Fortune 500 firms, in leading universities, on congressional staffs, and in the Washington bureaucracy. Iggies get around and spread their diseases. The congressional staff infection, for example, is now rampant in both the U.S. Senate and the House.

From these strongholds in Washington, hypoconomy has wreaked havoc in the media. The media seems convinced that it lives in a Third World economy — drowning in debt, riddled with poverty, and in dire need of more taxes and government regulations.

From the media, the infection has spread to the people. With an exemplary case of hypoconomy, they tell public-opinion pollsters that, while their own personal prospects have never been better, they foresee economic calamity for the country. Thus the circle closes, in an infinite regress of media mirrors, in which healthy and productive Americans see reflections of a wizened, woebegone America — definitely less than investment grade.

Clyde V. Prestowitz, a former Commerce Department official in the Reagan Administration, summed up the symptoms in his recent book *Trading Places*. He argues that, while the U.S. shuffles leveraged buyouts and junk bonds, the Japanese are taking over the world economy. In a glorious fever of fake disease, Prestowitz writes: "The power of the U.S. and the quality of American life is diminishing rapidly in every respect. We are becoming an economic colony of Japan."

The situation may be even worse than he thinks: What would he make of [this] junk-bond conference [being] held in a Japanese-owned hotel?

All these hypoconomists speak the same sickly tones. "Oh, my aching productivity, my atrophied manufacturing," they moan, after the six fastest years of manufacturing productivity growth since World War Two.

"Oh, my swollen national debt," they caterwaul, though U.S. debt, as a share of GNP, is lower than the OECD average and is about to be swamped with revenues from a Social Security tax increase and a rising influx of young immigrants.

"Oh, Lord, my crippled competitiveness, my rampant poverty, my wretched inequality, my slipping standard of living, my awful imbalanced trade."

On and on the pundits prattle, like some runaway national nightmare of a garrulous and hypochondriacal inlaw. But it is merely your friendly neighborhood economist at his usual podium on the networks, perhaps speaking ventriloquially thru your favorite politician or Chrysler executive. The disease has reached such a high profile that many of your best friends may have contracted it, as tough-minded entrepreneurs in non-Iggy firms start talking like Martin Feldstein.

Under such conditions, everyone should practice safe economics: Wear earplugs and smile. When you get home, assume the lotus position, and mumble quietly under your breath, "Supply creates its own demand" — until feelings of peace and serenity flood your mind and your interest rate drops.

As you may have guessed, I believe the American economy is worthy of new investment. But I would hesitate to call it an investment-grade credit. There are problems among the Iggies. They no longer dominate the world economy. But they still dominate the economic statistics.

Consider the issue of productivity. Whenever General Motors increases its output of cars or USX raises its output of ingots and Xes, the increment gets counted. The unit sales can be compared to previous units, and added to GNP and productivity growth. Since GM drastically reduced employment, its measured productivity rose still faster.

Like many Iggies with good government contracts, GM also benefited from trade quotas, which imposed a huge unmentioned burden on the economy. In the accounts of the hypoconomists, these costs are absent, [and GM becomes] an unalloyed source of productivity growth.

But how can you measure the output of a cellular phone or a creator of cellular phone systems? How do you gauge the output of cable-TV systems that turn the television from a lowest-common-denominator broadcast medium into a cornucopia of programs for a variety of tastes? How do you capture the investment and output of a software firm?

If you merely measure their revenues, you miss <u>most</u> of their <u>real</u> contribution to the economy and <u>all</u> their <u>potential</u> contributions. Not only are these new products worthwhile in themselves but they also enhance the value of the products around them — television sets, automobiles, and computers.

The more creative the economy — the more new goods and services and the more new companies — the less GNP and productivity data will measure growth. The investment-grade firms are mostly investment grade because their products are familiar, and their value easily measurable, and the capital equipment they use has a demonstrable relationship to output.

Iggy collateral is all comprehensible, even to Iggy bankers.

But new and creative smaller firms offer the unmeasurable collateral of new products, new ideas, new energies, new visions. In Iggy circles, these intangibles are known as "junk."

A further flaw of the statistics is that Iggy product-lines are mostly mature enough so that prices do not drop. Largely because of quotas, U.S. automobile prices are still drifting upward. But fast-growing companies, in general, are aggressive price-<u>cutters</u>. In GNP and productivity data, declining prices often signify declining output and productivity. Yet, in the most dynamic parts of the economy, prices drop precipitously (or else functionality rises, which is the same thing).

Year after year, all the fastest growing companies are radically improving functionality and lowering prices. Very few of these quality improvements make it into the GNP, inflation and productivity data. Until 1985, for example, the Bureau of Economic Analysis assumed no decline in the price of computing over the previous 20 years — a period when the cost of a [typical] computer function dropped more than 100,000-fold.

Today, new forms of software are the most important and productive capital in the economy. Software is almost entirely a non-Iggy or junk product. It is also mostly absent from investment data.

Apart from the real and disastrous problems of the U.S. educational system, the social complaints about the U.S. are also mostly bogus. The persistent claims of a surge of poverty and inequality — supported by the usual citations of relative incomes in the bottom and top fifths of American families — fail to note a crucial unknown fact. The top fifth contains 28% more persons and supplied 30% of the nation's total of weeks worked. The bottom fifth provided only 8% of the weeks worked. In proportion to work effort, the top fifth of families earned only twice as much as the bottom fifth.

The U.S. economic performance becomes particularly impressive when compared with Japan's. Despite the huge initial lead, U.S. industrial production during the 1980s has grown 19% faster than Japan's.

By most economic measures, the bottom fifth of U.S. families live better than the average of Japanese families. The U.S. bottom-fifth families mostly own their own homes. U.S. bottom-fifth families have twice the housing space of average Japanese families and spend a far smaller income-share on housing. U.S. poor families have more cars, TVs, toilets and other amenities than average Japanese families. According to a Census study, moreover, the bottom fifth of U.S. families actually spend three times as much money as they report as income.

The hypoconomists, however, would ponder such figures and treat them as yet more evidence for their forlorn faith in catastrophe. The U.S. poor live so well compared to the prosperous Japanese [runs the hypoconomic chain of logic] because the Japanese save and invest in the future and study for it. While the U.S. lives high on the hog and allows its economic leadership to slip away, these pundits say, the Japanese have launched a tsunamic wave of technological advance and productivity growth that is sweeping American industry aside.

Let us grant that the Japanese have made impressive gains in technology, particularly in manufacturing. But the litany of the hypoconomists is false. As well as the Japanese have done in relation to the rest of the world, they may actually have been losing ground to Americans during the 1980s, not only in industrial production but also in the information technologies so stressed by Prestowitz and others.

Total U.S. electronic production, estimated at nearly $200 billion in 1988, was about 80% higher than Japan's and more than all of Asia's put together. The Japanese have been gaining market-share during the 1980s and gained again in 1988. However, all the Japanese gains in share over the past four years [i.e. 1985-88] are attributable to the 90% rise in the value of the yen. Most of their gain in 1988 came from a 13% yen-appreciation during that year.

With any adjustment for currency gyrations, the U.S. has probably <u>gained</u> share in real electronic hardware since 1984.

In computers, for example, U.S. firms still hold 70% of the world market. In the all-important realm of <u>using</u> computers, the U.S. has an installed base of computer power six times larger than Japan's, and three times larger even on a per-capita basis...

But these numbers may understate U.S. technological gains and their promise for the future. Throughout the 1980s, value added in information technology has steadily shifted toward software and design. According to an estimate by *The Economist*, the U.S. share of world software markets, between 1978 and 1985, rose from under two-thirds to over three-quarters. Since 1985, all indications are that the U.S. lead has widened... Software is increasingly crucial to leadership in information technology. Even in telecommunications, 80% of the value added now comes in software.

In sum, the U.S. is focused on software and small computers at the very time the global information markets are moving toward software and small computers. Even in semiconductors — which Prestowitz and other hypoconomists give up as nearly a lost cause — the U.S. has been gaining share, adjusted for the currency changes. Except for the semiconductor trade agreement that doubled the value of Japanese memory output, the U.S. would have held share in 1988. In the most creative domains of custom devices and computer-aided engineering, the U.S. maintains a large lead.

Now the alarmists are crying out against a new Japanese threat: High-Definition Television. Unless we mobilize the U.S. government, and all the leading Iggies in the subsidized cartel, to catch up with Japan in HDTV, all will be lost.

The fact is: HDTV will be obsolete by the time it is introduced. In technological terms, television is already dead. Of course, its corpse will remain for a decade or so more, stinking up the living rooms of America. But, for video processing and entertainment, HDTV will come online at the very time that the whole TV industry is about to be blown away by computers.

With a fourfold rise in resolution, HDTV is said to be a revolution. It is a revolution only in comparison with the usual sluggish pace of television technology, which takes a step ahead every 25 years or so and calls it a revolution. Over the last 25 years, computer technology, centered in the U.S., has improved not fourfold but approximately 230 thousandfold.

American computer technology still is moving thousands of times faster than Japanese television technology. HDTV will still be chiefly an analog kludge for couch potatoes; the specifications of its signal will all be optimized for over-the-air and direct-broadcast. By the time it comes to market, the U.S. will be producing entirely digital solid-state computers linked to fiber-optic cables or to super new forms of optical disc. These systems will yield "perfect pictures every time."

Telecomputers will be cheaper to build than TVs and they will also allow the full interactive participation of the viewers. Thru their computer screens, people will be able to fly planes and visit foreign countries and play full-motion movies and connect to digital databases of information and entertainment — anywhere in the world, at any time. Such telecomputers, which can be built today, will leave the television industry in the dust.

The only hope for Japanese HDTV is a massive collaboration between the Iggy broadcasters and the U.S. government to save the technology for Japan, the networks, and other broadcast-dependent interests. Otherwise, the Iggies in the TV industry won't know what has hit them. They cannot even imagine a technology that improves several thousandfold every decade.

A dominant position on the frontiers of information technology might not make the U.S. an investment-grade credit — [not when] Iggies [continue to insist on] a collateral in big machines and tangible and familiar products. But it gives the U.S. the lead in the most critical source of value in the new world economy, an economy of ideas and human capital.

The main problem of the hypoconomists is that, deep down, they are mercantilists. They cannot imagine U.S. gains in competitiveness and market-share that are not accompanied by gains in trade.

But a truly healthy and innovative economy, full of unpredictable junk like the U.S., attracts capital from around the world. As long as the rest of the world suffers capital flight and emigration to the U.S., the U.S. will necessarily run a trade deficit. That's just a necessary cost of running the most healthy and competitive economy in the world.

Of course, that makes a lot of Iggies and economists feel sick.

Money, Morals And The Merger

Capitalism: How Faith Becomes

Capitalism [is] the system of giving. It's the system whereby investors give of their wealth and work without a predetermined return. It's a system that's open to the future, that doesn't predetermine results.

In a socialist plan, unless you know the results, you don't launch the project — and that is sterile, because all new knowledge comes from striking out into the unknown. Capitalism depends on striking out into the unknown, whether new technologies, or new modes of operation [or] new products. All of [these potential gains] are dependent on facing risk and having faith in the future...

Capitalism is the system of social justice — the system in which the good fortune of others is also your own, because you know that the success of others expands the market for your goods in the ever enriching spirals of economic creativity and growth.

So capitalism is the system of social justice.

1981 RATHER

Capitalism: Opposite Of Greed

[H]ow many economists have actually studied the behavior of entrepreneurs? If they did, they'd discover that entrepreneurs work harder than anyone else in general, and they have to learn more so they [also] study harder. Entrepreneurs have to raise money and build teams, so they have to cooperate, and then they have to respond to the needs of other people. In a capitalist system, you can't succeed without responding to the needs of other people. Building a company means forgoing consumption in order to pursue long-term goals.

So the actual behavior of the central figure of capitalism — the entrepreneur — is completely contrary to the greed models that everybody exalts...

Monetary gain <u>should</u> be a prime goal. It's just that monetary gain doesn't mean selfishness; it means the ability to achieve your goals. It means the ability to use your knowledge and insight to create more wealth thru yet greater service to the public.

Seeking profit doesn't mean selfish or greedy pursuits. Profit is really an index of the service being performed for others by a company. A profit is the difference between what inputs cost the company and what they are worth to somebody else. It's the index of the altruism of the process.

[I]mproving your service to others [is why] a business thrives. And it doesn't thrive by improving the service to the entrepreneur. As soon as the entrepreneur begins feeding on his company, you want to sell [that company's stock]. As soon as you see the entrepreneur on some kind of ego trip, you better get worried because that is just deadly to a successful enterprise.

It's always got to be oriented toward your customer, and toward your collaborators, and toward your role in service to the world. If you're on some sort of ego trip, you're just going to lose.

Everybody knows a few monsters who make good, but their making good is usually a result of their inspired knowledge of the marketplace and the technology. It's not the result of their voracity or something [of that sort] — those are usually <u>obstacles</u> to success.

The most greedy people [are those] who want something they haven't earned, who want wealth they haven't produced. Greed leads people to turn to government. Greed leads "as by an invisible hand" to socialism, not to capitalism. The successful capitalists, the capitalists who make capitalism thrive — and you can always have vicious people in any business — are the ones who give far more than they get.

Robert Noyce was a rich man, but his contribution to

the economy was immeasurable — at least a trillion dollars worth of U.S. assets are attributed to his contribution and to a small group of colleagues. They haven't received, in return, an infinitesimal portion of what they have given to the country. I think that entrepreneurs, in general, give comparatively more than they ever get back.

1990 UPSIDE

Capitalism: Versus Its Attackers

People on the radio this morning were all convinced that [the 1980s were] only a revel of greed. They constantly referred to the homeless as sort of typical harvest of capitalism. You know, it is a real question, a real enigma of capitalism — the distribution of wealth it creates. I mean, why does Harry Helmsley have a billion dollars while Harry Homeless sits on a rug on a steam grate?

All my interlocutors this morning were sure that it was because Harry Helmsley was so greedy — the greed of the capitalist causing the poverty of the homeless. In other words, theirs was the fundamental belief that wealth causes poverty.

That's really how you can sum up the theory of the Left, this belief that wealth essentially comes from stealing. It's a very popular position, both at prisons and at Harvard, that wealth essentially comes from stealing. Intellectuals want to believe it [so they can turn around and] disparage their competitive intellectual class, the entrepreneurs — and the people in prison want to believe it because it exonerates their own crimes.

But true greed is the desire for unearned benefits, and Harry Homeless...wants to live better than most of the people throughout the history of the world without giving anything whatsoever back to society. This is the very epitome of greed.

[By contrast] what the entrepreneur does is constantly give back to his society — that's his fundamental principle. His companies survive and prosper to the extent that they respond imaginatively to the needs of others. That's how an entrepreneur prospers.

Greed leads by an invisible hand to an ever-growing

welfare state — because the greedy person's best way to assure unearned benefits is to turn to government and have government steal from others to gratify his greed. Greed also leads, by an invisible hand, from the ever-growing welfare state to socialism.

But the entrepreneur really has to be altruistic in his orientation. The entrepreneur has to also understand the needs of others. He has to forego his own appetites to save — foregoing consumption, that's what saving is. He has to collaborate with others. He has to reinvest. And "investment" is another term for giving; When you invest you give your resources to others and you trust them to preserve or increase the value.

1994 RECAP

The idea...that Bill Gates is greedy while Harry Homeless is somehow altruistic is just complete nonsense. In proportion to their income and opportunity, entrepreneurs spend less [on themselves] than any elite in the history of the world. It's actually Harry Homeless who is greedy, in a real sense, because he wants to live better than most of the people on the face of the Earth [have] for most of human history — without giving anything whatsoever back to his society. He wants <u>totally</u> unearned wealth and income. He wants to occupy the most valuable real estate...from the centers of Manhattan to the beaches of Santa Monica — and receive completely unearned wealth. And...that is the nature of avarice — the desire for wealth that you haven't earned.

1993 BIONOMICS

Capitalism: Versus Its Defenders

The great enigma of capitalism has really been the distribution of income, and most of the hostility to capitalism has derived from the assumption that the driving force of capitalist growth is somehow greed. Even Adam Smith saw capitalism as essentially driven by greed. He depicts entrepreneurs as predatory and vicious people who, if they ever get together, necessarily conspire against the public. I mean, Adam Smith has paragraphs of vitriol directed against "men in trade." English intellectuals always are disdainful of "men in trade."

1993 BIONOMICS

Because of the centrality of Adam Smith and free-market economic theory, it is largely supposed that capitalism is based on selfishness and that this leads us to prosperity "as by an invisible hand." Some view capitalism as a Faustian pact — a deal with the devil — in which we gain wealth in exchange for giving in to the sin of avarice.

So it has led to the belief that capitalism is somehow based on sin [which, in turn, leads to a] profound ambivalence about capitalism: Being productive is somehow seen as worship of mammon.

I think [such a framework] completely misunderstands the dynamic of enterprise. Business investments are the most productive <u>charitable</u> gifts in any economy. Businessmen succeed by collaborating with others and by serving others. I think this is the heart of capitalism. It's not based on taking, it's based on giving. It is tantamount to gifts which are actually <u>good</u> for their recipients...

The success of capitalism is a great triumph of Christian virtue. Capitalism is the opposite of greed. Greed is the desire for unearned benefits. Greed is a refusal to serve others. Greed leads to demands on government to give unearned goods. Greed leads to an ever-expanding welfare state. It leads to socialism.

1994 ACTON

Creative Destruction

Conventional economics, with its "partial equilibrium" models — "holding all things constant" that never stay constant; with its usual Keynesian bent; with its elaborate supply-and-demand curves forever adjusting to equilibrium; with its very definition as "the science of allocation of scarce resources" — utterly fails to understand the entrepreneur. He does not adjust to an equilibrium, he creates and destroys equilibria. He throws the world into disequilibrium, creating new markets and destroying obsolete ones, in an act which [Joseph] Schumpeter called "creative destruction." He does not "allocate scarce resources" in a world of shrinking options, he creates <u>new</u> resources, hitherto unimagined, that expand the options for the entire human race. His offerings are gifts which, if accepted, will be reciprocated throughout the world in abundance.

1988 E-FORUM

How can an economic system which celebrates "creative destruction" create a stable family life?

Some things don't change, other things have to change. Essential family values, the differences between men and women, are permanent — they're part of our endowment given by God and by nature. That's fundamental and unchangeable. And if we imagine that we can overcome sex roles summarily thru a political revolution, we will be deeply disappointed. Families will break down, and when families break down, enterprise dies.

But some things have to change, and [have done so] thru all human history. Technology is the force of human imagination, and it's limitless in its dimensions and prospects. And, as these technologies improve, we have to discipline them and channel them to serve the higher values of a free society under God.

This is the balance, the dynamic tension, of a creative and productive society: The stability of family releases heroes to master the challenges of a global economy — and that's the crux of the spirit of enterprise.

1988 HILLSDALE

The value of a nation's products ultimately derives from the values upheld by the nation's citizens. And if those values are corrupted or degraded in one way or another, ultimately the foundations of production and wealth are destroyed. So I think all these areas really are a Unity, and theology <u>is</u> at the pinnacle of this unified perspective on men, machines, families, and the very luminosity of life.

1989 MONITOR

Entrepreneurship: Basics

Between 1978 and 1983, the number of new business starts rose from 270,000 to almost 630,000... Venture capital rose by a factor of 200 from the average between 1970 and '77. There are 60% more companies listed over-the-counter on the stock exchange — a tremendous upsurge of new technologies. The United States was applying high technology 50% faster than either Europe or Japan. There were 5,000 new software companies emerged during this period.

The first thing an entrepreneur has to do is be thrifty: He has to forego consumption in order to pursue long-term goals — in other words, he has to reject his own immediate greedy desires, in order to invest his work and his wealth in some project that may or may not succeed — some uncertain project... He has to begin by suppressing his own desires in order to respond to the needs of <u>others</u>.

And I don't think that's "greedy." I think greedy people chiefly want something that isn't coming to them. They want comfort and security. And they usually turn to government to give it to 'em...

Entrepreneurs do produce real value that makes the economy grow. Now of course there's [also] a lot of junk produced, but capitalism allows the junk to be rejected and companies that continue to produce it to fail. In a socialist system, the junk's all supported by the government and they never fail. The government goes on forever and continues to force the people to celebrate the junk. capitalism <u>does</u> have a system for rejecting bad products and bad services...

Entrepreneurship is mostly financed by disposable personal savings. That's the most important [source]. Even in Silicon Valley, high-technology companies — 90% of them — start with disposable personal savings, from the owner or his uncle or somebody who knows them. It's personal savings mostly, and not the money in insurance companies and pension funds, although they do make a contribution.

1984 KING

Gaining Responsibly

While researching *Wealth And Poverty*, I wanted to know why some people come from nowhere and succeed brilliantly, and others seem to lose their way. So I talked to scores of criminals in prisons. Nearly all of them had the same theories of economic success.

All wealth, they said, comes from stealing: Successful Italian restaurants are fronts for the Mafia; successful actresses, models and businesswomen are all really whores. Oil tycoon John D. Rockefeller, one man assured me, made his fortune as a member of the Jesse James gang, and founded Standard Oil as a front. Everyone steals. My informants were merely unlucky enough to get caught.

Okay, they admitted, wealth doesn't <u>always</u> come from stealing. Sometimes it comes from luck. People hit the lottery, or get born with talent, like Michael Jordan or Bill Cosby.

To sum up: Succeed or fail, you are not really responsible for your own life. So, obviously, to create something thru hard work is futile.

I went back to Harvard, my alma mater, to be a guest lecturer, and [to] learn more about success and failure. Wealth, the intellectuals told me, comes from stealing: Businessmen succeed by exploiting workers, polluting the environment, and selling shoddy goods for high prices. John D. Rockefeller was a "robber baron" who got rich by monopolizing oil. (Actually, Rockefeller got rich by dropping the price of oil 90%, making it a feasible fuel for cars.)

Sociologist Christopher Jencks (then at Harvard) declared that the only source of wealth was luck — being at the right place at the right time. Social scientists tell us that whether we succeed or fail, steal or live honestly, is determined by how "society" conditions us to act. We are not responsible for our own lives.

Like the prisoners, the Cambridge set sneers at those who plan, risk, set goals, and gain by serving others — as business requires. While the crooks admire the big crime bosses, professors and students lionize tyrants like Fidel Castro (who visited Harvard and wowed the campus with his denunciations of business and enterprise). Dons and dictators make others serve <u>them</u>.

1988 SUCCESS

Giving Responsibly

Giving is difficult. The chief fallacy of socialism is the idea that giving is easy: You just take from one person and give to the other to the benefit the community. But all of us know how hard it is to give without hurting. We encounter this problem all the time with our children, like during the holiday season. It's <u>hard</u> to give, and it takes an understanding of others to give successfully.

The true foundation of capitalist success is that it is <u>productive</u> giving, an investment that's a truly productive gift. It truly responds to the needs of others and truly helps others. This is really the heart of capitalist success.

1994 RECAP

It's easy to simply spend money on someone — and hurt their morale and future. In most cases, the investments of businesses are better charity than the official charities because an investment depends on the recipient also serving others. A charitable gift does not demand anything from its recipient; the recipient merely uses the gift — [but] capitalism results in ever-widening circles of service to others.

1994 ACTON

That's what investment is: Giving your money to other people, in a way that actually <u>helps</u> other people — unlike most charity, which actually debauches the moral fiber of its recipients — as most of us know when we think of how we're going to reward our children.

1993 BIONOMICS

Immigration: Charity plus Realism

[T]he thing that puts you at odds with much of populist thought in America today is that you say this genius would not flourish in this country without immigration. For people who didn't read [your 12/18/95 *Wall Street Journal* op-ed], could you basically recap your theory?

All of America's great achievements have come from immigration. We initially were a nation of immigrants, of course. That was the initial genius of America — that we received people fleeing persecution and oppression in Europe and elsewhere, who found a land of opportunities, new frontiers, in the United States.

This has been true throughout our history. New waves of immigrants have resulted in new upsurges of income, productivity, innovation and achievement. The spearheads of this achievement have always been this "genius class," as I roughly describe it. I do believe that genius is 90% perspiration. But it does have a genetic content as well. This is a class of people who are just enormously more productive than others, and they tend to go where they're welcomed, and stay where they're well-treated.

America has been their land of opportunity for most of the past century. Receiving these immigrants during the Second World War made possible the Manhattan Project, which produced the atomic bomb, which ended the war successfully and then allowed us to continue in the lead in the arms race. This was critical, because it was almost entirely immigrants who created the atomic bomb, the hydrogen bomb, the intercontinental-missile program, the space program. All were heavily fueled by immigration and the geniuses who emigrated to our shores.

Is it safe to say that the development of all these projects would not have occurred at all, were it not for immigration?

Yes. I don't think we could have had the Manhattan Project. The Manhattan Project was an achievement of European immigrants, a lot of them Jewish, who brought their genius to the United States and put together the bomb. There were some Americans, but mostly in relatively lesser roles.

Then, later, all our technologies fed on this input from outsiders — particularly the microchip, which is really the heart of the present, American global leadership.

George, longer than anyone I can recall (aside from those in the business directly), you have been touting

the relevance and importance of the computer to America's future. In your piece in the *Journal* you cite some of the key inventors of the microchip, developers of that technology, as also being immigrants.

The company that really founded the microchip industry in the United States, as the microprocessor industry evolved into the personal-computer industry, was Fairchild Semiconductor. When the parent company tried to control it too closely, the key people spun off and became Intel Corporation. The group at Fairchild and Intel were led by Gordon Moore and Robert Noyce, both of whom were American geniuses and inventors. But most of the other people at Intel, or at least half of the other major contributors, were immigrants.

Andrew Grove fled thru a field across the Hungarian border in 1956, barely escaping the Russian tanks. [Early] on in his career, he ran a couple of crucial projects at Intel that made them dominant in MOS technology — metal oxide semiconductor technology — which is really the foundation of the whole industry.

In every major semiconductor company, and every major semiconductor project, between a third and two-thirds of key contributors are immigrants. Americans have just not focused on these hard-core engineering skills.

But is that a lack of genius indigenous to America?

I think it's the result of a variety of things. In software, which entails similar degrees of genius, the numbers are not so high: Probably 10 to 15% of the major contributors to America's software predominance are immigrants. But they are critical contributors. It's not this overwhelming phenomenon that one discovers in microchips.

But both of them were absolutely critical to the personal-computer industry, which, in turn, is the driving force of American economic growth and the spearhead of world economic growth today...

Yet you still have, on the American political scene, this anti-immigration sentiment. And many of the people who are showing some moderate signs of success [by]

attacking this loss of manufacturing-sector jobs are conservatives. (Perot's slightly conservative on balance, you'd have to say, although he made his money in computers.) Buchanan is turning into a David Bonior in this area, when it comes to industrialized job-loss.

And people believe it. When they read you saying this, they're going to scratch their heads, because there are a tremendous number of citizens who believe we're losing jobs left and right; that the country is going south fast; and that we've got to build a wall around America. Yet here you are saying the worst thing we could possibly do is limit immigration.

Illegal aliens who come in and are prohibited from having employment, but mandated to receive welfare, are a problem — [actually it's] the welfare state that's the problem. We have a welfare state mandated to reach out to immigrants and induce them to take advantage of all the benefits.

You've been talking about this on your program. The welfare state is now an "enterprise," and it's "reaching out" to immigrants. The result is that today's illegal aliens and immigrants are being captured by the welfare state more rapidly than previous immigrant groups. And this is very destructive, because welfare destroys everybody it touches.

There's a rising tide of people who believe that the only way to fix this is to stop all immigration.

Rush, it makes no sense. I don't think it's very valuable to stop Mexicans from coming to the United States and doing the jobs they mostly do. *National Review* magazine, on the basis of alarms about illegal immigration, advocates a moratorium on all immigration, which would be incredibly destructive. It would mean that lots of high-technology companies just couldn't operate in the United States.

Let's construct a hypothesis here. There's a wall built around America: No immigration. We have embarked on a course of acculturating those who are here, who have

not yet learned Americanism. That's the strategy: Until
we can acculturate those who are here, we need to shut
down. Are you suggesting that, if this situation
occurred, there is not somehow an ability here to
produce the genius amongst those who live in the
contiguous 48 plus Alaska and Hawaii to continue this
high-tech revolution?

For certain key jobs and key inventive roles, there are
just a very few people in the world capable of performing
them. The numbers are small, and that small number tends
to be distributed all around the world.

So any company that wants to be absolutely on the
leading edge, to get the best people in every field working
together to produce some new product — whether it's a
new kind of fiber-optic application for a broadband Internet, or whether it's a new kind of digital disk, or a new
Internet computer, or whatever it is — those people [and
their companies] have to command the best in all these
fields.

If they can't get the best people to come to the United
States, they have to go to the best people. That's just a fact
of life.

And it's not new. It was true about Henry Ford, when
he was starting Ford Motor Company. Ford was the
leading-edge company in the world economy, and he "imported" a whole bunch of people from Scotland, England
and Germany to help him build his cars. Key advances in
Ford Motor Company were attributable to immigrants.

When you are leading-edge, you are effectively the
spearhead for the entire planetary economy — [so] you've
got to get the best, wherever they are.

1996 LIMBAUGH

Internet: And Porn

Saying that the Internet is somehow a prime source of
pornography is ridiculous. When you go to every hotel
room [and] about half the films are pornographic, and [can
walk into] any convenience store...pornography in various
forms is everywhere available. But it's a tiny, tiny share of

the total hosts on the Internet and to use it as a pretext for regulating the Internet is quite ridiculous, I believe.

1997 CATO

Life Before/During/After Television

If we think of life <u>before</u> television as the age of the amateur (with social life focused on the family piano, on amateur theater groups, on sandlot baseball games), and life <u>during</u> television as the age of the professional (with social life organized around boob-tube performances by millionaire actors, comedians, athletes and politicians), how should we think about the quality of life <u>after</u> television? Will it help us [move] back to the idyllic past of the amateur? Or will it be better than our past as well as our present?

I think it will be better. I think the culture will take a form more resembling the book culture than the TV culture. There are 55,000 books published in the United States every year. There's a religious book market as big as the trade book market, and each of those markets amount to about $2.5 billion. There are a huge number of successful technical books and career books, and there's a wide diversity of literature.

I think the book market is a much better reflection of American culture than the TV market, which I think is a perversion of American culture. In general, the interactive media culture will resemble book culture and literacy culture more than it will the current mass culture.

You know, the people who produce mass culture are the ultimate elitists. I've often debated with them, and they'll say to me: "You don't understand, George, the reason that the boob tube is an idiot box is that people really <u>are</u> boobs. We've done market research. We know they're boobs."

Well, I think they just don't understand the business. Of course, confronted with the boob tube, we're <u>all</u> boobs. When I get into a hotel room late at night and start clicking thru channels, I get distracted by the shocks and sensations just as anyone else would.

The critical fact is that a mass medium is no good whatsoever at conveying educated ideas; if it happens to convey a sophisticated idea, that's just an accident.

I think the French were perfectly right in trying to exclude U.S. television programs, because for the most part such programs are the ultimate realization of mass taste, and they are depraved and destructive. They are deeply destructive to American society, particularly to any effort to educate anyone in it. And yet the schools increasingly try to simulate the TV culture, which is their worst betrayal!

Simulate TV culture in what way?

By having students read dumb books that seem to be simulations of TV sensibility. By avoiding anything difficult. By trying to pander to the kids, to entertain them rather than teach them...

Have the 55,000 trade books published last year in the United States produced a better general culture? Or has the culture been affected by the small number of books — and movies and television shows — that were hyped into bestsellerdom?

I think that America is still the world's leading economy and it produces a tremendous amount of art and literature that elude the elite media and elite institutions and elite critical vessels. If American culture were really summed up by TV culture, there would be no leading software company, no world-leading scientific/educational enterprise, no globally ascendant computing industry. Bioengineering wouldn't be centered in the United States, and so forth.

So I really don't think this elite mass culture — and I believe it is elitist, contrived by elites to pander to mass prurience and anxiety — can generate anything worthwhile, and I don't think it does. The actual success of the United States does not stem from what the media generally treat — in other words, phenomena like the personal computer are incomparably more important than phenomena like Madonna.

1994 EDUCOM

In network TV, it takes increasing amounts of advertising to support less and less substance and content. They really are gripped by this sort of lowest-common-denominator market. And, in appealing to the lowest common denominator, they've got to target prurient interests and morbid fears and anxieties that we essentially have in common as a mass market — all of us. They get the illusion that people are that way...

And I think movie people have the same kind of illusion. They live in this world of mass media, which leads them to a deep cynicism toward people's tastes and curiosity and intellectual capabilities.

For a long time, people have said you can never go broke underestimating the intelligence of the American people. Well, I'm saying that creators of entertainment and movies and other amusements are going to start going broke underestimating the intelligence of the American people. Particularly the upscale markets where all the new tastes are formed and developed — these are quite sophisticated and exacting markets, and I don't think Hollywood understands them or addresses them...

What about that shared experience? What about the idea that we go to the water cooler and we talk about that episode of *Roseanne* last night?

I don't know. I think there is a big exaggeration of that. As a matter of fact, it's this stultifying TV experience that separates us as a nation, that sort of leaves us in a stupor on the couch and turns us into potatoes.

On the other hand, I think the computer creates really active communities. On a computer bulletin board, you have intimate exchanges with all sorts of people with common interests around the world. It greatly enhances communication and connection and sociabiliy and socialization. It's TV that, almost by definition, stifles [those], or tries to.

So I just don't accept any of the premises of that question. I think TV was great in the beginning, but it has had its day, and it's now fetid.

1994 REPORTER

As for the descendant of television, the dominant traffic of the future will be store-and-forward transmission of digital data among millions of telecomputers. These machines will be capable of summoning or sending films and files, news stories and clips, courses and catalogues anywhere in the world. The same couch potatoes who, in the absence of a better choice, now settle for a *Donahue* show on lesbian nuns or for a sanguinary stew of cops and prostitutes, will turn to favorite films or local sports or career-education. Many of the same people who now sink into a passive stupor before the tube will find themselves using teleputers to travel around the world, taking courses, conducting transactions, and shaping their own programs and software.

1993 ECONOMIST

Millennial Key

The key to understanding the promise of the 21st Century — to overcoming all the superstition which has afflicted this century, and resulted in a long stream of wars and holocausts and terror — is the understanding that the good fortune of others is also your own: Capitalism depends on the success of others.

And, above all, the largest "unserved market" is always the poor people. So capitalism depends on the prosperity of the poor. It depends on serving others.

Lots of people don't like to serve others; they think it's below them to serve others. They regard their own self-expression as the prime value. Even if other people don't want their art or their unwanted produce or their bureaucratic plans, they insist on imposing them on others.

[Such] self-interest leads not to an evermore prosperous society [but] leads, as by an invisible hand, to an ever-growing welfare state: If you're truly self-interested, you turn to government to give you what you have not earned by your own service of other people — [service which would be] defined by the voluntary choices of other people in the marketplace...

Capitalism accepts the judgment of others, and thus is the system where people thrive by serving others. That's the crucial source of the wealth that gathers here, and it's the crucial fact that makes the unlimited horizons of the 21st Century so benign.

1997 TCSM-CONF

People, Companies And Strategy

Apple Computer Corp.

Apple...really should move down market. I know it is not a popular view in Cupertino [but] Apple should understand that it is largely a software company. It should focus on providing a wide array of critical software functions that will be necessary to move toward the telecomputer.

Apple is very well situated to be a pioneering firm in this era. It is oriented toward image-processing. It commands the adherence of lots of hackers and software-producers and multimedia artists. All are oriented toward Apple, and that is its greatest asset.

Whether the box has a 68000-family processor in it, or is even manufactured by Apple, is less important than making sure it maintains this leadership in user-friendly image-processing software and multimedia capabilities that will be so important in the coming era. At the high end, Apple should be oriented toward retaining the loyalty of this large community of multimedia software producers.

At the low end, it should be developing machines like Fujitsu has. Fujitsu has produced a cheap Mac-like box — inasmuch as it's bit-mapped and has a very vivid high-resolution display that rivets your attention. I think Apple has got to be ready to compete in the low end and tend to a new generation of hackers and multimedia artists who are emerging now in the schools and who are increasingly turning away from Apple.

KARLGAARD: Apple's big advantage is that people say they love their Macs.

They should take advantage of that. They shouldn't gouge these people who love them. They should have let companies do Mac-compatible machines to begin with — they should really encourage that. I think they are.

1990 UPSIDE

Apple: Plus Microsoft

LIMBAUGH: What does this do for Apple?

Well, it helps Apple in the short run. But I think it's too bad that [Larry] Ellison and Sun [Microsystems] both failed to purchase Apple and transform it into an effective [force]. They both announced it, but I'm afraid Gates showed he could outmaneuver those two.

Yeah, but Gates offers so much less, in terms of dollars, than those two. They were offering to buy the whole company; he's got $150 million invested, but he can't vote any of it.

It's now $250 [million], and they've traded all their software licenses, and they've agreed to run the Microsoft browser as the default browser on Apple. They've really turned Apple into a Microsoft lapdog — at the very moment that Ellison joins the Apple board! From that point of view, it's really an amazing coup that [Bill Gates] has pulled off.

Well, if you were an Apple user and an excited [one] — let's say you like the platform —

I am!

Okay, well, what do you think now? Forget for a second, George, what you think is gonna happen with the network computer. Let's say you like your Apple and you hope that it survives and you hope that it grows. Is there any chance of that now?

There's some chance that Rhapsody — the new Apple operating system — will be a success. And I think they can nurse it along as a kind of a pseudo-competitor in operating systems to Microsoft. But the real action is the transformation of the entire industry that's underway thru Java.

1997 LIMBAUGH

Ascend Communications

Some 85% of its revenues come from its MAX 400X product that allows ISPs and Intranets to accommodate some 96 ISDN lines and "bond" groups of them, with compression, into 512 kilobit-a-second channels. An expanded product is coming soon called TNT. Competition has just arrived from Cisco, which is launching a rival machine called the 5200 that duplicates most of the MAX features.

Almost all this equipment is based on complementing the telco monopolies, linking analog modems or complex and expensive narrowband ISDN to even more costly telco T-1s. It is oriented to a lobbied and regulated world of no competition.

But competition is breaking out all over and regulation is being radically changed. Who will want 128 kilobits per second when cheaper links at 1.1-to-2 megabits per second will be available from Tut and others? Yet Ascend's market cap is nearly $6 billion or close to 212 times sales that reached a $500 million run-rate in the last quarter...

1996 NEWSLETTER

AT&T (plus 3DO)

AT&T has been excessively preoccupied with games. There's been this preoccupation with TV and games on the assumption that those are really popular, mass markets — [while] the PC is a specialized business and elite tool. Despite it being a computer company, AT&T has preoccupied itself too much with Sega, 3DO, Nintendo and all those other companies it has had affiliations with over the last couple years. And that's 3DO's big error as well. They want to be a peripheral to the TV rather than the computer. They may well have to correct that mistake before they succeed. Just think: 3DO could have been Creative Labs.

1994 UPSIDE

Bandwidth

As Andy Grove says, infinite processing power will get you only so far with limited bandwidth. The key to the next generation of computer development is coupling the personal computer with broadband networks.

Today the personal computer is crippled by its need to devote most of its MIPS, or a large portion of them, to compressing and decompressing any image that it urges. Thus teleconferencing, for example, and video telephones are so drastically unsatisfactory because all the computer MIPs are devoted to compressing and decompressing, rather than to real computer functions.

Once the PC is connected to broadband networks, it will really ascend to its dominant level in homes as well as offices. And that will be the crucial opportunity for educational materials as well.

1994 EDUCOM

Banks

Banks are ultimately an information system and — as Warren Brookes put it in his last major article — any information system can effectively become a bank, including your laptop computer. This is increasingly becoming evident [and it] does pose a real threat of "disintermediation" for banks. It's already happening. All the various functions of banks are now being unbundled in various ways: From mutual funds to real estate, a whole array of banking functions are all being disintermediated and increasingly performed by individuals. And this process will continue as the Internet evolves into the new central nervous system of a new global economy.

1997 CATO

Books and Chips

Publishing books and making chips is roughly analogous: The value of each is not in the material but in the intellectual content.

Printing, in the early days of that technology, was the

highest technology in the world. It transformed the world's economy and began much as semiconductor technology began — with the publishing of a few commodities: Bibles, manuals, whatever they were. As printing became a routine process and widespread around the world, you had a tremendous diversity of publications. This has reached its pinnacle in the last decade, with desktop publishing.

Semiconductor technology is moving in that same direction. We've seen an explosion of chip-designs; last year there were more chip-designs than hardcover books. As years pass, custom chips will spread ever more widely and, at some point, they will be distributed broadly enough so that the printing of chips will be almost as routine as the printing of books.

KARLGAARD: But aren't you stretching the analogy a bit? Desktop publishing, combined with a little printer and a bindery, can produce a book. But it takes a multimillion-dollar fab to produce a chip.

I admit it's hard to envision advanced chip technology reducing to the kind of desktop publishing form we see today. [Still] it's a mistake to look at the semiconductor industry chiefly from the point of view of the wafer fab.

1990 UPSIDE

Broadcasting

Particularly the broadcasters are [living on] totally unsupportable "dog" technology. And dog technologies mean that the kennel is always in an uproar, and the politicians always hear the howls from the kennel. Since the politician is the dog's best friend, they are always propping up the past in the name of progress. You see this frenzy of effort to prop up the broadcasters — anything to keep this totally obsolete, useless source of industrial pollution [going]. Whenever you see a broadcast tower, just think of a smokestack with no filters.

And what the broadcasters are promising to do is, "We'll apply filters, so we'll [deliver more] children's programming, news programming, free political ads — any-thing you want." Essentially this obsolete industry will be nationalized, by default.

1997 CATO

Bulletin Boards

The bulletin-board experience is very special and unique. It's launched this period as a golden age of text communications. It's a return to epistolary exchanges, but it's different because of the instant response. This will encroach to some extent on the time people currently spend pouring thru TV programs or real-crime stories. At the same time, people will want to have — amid this mad cornucopia of information products — places to go where they are comfortable and know what to expect...

It seems to me that local newspapers can supply this, as well as magazines and other such familiar vehicles that can move on-line pretty effectively. As a matter of fact, they will benefit more from higher-resolution screens than will the video people. The current computer screen is equivalent to 72 dots per inch, and you really need 300 dots per inch to read readily. In the next few years, screens will routinely have that kind of resolution and contrast, and all sorts of different news panels and other such technologies will emerge that will allow you to read from a screen.

1994 UPSIDE

Cable Industry: Monopoly

I think the cable television companies will lose their monopoly. Their particular network is so much less effec-tive than a digitally switched video network that they will lose the competition and will retreat increasingly to supply-ing programming, and such functions would be valuable to you: The more programmers there are, the better it is for the telephone industry, if you are going to transmit the video.

Some of them will try to get into the telephone business, I would suspect. But I don't see them as a very powerful entrepreneurial force myself. I think that, like HDTV, cable-television companies are essentially a dog business. The only reason they survive is [because] the politician is the dog's best friend. They really do focus on politics. They bribe so many politicians they can't keep it straight any more, and they're actually paralyzed in many cities because so many people have been bribed [that] the city agents can't award the contract to any particular company without risking some exposure.

Cable companies are getting increasingly unpopular, and you people should be able to bowl them over if you use resourcefully the technology that you command.

1990 LONGBOAT

Cable Industry: Plus CDMA

I'm an advocate of cable. It's been one area where I've apparently been wrong, so far. The stock market says I am wrong. But I think I will be saved again by CDMA.

Are the cable companies using CDMA over coax?

Not now, but they will soon. CDMA is great for a noisy channel, and cable upstream is the noisiest channel there is. @Home (which offers high-bandwidth Internet access thru coaxial cable lines to the home) is TCI's effort to transcend this problem.

Aren't they supplying the big-pipe, little-pipe model?

They were. But in order to have a good data solution for home offices and small businesses, they now seem to have gone with the LANCity technology. It was originally a Digital project with LANCity to do Ethernet over cable thru a metropolitan area. And the LANCity solution is a two-way, symmetrical, 10-megabit-a-second system.

What is the secret to making the two-way work?

I believe that ultimately all the cable companies will turn to CDMA for two-way technology. A Silicon Valley company called Terayon, backed by Cisco Systems, uses a CDMA variant to get 60 megabits a second of bandwidth out of the bottom 40 megahertz of a cable line, which are so noisy that today they are hardly used at all. Terayon will save the cable industry as much as $20 billion by allowing them to use current plant, without upgrades, for broadband Internet access.

As usual, everyone is now in the CDMA denial stage — "it violates the laws of physics," and so on — but sooner or later everybody is going to go to CDMA to harvest the lower 40.

The other available area for digital is above either 500 MHz or 750 MHz, depending on the quality of the system. Here you can devote some 300 MHz to digital communication that escapes the huge mass of competing noise that applies to the "low-split" channel. So the low-split channel has less bandwidth and involves lots of digital tricks and error-correction and compression, and the high-split channel is really the ultimate broadband solution, but it involves costly upgrades.

The spectrum space above 500 MHz is available now in maybe 20% of all cable plants, and it's expected to be in a third soon — although TCI, because of financial problems, has recently cut back drastically on its upgrades, thereby creating a huge opportunity for Terayon in the low-split space.

So you're saying there's not any one solution?

That's right. Cable at best currently connects to 60%-plus of US homes, roughly two-thirds. Of those, 20–30% are upgraded suitably. Perhaps many of the rest can use CDMA as it rolls out. So let's say that 40% of the total homes can have broadband connections provided by cable, reasonably speaking, over the next three or four years. Cable is then contributing a lot of bandwidth, particularly to up-market households, which are those most likely to want broadband Internet connections anyway. The technology has to take off with the top 10% of homes.

But doesn't that turn the cable companies into ISP monopolies?

I don't think [they become] monopolies, because the RBOCs — as well as MCI, Sprint, AT&T, and hundreds of others — are all going into the ISP business.

But if the cable company owns the cable network, which

is the really high-bandwidth entrée into homes, aren't they the ISP of choice?

They may be the ISP of choice, great, until they really overcharge you or start supplying bad service or whatever, at which point you use a direct-TV satellite dish on your roof connected to some upstream connection thru the phone network or wireless cable, as they call it, at 18 to 28 to 38 GHz spectrum, which is increasingly being exploited and demonstrated for two-way communications.

There just isn't going to be one monolithic solution. The lawyers in Washington believe that unless the government regulates every portion of this process — [the process] of the transition to a new, broadband Internet — some vast, new monopoly is going to emerge. I think the technology is moving too fast for this; the old telephone model simply does not apply anymore.

The model now is the dynamic computer-industry model, where radio technology is coming on, infrared technology, broadband, select and switch technology, satellite channels, DSL data-compression technology, wireless technology, and things we haven't even thought of yet are coming on.

1997 IEEE

Cable Industry: Plus Phone Companies

If it was legal for the phone companies to collaborate with cable companies, then they could just run the fiber-optic lines to the coaxial cables that connect to the homes. The coaxial cables are one gigahertz-wide in bandwidth; that's a tremendous bandwidth of a connection to the home — it can accommodate the entire digital revolution.

1992 NIGHTLINE

Cable companies possess the advantage of already owning dumb networks based on the essentials of "broadcast and select" — of customers seeking wavelengths or frequencies rather than switching channels. Cable companies already provide all the programs to all the terminals and allow them to tune in to the desired messages.

But the cable industry cannot become a full-service supplier of telecommunications unless the regulators give up their ridiculous "two-wire" dream in which everyone competes with cable and no one makes any money.

Cash-poor and bandwidth-rich, cable companies need to collaborate with telcos — which are cash-rich and bandwidth-poor — in a joint effort to create broadband systems in their own regions.

1997 NEWSLETTER

At the same time that [John] Malone has to retrench because of the new DBS competition, Continental Cablevision says it can expand — you know, can continue on course. The key difference is that it's allied to U S West. And I believe that these two suppliers of infrastructure have to collaborate. The cable and telephone industries are quite complementary. The big error the government has made is to block collaboration —

GREGORSKY: In the same region.

— beginning with Bell Atlantic and TCI. If Bell Atlantic could've collaborated with TCI in its own region, that would have been a great merger.

But as soon as it turned out that they couldn't, it became [a case of] two complementary technologies that were barred from integrating with their complements. It became just horizontal expansion rather than any integration of the functions of those two companies.

It's like you got a bunch of people with bulldozers and [also] a concrete company, and you're saying, "Go build this highway — but you have to do it in different states." They literally can't go together.

Right, right. That's a good analogy.

1997 FRAGMENTS

Cable Modems

Cable modems [will] be the dominant way information reaches the household by the year 2000. Now there is a lot of fashionable disparagement of cable modems and the cable industry in general. But the companies building these modems are not cable operators, they are companies such as Motorola, Intel, Zenith, Hybrid Networks, and a whole array of entrepreneurial companies supported by venture capitalists that can actually bring their products to market.

I think cable modems are going to roll out fast because of DBS technology, which has essentially eclipsed the future prospects of the cable industry. DBS is known at TCI as "Death Star," and this is for a reason. And it's this competition from DBS that is driving the transformation of the cable operators into an industry serving the Internet.

I hope that phone-company money will also pour into this area. Under existing legislation, phone companies are already allowed to purchase small cable companies in rural areas. So, in general, to make this all happen fast, you need to combine the bandwidth of the cable industry's installed base with the capital of the RBOCs. I think that may end up happening.

1996 HERRING

Cable Pipes: Into Schools

What would be a big help is if school systems demand that the government give the cable industry money to connect the schools. The government constantly says they want the school systems connected — well, cable is the way to do it. If you can do fiber to the school, that's a little better, but it's not hugely better than the best modern co-axial that cable companies deploy.

Don't get me wrong — coaxial is not a replacement for fiber for long-haul applications. But, for a connection from the network to a school or some other institution, cable is a one-gigahertz pipe — that is, one billion cycles a second. It's a really serious kind of pipe and it would be ample to supply schools.

1994 E-LEARN

Campbell, Gordon

Gordy Campbell, although he has his detractors, was from the beginning always ready to explain his technologies and his company's strategies in a way that many other people in the industry could not. His openness to ideas, his flexibility, his optimism and his entrepreneurial vision all appealed to me from the beginning — at a time when he was very unpopular. I was seeing people from all around Silicon Valley telling me what an airhead Gordy Campbell was. But he wasn't airy with me. He was always right down to business and was always explaining the technologies and the strategies, in an intellectual way that excels most of his critics.

1990 UPSIDE

Chapman, Bruce

Bruce Chapman has had a long and distinguished career. He's been a member of the Seattle City Council; Secretary of State of Washington State; director of the U.S. Census Bureau; Ambassador to the U.N. in Vienna; and director of the Office of Policy, Planning and Evaluation under President Reagan. Today he is President of Discovery Institute in Seattle, where he explores with me the interplay of politics, technology, science and society. He is also my college roommate, and best friend, and co-author of my first book, *The Party That Lost Its Head,* which was our tale of the 1964 Goldwater nomination.

1997 TCSM-CONF

Ciena Corp.

I predicted [this past winter] that the initial public offering of an obscure company called Ciena Corp. that most people never heard of would be bigger than Netscape's IPO. Everybody thought that was ridiculous. Ciena came public and it <u>was</u> bigger than Netscape; it was valued at a market cap of $3.8 billion — [because] it commands this wavelength division multiplexing technology of many bitstreams down a single fiber thread. It has allowed Sprint to deploy a 40-gigabit per second backbone for its long-distance capacity; and MCI has also laid such a backbone. And what this has allowed is...an explosion of Internet traffic.

1997 CATO

Clipper Chip

I think Clipper is a premature standardization. It's not perfected, it's not simple, it's not cheap, it's not effective, and it shouldn't be adopted... I do think that the problem they're addressing is a real problem — that terrorism and other such crime is a real threat and the National Security Agency is, in some sense, in an arms race with nuclear renegades and terrorists (bioengineers or whatever) — and they're going to have to use lots of new technologies to meet this challenge. But they're not going to have a sort of one-size-fits-all magical chip that will solve their problems... I think they should be able to figure out how to chase the bad guys without ensnaring all the good guys in the computer industry in the process.

1994 MICROTIMES

It's the wrong mindset. There is no mechanical solution to an enormously dynamic environment. I gather there is a real dispute between the NSA and the FBI about this stuff. The NSA has all the encryption technology, but it isn't allowed to share it with the FBI, so the FBI wants to control everybody with the Clipper Chip — even at the cost of losing the industry overseas! Well, the NSA understands that it is very desirable to have American companies introducing and controlling these technologies, and the <u>worst</u> thing that could happen to our security in general is for the entire technology industry to move to China. So I think the NSA and the FBI need to get together and share technology, and work this stuff out.

1996 HERRING

Computer Industry: Refocus

Now addicted to the use of transistors to solve the problems of limited bandwidth, the computer industry must use transistors to exploit the opportunities of nearly unlimited bandwidth. When home-based machines are optimized for manipulating high-resolution digital video at high speeds, they will necessarily command what are now called supercomputer powers. This will mean that the dominant computer technology will emerge first not in the office market but in the consumer market. The major challenge for the computer industry is [therefore] to change its focus from a few hundred million offices already full of computer technology to a billion living rooms now nearly devoid of it.

1997 NEWSLETTER

Computers: Versus TV

The TV industry is dominated by about 20 big global companies. The computer industry has about 20,000 companies, in the United States alone — a vastly greater entrepreneurial force. TV is a dumb receiver; it can just receive signals. The computer, the digital computer, is not only a receiver; it can receive full-motion video over fiber-optic cable — actually can <u>better</u> the TV set as a receiver. But it's also a <u>processor</u> of video images. The computer can originate digital video images, and [do so] much cheaper than the current movie industry or the current TV technology. And digital computer technology can also <u>transmit</u> video...

So, rather than having a hundred channels at best, one-way channels, the computer will have an unlimited number of potential channels. Every desktop is a potential broadcasting station. The computer is an immensely more powerful tool than the television set. The desktop publishing industry, which has resulted in some 10,000 new publishing companies in the United States in the past decade, will become a desktop video publisher, and transform the nature of video.

1990 HILLSDALE

The computer industry has got to see itself as TV-killers. It's not their only target, but the key target of the computer industry is to wipe out the TV.

1990 UPSIDE

At Intel, they point out that transforming a PC into a television is simple: You merely add one layer of functionality. But to transform a TV into a PC runs against the grain: You have to add thousands of functions and features in a race with the fastest moving technology on the face of the Earth, while retaining backward-compatibility with one of the most sluggish. It is a lost cause.

1997 NEWSLETTER

[Y]ou have written that the current TV/telephony infrastructure will cease to exist.

Yes. I mean TV and telephony — "telephony" defined as a centrally switched voice-optimized network, and "TV" as analog broadcasting. These are not going to be the important communications channels by the beginning of the next century. The Internet is going to take over. TV broadcasting in particular is going to be an orphan technology by that point.

Won't they also broadcast 10 million TV channels for people to tune into?

Then this wouldn't be television. The very nature of television is you have dumb receivers, and you broadcast a selection of channels chosen by the broadcasting companies. To the extent that you can find the stuff you want around the globe, store it, time-shift it, and interact with it, it's no longer TV.

That's the triumph of the PC. I think TV will be a subset of computer technology, and you'll be able to watch the Superbowl on the appropriate screen that you choose. There will be a variety of different display technologies available, and portable computing devices will be able to connect to those displays probably thru some infrared or RF link. The whole idea of the TV box will disappear, although there will be displays that look like TV displays.

When Tim Berners-Lee created the web, he intended authoring and editing to be as fundamental as browsing. Somehow, that got lost in the initial generation of browsers, though it seems to be coming back. Will creative interactivity win out over the passive WebTV model?

I think this is implicit in the triumph of the PC or network computer — what I call the teleputer. My favorite description of this outcome is that one person at a workstation will have more creative power than an industrial tycoon of the previous age, and more communications power than the broadcast tycoon of the television age. Certainly the same technologies that make possible the evolution of the Internet to this new broadband nirvana also will endow the terminals on the Net with fabulous creative potential, and you'll be able to make whole <u>films</u> on single workstations at costs that are radically below the cost of the typical Hollywood <u>television</u> offering.

1997 IEEE

Computer networks respond to all the human characteristics that television networks defy. Computer nets permit peer-to-peer interactivity rather than top-down broadcasts. Rather than a few "channels," computer networks offer as many potential connections as there are machines linked to the web. Rather than a system in which a few "stations" spray images at millions of dumb terminals in real time, computer networks put the customer in control. Television will die because it affronts human nature — [in this case, the] drive to self-improvement and autonomy that lifted the race from the muck and offers the only promise for triumph in our current adversities.

1993 ECONOMIST

Drucker, Peter

Speaking of business writers who are conservative yet

misunderstood [by most people on the right], tell us the
story of your near-interview with Peter Drucker.

I was originally assigned to do that interview [of
Drucker that *Inc.* ran in November 1985]. So I read almost
all his books, which was wonderful — his novels, his early
books, and [the autobiographical] *Adventures Of A Bystander*,
a masterpiece of a book. I spent an enormous amount of
time figuring out what questions to ask him. And he had
agreed to the interview — until he learned I was to do it. He
said: "Oh no, Gilder just wants to come out here to argue
with me."

**And, in the interview [with Tom Richman] that *Inc.*
eventually used, he takes a shot at you.**

He also took a shot in *Innovation And Entrepreneurship*
[which was published the same year].

**But since then you've been paying homage to him in
print?**

I always did. *The Spirit Of Enterprise* [published in 1984]
acclaims Drucker. He is, however, a big-business pundit.
His understanding of entrepreneurship and technology is
less powerful than his grasp of management in large companies and institutions. No one beats him, though, for a
general understanding of human history, motivations and
organizational perversities. He is in many ways our leading
intellectual.

**But there's another guy conservatives don't understand.
We never tried to coopt him, except some of the business
types. You're essentially walking some of the same
ground Drucker walked in the 1970s — being
understood only by the non-political parts of the
coalition.**

Right. That really is true, and quite strange. I'm a deep
conservative. All my emotional ties are with them. My
whole career, I've imagined that I'm working for them. But
the people who enjoy my [more recent] stuff tend to be
social liberals who like technology!

So your base is schizoidal.

I don't have a conservative base. I almost never give speeches to conservatives. I get bashed [for having written against feminism] by the liberals all the time — so I pay for being a conservative. But most conservatives really don't like the technological stuff, or my "altruism of enterprise" stuff. Many are suspicious of supply-siders. I'm doing fine, having a ball, but kind of mystified.

1992 GREGORSKY

Dumb Networks

NEE: You advocate the building of "dumb networks" as opposed to smart networks. How did you arrive at this theory?

About five years ago, I was talking to Jay Keyworth, President Reagan's chief science adviser and a leading physicist at Los Alamos for a while; he's also on the board of Hewlett-Packard. And somebody was saying to him that we were going into the era of smart networks, and he said, "No, networks should be as dumb as a stone." I began thinking about it, and I became alert to signs of dumb networks.

Before, I had been perplexed by the amazing resilience and robustness of Ethernet. So I saw that dumb networks were prevailing there. And then I met Paul Green, the IBM advocate of "dark fiber" who invented the first complete all-optical network. It is still experimental, but they have functioning prototypes in Geneva [Switzerland], all over Westchester County [NY] and in Japan.

All these ideas came together, and I began to get a real picture of the dumb network.

What do you mean by a dumb network?

Smart, centralized networks all emerged during a time of dumb terminals. To have dumb terminals, you have to have intelligent networks. In the TV world, you had a stripped-down receiver that could be cheaply manufactured by the millions and that relegated almost all the intelligent functions to the station. If you were a telephone company, you had all the intelligence in the central switches and the telephone was a dumb terminal.

Even in the computer world, until the last decade, you essentially had smart centralized mainframes with a lot of dumb terminals attached to them. It was the same model in the computer world, the television world and the telephone world.

Now all those models are collapsing. Moore's Law assures that with the doubling of capabilities every 18 months, you will have supercomputer terminals. When you have supercomputer terminals capable of sending out huge floods of bits, what you really want is just dumb bandwidth to accommodate it. This kind of dumb bandwidth is now increasingly available in what's called dark fiber.

Until recently a fiber-optic system could not function any faster than the electronic amplifiers and repeaters, which had to be installed every 22 miles to amplify and regenerate the photonic light signals. The repeaters couldn't really function much faster than 2.5 gigahertz. And that capability is not rising very fast. So the fiber-optic system was constricted to the switching speed of transistors.

But the intrinsic capability of fiber-optics is not 2.5 gigahertz, or even 25 gigahertz, which are all the frequencies currently used in the air. It's a thousand times that — it's 25,000 gigahertz. Three frequency windows in fiber can accommodate infrared pulses, and each one of those windows is approximately 25,000 gigahertz wide — enough capacity to hold all the phone calls at the peak moment on Mother's Day in America. New all-optical amplifier technology has been developed for two of those windows that allows you to exploit that capacity.

How dumb a network are you talking about? Wouldn't it need some switching or routing capabilities to be a national network?

There are a lot of passive optical components being developed to perform a lot of the functions that active switching components perform. So messages can be routed thru the system using passive components. Even with 25 gigahertz, you still run into bandwidth problems if you are really shipping all the things that are exchanged across a national network.

So it's unlikely that we will obviate all switches. But, in general, bandwidth is a substitute for switching. If you have enough bandwidth, you can simulate any kind of switching topology.

Is the main problem with switching that it slows down the network?

Yeah, it slows down the network, and it also requires the network to adjust to it. Now, I don't think this [change] is going to happen overnight. It's a long-run direction that is possible as the full capacity of fiber is realized. There will be an era of ATM [asynchronous transfer mode] switches that intercedes. I am not sure that ATM will be a single omnivore kind of protocol but, because of its ability to handle various multimedia forms, it will have a good ride.

So you think that ATM makes sense as the next step.

It's just really catching on. Everybody is making chips for it, and increasing numbers of computer companies — like Apple, Sun and some IBM machines — will have ATM interfaces. Sprint, Wiltel and some of the big network systems are already rolling out ATM functions in their long-distance networks; Time-Warner is using ATM to distribute films in its interactive TV trial in Orlando.

So there is no question that it is happening and will be the next network that is dominant. And it is a step to a dumb network. ATM is dumber than frame-relay, which has variously sized cells and requires more software control. The point about ATM is that all the cells are 53 bytes, and they can all be processed in hardware. This is the first step to a dumb network.

The general evolution of networks will be toward having more intelligence relegated to servers on the edge of the network (which can be used for very specific applications), and more of the middle of the network will be raw bandwidth.

This is happening even in the wireless domain. The people with phone-company mentalities focus on very rigid standards in wireless. They think there is going to be one standard that all PDAs [personal digital assistants], phones and digital cellular devices will use. But Steinbrecher radios really transcend that model. They are indifferent to the air standard. They process it all on the edges of the network in the DSPs [digital signal processors] that analyze the variety of radio signals in a particular band. That means radios don't have to be modular and can completely exploit the advances in digital electronics.

Increasingly, that will be the model. This idea that we will be able to standardize everything and have one kind of network everywhere is an illusion. Rather than abolishing the standard zoo, we have to domesticate it. So you have dark fiber and dark air — the atmosphere and the fibersphere — and intelligent devices on the periphery sort thru the variety of standards. And you use the computing intelligence to surmount the problem of multiple protocols and modulation schemes.

All around the world, different countries are developing different video standards and TV standards, and you are not going to change that. So let the viewer identify what kind of material is being received — and channel it to the appropriate DSPs to decode it. The whole move toward open systems is based on that vision. It is contrary to the visions of the phone and television companies, which have managed to impose one standard.

In the past you said that Ethernet will outlast ATM. Do you still believe that?

Yeah. The original Bob Metcalfe vision was of the ether. The first Ethernet was Aloha, which was a wireless network started by the University of Hawaii, interconnecting all their various campuses across the Hawaiian islands. And it was the simplest of networks, where you just send. If you don't get an acknowledgment you send again, until it gets thru. Ethernet evolved from Aloha, and it's the ultimate dumb network. All the intelligence is in the periphery. The medium itself is dark, essentially. All the information needed to make the network work is acquired by the terminals themselves, rather than transmitted from any central point in the network.

So Ethernet is the model of the dumb network for smart terminals. Ethernet has faced new challengers steadily over the years and survived. Token Ring got a tremendous push from IBM and was expected to blow away Ethernet, but Ethernet is still expanding its market-share. The reason Ethernet did succeed, contrary to all expectations, was that it was dumb. It allowed you to take advantage of Moore's Law in the terminals. It didn't require the terminals to await adjustments in the software provided by the switching company.

And it didn't specify the medium.

It didn't specify the medium. You could do twisted-pair Ethernet; you could do coaxial Ethernet; you could do shielded, unshielded, 10-base T. It left a lot of room for creativity.

But Metcalfe and others now think Ethernet might have seen its end. Why do these guys who are immersed in the technology disagree with you?

Metcalfe says that, to some degree, it's a matter of where you focus your vision. If you are talking about multi-media, he believes ATM will dominate. If there are collision and congestion problems [using Ethernet for video, voice and data] and you can't be sure of the isochronous arrival of voice and video [then ATM is preferable]. But when bandwidth gets sufficient and you can send multimedia with good assurance that everything will arrive at the right time, things will change. Nothing fundamental about the dumb-network model prohibits sending isochronous data.

It does appear that the opto-electronic technology and the fiber technology will not come on-line soon enough to usurp this ATM solution. ATM is a compromise; it's not the best solution by most standards. The ATM 53-byte cell is the largest possible cell that can handle voice — that's why it was chosen. Anything bigger and the timing for voice com-munications is disrupted. Anything smaller and the over-head for data-transmissions becomes completely dominant.

Does ATM have any other advantages?

It does have the virtue, which is hard to underestimate, of being entirely realized in hardware. Having all the pack-ets the same size is really the arrival of the RISC model in communications. A key to the success of RISC is that all the instructions are the same size, so they can be managed more efficiently by the hardware. ATM is a form of RISC architecture applied to networks.

But, just as the RISC architecture is not driving all complex instructions from the field, ATM is going to have to live with a lot of Ethernet as time passes because networks will move to the real ether, which is the air. And the real ether nets have to be dumb.

That's why I think the Steinbrecher radio is the single most important technology that I have seen developed in the past 10 years or so. Radios are no longer tied to a specific air standard. And that emancipation of radio from a specific air standard can afford the same kind of gains that have been achieved thru open systems in the computer business.

1994 UPSIDE

It takes smart men to create dumb networks... It's the architecture that's dumb, not the people who have to manage the transitions, maintain the connections and integrate the software. I don't think network management will be obsolete. It will change, but it will move to different points on the network. There will still be plenty for [Chief Information Officers] to do.

1994 CIO

Gosling, James

James Gosling essentially decided on a new tradeoff. He decided that computer cycle-time was abundant while programmer time was scarce, so he was willing to accept the slower effective implementation of instructions — in exchange for improving the productivity of programmers by a factor of between three and five.

And, in fact, reports show that the productivity of programmers using Java does increase by a factor of between two and five. This is because automatic memory-management, automatic garbage-collection, the prohibition of pointers to memory addresses, and object-oriented

memory-organization — all bar the kind of memory conflicts that are a major problem for most computer programs.

Mr. Gosling traded memory-access time for programmer
time, and programmers are eager to accept that deal, particularly as all the wealth in the industry migrates toward
Intel and Microsoft. A new model beckons programmers
and developers around the world, and they are flocking to
it.

1996 INT-ENG

Grove, Andrew

I like Andy Grove, even though he is hostile to much of
what I have been telling you [about trade and the Japanese].
Andy Grove is somebody who emerged from battles of
actually producing devices. He leads a major company, and
he continues to keep in command of the details of how Intel
operates. He is an extremely powerful intellect and an
extremely exciting and combative conversationalist. I'm
very much impressed with him, even though I am occasionally worried about some of his positions at Intel.

1990 UPSIDE

High-Definition Television

People in the HDTV business talk about having $3,000
systems in 1995 or something. I think in 1995 there will be
$3,000 computers capable of affording all the benefits of
computers and also the benefits of full-motion video. If you
can have a smart system that can manipulate the video in
every feasible way — window and zoom and whatever you
wish, from your seat — why would you settle for some
HDTV transmitting the same few programs that you get
today?

1990 UPSIDE

When analog HDTV was introduced by the Japanese
several years ago, there was a general outcry that this
would be the end of the line for the American electronics
industry, and [therefore] we needed a massive government
program to save it. At the time, I said analog HDTV was a

dog, and the only reason anybody is interested in it is
because the politician is always the dog's best friend. Government is always propping up the past in the name of
progress.

1994 MARSHALL

Hollywood: Timing

[T]he new technologies give the power to the people.
Each individual with a computer workstation commands
more power than a factory magnate of the previous era and
more communications power than a broadcast executive
today. Each individual takes power over his own education
and his own entertainment.

**What does this mean? What is the right training for the
entertainment world? How far off? Are you talking 10
years? 20 years?**

This is happening right now. This is something that is
happening every day. This is a point I always have difficulty making. This is something underway now, all over the
place. It is just happening. And it will keep happening and
it will gain increasing momentum and finally it will become
a kind of tsunami that will be noticeable even at Hollywood
and Vine.

But it's already having its effect: While the Internet
grows 15% per month, and the number of CD-ROMs sold
rises from a few thousand to 5 million this year, and on-line
data-base computer-service businesses rise almost 500% in
four years, at the same time Hollywood is pretty flat. All
they're doing now is tearing their products apart and re-
packaging them — that's their idea of radical innovation. It
actually does yield some further income, but it doesn't
solve the basic problem and need.

1994 REPORTER

Interactive TV

Making the boob-tube into an interactive hive of theater,
museum, classroom, banking system, shopping center, post

office and communicator is contrary to the nature of the box.

1994 BERKSHIRE

When you look across the landscape of the last several years, at various experiments, initiatives and developments, you find that most of the ones associated with interactive television have failed... And Gates himself has said interactive TV is a very bad way of thinking about the new kinds of computers we are going to provide...

A lot of the stuff about HDTV and interactive TV and set-top box TV is all just hype. The really interactive information superhighway systems will be spearheaded by networked personal computers. As soon as the cable systems become accessible by computer users, it is going to radically change the industry. When you have a six-megahertz cable channel to tie to your computer, you change the whole nature of the computer.

1994 UPSIDE

I think interactivity is almost by definition a computer function, and interactive TV is nonsense. By the time the TV gets interactive, the computer will be 50 times more cost-effective and will be on a learning curve that continues to double every 18 months. The TV people will always be hopelessly behind — and all of a sudden their market will go over a cliff. So many people will have computers that they won't even contemplate using their television interactively.

1994 REPORTER

ISDN Versus ADSL: Neither

The Integrated Services Digital Network [ISDN] expands by seven to eight times the carrying capacity of existing copper lines, thus allowing digital signal transmission without fiber-optics. Is that significant, or just a bandaid on an existing structure?

ISDN means digital lines reach right to your own home;

and you can connect your computers to them, making something like [the Heritage Foundation's] Town Hall [computer network] much more efficient and responsive. It's a step forward.

Not a detour or delaying tactic?

Neither, in my judgment. Some people think so, but I don't. It's significant, but fiber-optics means — literally — scores of thousands of times more bandwidth than the current copper lines. And here we're talking seven or eight times expansion?

To the extent the phone companies think they can deliver full-motion video adequately thru the current copper plant, they will be disappointed. They will merely provoke the cable people in making the needed investments and alliances to compete successfully. That's all they'll succeed in doing — provoking a full-scale response from the cable people — which is good. At which point, the phone people will see that they have to do fiber — all the way. If not to the home, then to the curb.

1992 GREGORSKY

The very same trumpets that blared ineffectually for 10 years for ISDN now toot for an amazing new redeemer of twisted copper called asymmetrical digital subscriber loop (ADSL). As developed by a tiny California company called Amati and adopted by Northern Telecom, ADSL sends a stunning six million bits per second of full-motion video down a conventional telephone line.

As a technological breakthru, ADSL is stupendous. But it resembles the varistor, a brilliantly crafted device excogitated in the late 1960s by the vacuum-tube people at RCA in the face of the new threat of silicon transistors. Even in strategic terms, it is a distraction. ADSL provides a new weapon for a losing fight with cable and satellite firms sending hundreds of channels of pay-per-view films and games to the household. A dying telephone technology clutches at a shiny new broadcast-industry death rattle.

1993 ECONOMIST

The world of communications technology divides into

two parts. On one side is a parasite farm, feeding on the archaic tariff structure of the telcos with its $1,000-per-month T-1 lines and narrowband ISDN (144 kilobits per second) hyped as "new technology." Any companies accommodating the telcos' absurd plans to link businesses to the Internet at 144 kilobits per second and call it progress are part of the problem. This includes many of Wall Street's favorite "Internet" stocks, such as Ascend, Shiva and US Robotics, and IPO prospects such as Livingston Enterprises.

The [alternative] strategy is to overthrow the parasite farm and create an entirely new market-based pricing structure for communications... All the communications companies soaring on Wall Street under the sheltering wings of telco tariffs must face a world of competition where the current telco price-structure collapses.

1996 NEWSLETTER

IBM: At The Bottom

I think [Mark] Stahlman's article is definitive. It really does tell the story well. And it remains supremely relevant, because IBM is completely failing to respond to that message.

Creating a new organization with nine manufacturing companies and then channeling those products into four geographically organized marketing divisions are mistakes. Each of those product companies should have its own sales and marketing force.

IBM's blindness to the customer, and estrangement from the computer-buyer, remain just as acute as before. As Stahlman points out and his critics fail to grasp, IBM's problem is not the mainframe computer. Mainframes remain a key IBM strength.

IBM has accepted the general critique that they don't make enough small computers and underestimated the desktop revolution. But they haven't responded to Stahlman's critique, which shows that the industry really has divided into a large number of different industries requiring different marketing channels, different customer relations, different manufacturing technologies and different R&D efforts.

IBM sort of understands the need for different R&D and manufacturing, but they don't comprehend the need to have separate sales and marketing organizations. It's desirable to give full profit responsibilities to some of IBM's individual units as well. IBM has to get people who are specialized in one type of computer selling those computers, even competing with other types of IBM computers if necessary.

If a customer wants to deal with "one IBM," the company should be able to supply that kind of sales or system-integration function. But I think there are fewer and fewer of those types of customers. Most customers look at products from IBM, Sun, Apple and a range of other suppliers. Very few want to deal with just IBM.

The real flaw in the U.S. semiconductor establishment has been IBM. It's the biggest producer of chips, but it has failed to expose its production to the market, and refuses to supply chips to other American computer companies. People constantly complain about Japanese computer companies possibly monopolizing DRAMs and withholding them from competitors in the United States. Well, that's what IBM does. So the problem isn't Japan, it's IBM.

It would be a very important step forward if IBM does begin aggressively marketing their chips. But that would take a reorientation of their semiconductor operations. IBM has all these bizarre components and specialized technologies that just can't compete against open systems and commodities. The semiconductor operations should definitely be made to compete on the open market. I've been advocating this for 10 years. This has been one of IBM's biggest failings.

IBM's incredibly misconceived reorganization suggests that [CEO John] Akers has profound responsibilities for the company's problems. If he had started doing things slightly right, he would have been less culpable. But it's clear he still doesn't understand the situation. And that's what Stahlman's article really does. It gives you a way to comprehend Akers' responsibility and Akers' failure. Most of the other critics haven't done that. They talk about IBM's bureaucracy. IBM is bureaucratic, but that's not really a stunning revelation.

I would expect that the person who replaces Akers will follow Stahlman's strategy. It's not particularly helpful to tell IBM today that they underestimated personal computers and workstations. They understand that vividly. That just isn't a novel or significant insight. And that's what most of the critics have said. IBM understands that well by reading their P&L. But, by reading Stahlman's piece, they will understand what they need to do about it. It should be must reading all thru IBM's headquarters.

I would like to see John Sculley replace Akers. He understands the new computer markets, but needs the resources IBM commands to exploit them. Sculley sees the opportunities, but at Apple he is forced to collaborate with the Japanese to fulfill them. If he ran IBM, he could really address the consumer-electronics market.

1993 UPSIDE

IBM couldn't even get rid of OS/2. It just had too much NIH [not-invented-here syndrome] to get rid of OS/2 and embrace the Mac operating system. If IBM had done that, it would have changed the whole industry, and it would have been a perfectly appropriate strategy for both IBM and Apple. But they were just too obtuse to do that. And now IBM thinks it is so smart because it has a whole division devoted to the Internet...

What about IBM's acquisition of Lotus?

IBM was paying $3.8 billion for Lotus at a time when it could have bought the whole Internet for that much!

1996 HERRING

Kurzweil, Ray

Ray Kurzweil [is the] peerless inventor of such brain-extenders as reading machines, speech-recognition and music-synthesis. [In *The Age of Spiritual Machines*, he] has now reinvented the book as a luminous synthesis of mind and machine... This is a book that makes all other roads to the computer future look like goat paths in Patagonia.

1998 FRAGMENTS

Kyocera Corp.

The whole U.S. semiconductor industry has been dependent on Kyocera for 20 years for most ceramic packaging for advanced chips. Nobody has been "held hostage" yet. They operate intensively in the United States. Their leadership is quite oriented toward the United States. The only thing that could drive Japan into some nationalist posture is the kind of panic about Japan which we see widespread in the U.S. It is a terrible mistake for the U.S. electronics industry to encourage this Japan panic that the politicians find favorable to indulge.

1990 UPSIDE

McNealy, Scott

The most common personal computer of the next era...may not do windows. But it <u>will</u> do <u>doors</u>. Scott McNealy has even got a Java ring here that'll do the car door, the garage door, and open doors to the future for computer architecture and opportunity. For 10 years, Scott McNealy has been the spearhead of this new paradigm — of the network as the computer, where the previous central processing unit becomes peripheral and the network is central. This has rendered Scott McNealy and Java as the central figure [and technology] in the computer industry today.

1997 TCSM-CONF

Mead, Carver

[A]s I went all around Silicon Valley while covering the industry for Esther Dyson and the *Rosen Electronics Letter* (which Esther took over), there was always a copy of Carver's book — *The Mead-Conway Text On VLSI* — in the very small bookcases that were in every entrepreneur's office. I'd ask them about it and they would always say, "You don't need to read that. It's pretty good, but Carver is a little irresponsible." There would always be some slightly disparaging comments when I inquired about this book, but I kept seeing it, again and again, in all these offices.

Finally, when everybody disparaged him, it seemed to me to be a vote of confidence — since I was kind of contrary... Lots of the most innovative companies were run by students of Mead or were following the Mead-Conway paradigm. Thus, it seemed to me that the most creative work in Silicon Valley all ultimately derived from Mead's students. And then I met him, and we just got along very well, and he exceeded all my expectations.

1990 UPSIDE

I came to meet Carver as a result of a long peregrination thru the semiconductor industry. I was looking for the best and most exciting new companies in the industry, the new frontiers in the industry. And, every time I came to a young entrepreneur or engineer who really had the fire, I'd ask him where he got his essential push. And, incredibly often, I would hear that he'd gone to a lecture by Carver Mead, or had been taught by Carver Mead, or was a student of Carver Mead.

And then I would go and talk to the established people and ask, "Tell us, who is this Carver Mead anyway?" And they said, "Awww, don't worry about him — he's not very significant." For some time, they persuaded me — because, when I first started writing, I was overly impressed by huge companies.

Finally I looked him up, and thus *Microcosm* is based, to considerable extent, on the long career of Carver, beginning with the invention of the first gallium-arsenide transistor and moving thru the first silicon compiler...and moving on now to massively parallel analog processing...

And perhaps the first thing he told me that really riveted my attention was how crucial it is to listen to the technology, and find out what it's telling you. You can't force the technology — you gotta listen to it and respond to it, respond to the medium. Just as this injunction works for actually developing new devices, it's also crucial for societies to listen to their technology, and understand the potential of it, and its ultimate meaning.

1987 CALTECH

During the '70s, he foresaw that chips were gonna become much more dense, and that it would be necessary to computerize chip-design. He developed ways to computerize chip-design [and taught them to] his students year after year...despite the resistance of all the rest of the industry, which didn't want to move the power of chip-design away from the chip companies to just ordinary people.

Mead's students started literally scores of companies, which transformed the whole industry during this decade. During just five years in the mid-'80s, the number of chip designs produced in the United States rose from just 9,400 to well over 100,000 — a complete upsurge in the creativity of chip-design in the United States.

And this all started with one professor teaching his students, year after year, who went out into companies and transformed those companies and diffused this new technology. U.S. creativity surged — but most Americans have never heard of Carver Mead.

1990 HILLSDALE

Microsoft: At Risk

[T]he PC paradigm is suffering problems. For example, software is widely seen to be in crisis. Ted Lewis, the seer-sage of *IEEE Computer* magazine, reports that, while hardware in general advances at a pace of Moore's Law, around 48% per year (doubling every 18 months), microprocessors double their performance every 15 months (56% per year). But software functionality ekes out 4.5% per year, while sprawling imperiously across the exponentially growing space on hard drives.

Microsoft Office, for example, currently occupies some 50 megabytes; the Windows 95 operating system usurps 15 megabytes. Of course, these numbers probably mark a record low as a proportion of average disk space. The problem is that these programs are maladapted to the new machines.

The programs depend on constant reads and writes to working memory. Yet, for all the continuing surge of memory capacity, memory speeds are rising just 7% per year. Since the early 1980s, the ratio of CPU speed to memory speed has risen from essentially one-to-one to approach 20-to-one, with CPU clock-cycles at 3.5 nanoseconds and DRAM access times at some 60 nanoseconds. Operating software, independent of content, squanders the scarcest resource — the memory-processor link — at a time when this bus is also under increasing pressure from the network.

The chosen solution is to multiply memory and pile up caches of fast static RAM. But increasingly the bulk of content resides on the network.

In the Wintel system, network-access entails several further layers of operating system software and protocols, including unstable mazes of protocol stacks, comm ports and DDL files. Microsoft is now trying to absorb all this complexity into a "thick client" operating system. Bill Gates still assumes that the old paradigm prevails — that the desktop is the center and can adapt the network to its legacy systems. He sees Internet standards as a way for Microsoft to reach out and usurp the local area network in new Intranets based on the NT operating system...

With 80% of the desktop software market and an array of Internet ventures, Microsoft can afford its games for some time. But the new paradigm will not roll over the LAN and the client-server model without gaining the momentum to roll over the desktop as well. In the new paradigm, the installed base is your enemy. You cannot see the future thru Windows.

1996 NEWSLETTER

It is not desirable to integrate all sorts of content and communications protocols into this gigantic operating system growing ever more complex year after year. That model collapses of its own internal conflicts and contradictions.

What you need to do is deliver interfaces that are robust and that can accommodate software components [and] that can epitomize the Internet model — where you have a few crucial standards that are enforced and [thereby] permit the effluence of complexity on the edges. The efforts to absorb these communication systems into the OS is a mistake. You create a system that does everything poorly.

1997 NC-ONLINE

Microsoft: No Antitrust

It is not possible for antitrust to function quickly, or intelligently, enough to accomplish the goal of a disaggregated Microsoft without damaging it seriously... Such an effort would bring government into an area in which it is incompetent. [Also, by the time] the political and judicial system could accomplish anything, the entire industry will have changed so much that the original decision would be irrelevant.

1997 NC-ONLINE

Microsoft: Predictions

I actually think Microsoft will figure a lot out and contribute to the triumph of the Internet model. But this new model means that Microsoft will be less menacing and won't be able to control and dominate the computer industry. As a result, Microsoft may never exceed its peak market-capitalization of $60+ billion when the stock was trading at $109 per share with a P/E of 38 (or something like that).

1996 HERRING

My imprudent prophecy [during] a speech to Andersen Consulting in June that Microsoft's market cap would never exceed its summer peak, based on a stock price of $112, seemed to rocket the Redmond giant to new highs. The shares stood at $133 when we went to press. Oh well, the higher they rise, the harder they'll fall.

1996 NEWSLETTER

Microsoft: Versus Java

The fight between Java and Microsoft is a clash of paradigms. Java began with the Internet paradigm and has flourished with the spread of the multiplatform web. ActiveX began on the desktop and is withering on the Net. The winners will observe [Einar] Stefferud's model, relegating complexity to the edges, preserving openness and simplicity in the core, and relying on bandwidth to improve it.

If Microsoft cannot accept the industry's commitment to achieve openness thru Java, it will be time [to] short [the stock]. If Microsoft does devote its huge resources to fulfilling the Java promise, however, the company could well achieve its $500 billion destiny. The margins will be lower, but the profits will be greater — in a global economy based on the Internet as its new central nervous system.

1997 NEWSLETTER

Before, they pretended to support a new paradigm, where programs could exist anywhere on the Net and be downloaded into your machine safely — that's the Java promise. Until recently, they pretended to support the Java promise of platform-independent programs. They'd agreed with Sun to support Java in general as a cross-platform solution for the Internet...

Now they denounce it, and this is the big news of the past week: Microsoft, after pretending to support Java for several months, has now come out emphatically against Java. They're trying to change the Java language into a mere tool for writing Windows programs.

1997 LIMBAUGH

[Microsoft is at] an unfortunate point in its history when it will have to change more drastically than those at the helm want... [What the company needs to do is create] a platform-independent Java component system working across the network and breaking away from the bloatware it is currently selling...

I think that Gates will turn to Java to save Microsoft, and I think his contribution will be very valuable. But if he tries to wage a tactical war over Java and to prevent Sun from benefiting from Java, it's unseemly, perverse and a tactical mistake he will regret. He didn't invent this technology, and he has to deal with the companies that <u>did</u> invent it. And he can live with that.

1997 NC-ONLINE

Milken, Michael

NEE: What's fulfilling the role today of real risk investors?

I think venture capital is coming back some.

But those are small investors.

The big investments are not happening. The telephone companies were providing the source of this capital, so that's why the collapse of the TCI-Bell Atlantic relationship was somewhat portentous. It meant this telephone money might be institutionalized in some way, instead of going out and creating new ventures. There is really not an evident source. Junk bonds are returning, but they are being used much more cautiously than they were before.

Michael Milken financed the cellular telephone business, $2 billion to McCaw; financed the first national fiber-optic system, which was MCI, another $2 billion; financed the cable-TV industry, another $2 billion to TCI; financed the cable-production business and programming business, Time-Warner and Turner, which were also investing in cable as well, and Viacom. All these companies that today are considered leaders in the Information Age were represented as part of Milken's evil Ponzi scheme in the 1980s.

It was possible, back then, to say Milken was making wild-eyed investments to earn big fees, resulting in big losses of employment in these teetering, sleazy firms based on debt they could never pay back. All these images were conveyed in the literature that demonized Milken. But today these are the spearhead companies for the whole economy, constantly in the front pages of all the newspapers; TCI and McCaw have been valued this year at $50 billion between them.

So it's impossible to make that charge against Milken anymore.

He was really a risk-taker. He was willing to plunge $2 billion into a company with $100 million revenues — he had a great eye and really did it brilliantly. The people who prosecuted him did not understand what he was doing at all. It was mysterious to them and he was making too much money to be legal [laughter]. And they believed [Ivan]

Boesky. Milken went to jail and learned how to teach math. The first thing he wanted to do when he visited us was to teach our kids math games.

You're good friends with him?

Yeah. I met [with] him recently, and I saw him now and again before that. Contrary to what some people say, I have never received any money from him, except for some money I received for a speech to the junk-bond conference. But absolutely no financial interest. I don't even hold shares in any of the companies I mentioned. People can't accept my arguments, so they try to say I'm just a paid flack for Milken, which is wrong.

But Boesky gets out of jail and he leaves his wife and he runs off with some bimbos on a boat and hasn't been seen since. So there is quite a difference in the two characters, and the fact that the prosecutors all believed Boesky. It is true that Milken didn't talk while Boesky was willing to chatter, and that did make a difference. Milken had all this high-priced advice that told him not to talk. He would have been better going by his own instinct. A big risk-taker in the economy, but not when it came to his own defense. He got a lot of bad advice.

Anyway, he really was important to the information highway.

1994 UPSIDE

Nanotechnology

What about nanotechnology — building from the bottom-up?

The nanotechnology movement is a sort of hype. I think chip technology is nanotechnology. There are lots of fascinating things done with micromachining, and perhaps they will bear fruit sometime in the future. But this silicon technology is better as an information tool, and information is increasingly powerful — so the effort to create little gears and machines seems to me to be a niche, but not a basic advance.

1994 MARSHALL

NextWave

Without collateral beyond the ideas and entrepreneurial confidence of its creators, NextWave violates the materialist superstitions that govern most investment and that underlie old-paradigm economic data...

A supreme vessel of the CDMA wireless technology paradigm that [Allen] Salmasi has been pursuing since his time as a college student in engineering at Georgia Tech, Purdue and [Jet Propulsion Laboratories] some 25 years ago, it substitutes bandwidth in the two-gigahertz microwave band for power and processing. In the face of what analyst Carl Aron calls "The Coming Wireless Ice Age," NextWave is committing itself to a project that will ultimately cost tens of billions of dollars to consummate around the world.

This is the kind of venture that is utterly absent in Europe and rare anywhere outside the U.S. Together with Globalstar and Qualcomm — earlier Salmasi companies — it is a sword of creative destruction aimed at the existing telecom establishment...

1997 NEWSLETTER

Perot, H. Ross

Perot's proposal for town-hall democracy is reactionary: It's an unscientific public-opinion poll. Today's polls use diverse techniques with different questions. The Perot "instant town hall" makes them look like brilliant displays of wisdom, sagacity and insight. This business of pressing a button, immediately after hearing some stilted presentation of options, is *Ochlocracy* ["Government by the mob; mob rule; mobocracy"]. It's the opposite of what computer technology offers — the opposite of a mob: All sorts of individuals contributing their own special insights. It empowers individuals, rather than submerging them in a mob. Perot wants to submerge us in a mob.

But he hasn't been an advanced force in the computer industry for 30 years. He's a representative of the mainframe establishment, which has been laid low by the personal computer. He lost complete interest in Steve Jobs's NEXT as soon as they stopped manufacturing in the U.S.

and focused on software, which was their chief strength in any case.

1992 GREGORSKY

Public Utility Commissions

NEE: The state PUCs are a barrier as well. Many of them are operating as if nothing had changed.

We have got to channel them off into fields that don't mess with communications. Some of them are trying to adjust. New Jersey, Iowa, North Carolina and Tennessee — a number of states — have been pushing their RBOCs into more rapid adoption of broadband networks. California has one of the real reactionary commissions, I gather. It's dominated by consumer forces, which really are deadly to the interests of consumers. They halt progress in the name of customers; ordinarily, customers benefit from technological progress.

1994 UPSIDE

RBOCs: Business Model

NEE: The phone companies grew up in an era when the intelligence was on the network and the devices were dumb. If we are moving in the opposite direction, what will the business model of the phone companies become?

That's the big challenge. You've got to have a business model that charges appropriately for provision of bandwidth.

But they are not going to make as much money doing that as [by] providing the switching and intelligent networks.

The idea that by charging more you make more money is probably a false assumption. The plummeting price of transistors has built a $360 billion computer business around the world. You make far less money on each PC than you used to make selling mainframes with all the services and peripherals surrounding them. But the overall computer business is now much larger.

Similarly, as bandwidth plummets in price, it will become ubiquitous — the central nervous system of the global economy. As more and more of the U.S. value added flows thru this conduit, getting a relatively small portion of these transactions will be a bigger business than the existing phone business.

To build the ultimate dumb network in the sky is going to take a long time, so I see all sorts of interim stages, where different combinations of hybrid networks develop with different amounts of switching. But I think the gravitation of switching, out of the network, is underway today. It is being demanded by corporate customers all across the country. This has brought a crisis to Northern Telecom. They recognize the complex, function-rich switching systems they previously produced are just no longer acceptable, because the thousands of lines of software code cannot be upgraded to respond to the constantly changing needs of an industry governed by Moore's Law.

It is very interesting to watch the evolution of the advanced intelligent network, the AIN, which is the "official" vision of the entire phone industry. AIN originated as a feature-rich central-office switch mode and has evolved to a client-server vision. All intelligence and special services are now modules on the fringes of the network rather than part of the switching fabric itself.

So I think the general model I proposed — from dumb terminals and smart networks, to smart terminals and dumb networks — is a true perception. The force of this general technological trend is being increasingly manifested in the computer business, the telephone business, the wireless business and the video business.

Do you see the RBOCs moving toward your ideas?

They definitely are changing. In the executive suites of the RBOCs and Bell Laboratories there is some skepticism of a complete fibersphere vision, and they may be right. There is a lot of debate about how fast digital technology will advance, so I accept the idea that there will be various combinations. But I see a continued evolution toward this model of dumb air or dark fiber.

At the same time, bandwidth, although it will be abundant, will not be unlimited, so there will be switching and routing and other such functions.

Why are telecom executives resistant to your ideas? Is it because of the technology limitations or loss of control over their present business model?

Everything. Cannibalizing your installed base is a desperately hard decision for a company to make. Then there is the business-model problem. I am just guessing wildly, but probably half the people in a phone company are devoted to the existing model of regulation and bill-collecting and tariffing of communications. If that model is changed, their skills will have to be reengineered, and that is not a happy prospect, understandably, for many people. And their current system works and continues to be profitable, so there is no reason to scrap it.

So [the RBOCs] will be too slow, and bypass technologies will have a larger role. I think bypass technologies are going to employ the dark model first.

1994 UPSIDE

RBOCs: And '96 Telecom Act

As I understand it, [Bob] Metcalfe had three main arguments: First, that current data showed collapse [of the Internet] was inevitable; second, that intranets were sucking up resources while adding a load to the Net; and third, that the Net needed to be managed so that investors could realize returns. You never said much about his third argument.

That's because I'm pretty much in agreement with it, although unlike Metcalfe I don't think the Net has to be centrally engineered. Each portion of it is elaborately engineered. That's what Cisco Systems is doing; that's what all these people are doing in the network equipment industry. They're engineering various portions of the Net.

I suppose what Metcalfe is implying is that, for this kind of equipment, the process of somewhat diffused engineering governed by the market is distorted by the pricing anomalies that prevail throughout the phone system. And I agree that these anomalies are a real problem. That's what the Telecommunications Act of 1996 addressed and tried to alleviate, but failed to accomplish because of foolish errors made by the FCC in interpreting it.

As I understand it, under a concept called TELRIC (total estimated locally regulated incremental costs), the regional Bell operating companies have to charge incremental costs to their competitors for upgrades of the network. In other words, if the RBOCs install a lot more fiber and huge new switches and extend the bandwidth of their networks, they will have to then lease the additional capacity to their competitors at cost.

Of course this is preposterous. It means no RBOC will ever upgrade its network again, and to the extent that this kind of insanity prevails, the Internet will have to move off the local phone networks — and that will be a real problem.

There are solutions to it, though. There are ways of circumventing the central office switch and running right thru the central office without connecting to the 5ESS or DMS-500 switch that runs it, thus avoiding some of the requirements that the new law imposes.

But it's still a very unappetizing picture for the RBOCs, and I think this effort to create a "level playing field" is quixotic and stupid. In law schools they can talk about level playing fields, but out there in engineering there are no level playing fields. The RBOCs have some advantages, the long-distance companies have other advantages, so let them compete.

This idea that the 65 million tons of copper wire commanded by the RBOCs is an insurmountable barrier to entry for other companies is nonsense. It's actually a barrier to entry for the RBOCs, a "copper cage" that keeps them out of the huge new markets for broadband Internet. There are plenty of ways to bypass them with wireless. So if we have to bypass them with wireless, and cable, and satellite, we will — and that is part of my answer to Bob Metcalfe.

1997 IEEE

Rothschild, Michael

Michael Rothschild [in his 1990 book *Bionomics*] gave me a crucial new sense of biology, which I'd really neglected until that point. He showed me that the evolutionary perspective does not necessarily entail the acceptance of the materialist fallacy — [a fallacy which includes the notion] that somehow ideas are generated by material rather than being a separate domain, higher up the hierarchy. The sociobiologist in a sense reduces his own theories to an artifact of genetics and thus, in a sense, subverts the very authority of his own voice.

Michael shows that bionomics is [instead] a mandate for human emancipation, and this is his crucial and most powerful insight. A lot of people who've addressed the biological model have used it for various traps of determinism, and I think his understanding that biology affirms <u>liberty</u> is absolutely central and crucial to his message.

1993 BIONOMICS

Satellites

The problem with satellites is the limited bandwidth you can get out there on those birds. And there are delays [in getting signals] from the geosynchronous satellites to the ground. It takes a quarter-second to get up there and a quarter-second to get back, so you get a half-second time delay, which is really noticeable in conversation. The bandwidth is more limited from satellites than it is thru the fiber, so whatever you can accomplish thru satellites can probably be exceeded by fiber systems on the ground. Satellites will always be a supplementary system.

NEE: Used mostly for areas that have low populations, where no one is going to lay fiber line.

Everybody [out here in the Berkshires] does have a dish. If you drive up and down the valley, you'll see these big blue dishes. I still see satellites as a supplementary technology, even these LEOs — low earth-orbit satellites — which solve the time-delay problem. LEOs are close enough to earth that there is not a detectable delay.

So Is Motorola's *Iridium* project feasible?

It probably is feasible. A lot of its competitors are also being launched that promise [user] costs of a quarter to a tenth of Iridium. These other systems may not prevail, but they will force Iridium to adopt cheaper technology than was initially proposed. Iridium's costs now are too high. The [U.S.] satellite business has been retarded by very bad management by NASA. But now the Japanese are getting in the game, and I have a feeling they are going to give NASA a real kick. Launching satellites will become a much more efficient and routine task than it is today.

Is that a big proportion of a satellite's cost?

It's expensive because our launchers are so expensive. They are military missiles, and we've used national-security arguments to stop a number of proposals to create cheap, functional launchers. That [cheaper] technology is spreading around the world. But still, this will be a backup system for when you're in the boondocks or in a foreign country and you don't want to go thru their phone system. There's probably a big business in LEOs, but I don't think there's a big business for lots of LEO companies. There will have to be some sort of decision on what's the best technology.

1994 UPSIDE

Satellites: Relieving Internet

If there are all of these new technologies, and bandwidth is, as you claim, doubling every year —

I think it's going to double more often than every 12 months.

— why are we having brown-outs?

Because Internet traffic rose 16-fold in 1995. Then in 1996, after Metcalfe made his big publicity campaign about an Internet crash, between August and the end of November Internet traffic rose another 54%. And it probably rose even more, because that figure applies to the National Access Points (NAPS) only. Meanwhile, some of the Cisco Systems routers were malfunctioning.

However, recent data reported by Merit, which Metcalfe stresses, shows between a 70–90% drop in router instability at all the NAPs from around September 1 thru the end of December. This improvement, if the data proves out, is especially dramatic in the face of the 54% rise in traffic during this time.

But your "law of the telecosm" says that bandwidth capacity will always exceed the traffic, because as new nodes are added on they add the resources necessary to carry the traffic.

That's true, it's just there are sticky points, there are snags and glitches in the marketplace for bandwidth. And that has two different effects. The first is that extension of bandwidth will be very lumpy. There will not be a kind of linear, Moore's Law "revelation of bandwidth." Instead you have a new move of deregulation that results in a huge increment of bandwidth being deployed.

One such huge increment is satellite, which I think is going to be available for the Internet in the next year. One giant digital satellite can transmit downstream about 270 terabytes a month, which is the total capacity of all the U.S. Internet traffic, at least up until about August. Traffic thru the NAPs for the month of August was about 270 terabytes.

Do you predict that ISPs next year will be turning to satellite service and bypassing the RBOCs?

Well it's a complicated engineering problem to solve. Hughes has a solution in DirecPC, which offers Internet access via satellite network to your PC. They devote a couple of transponders to Internet access, I believe, on their Galaxy-5 satellite, which is mostly devoted to their VSAT [very small aperture terminals] network that offers private corporate connections for high-speed data-transmission.

At present they don't have much incentive to expand their Internet offering, because it competes with VSAT communications, for which they get compensated much better. But by the time your magazine comes out, they should have shifted their Internet offering from a VSAT satellite to one of the DBS-TV satellites (although I hear they are foolishly reconsidering this move).

When they do move their Internet channels to DBS, rather than competing with the VSAT network, they'll be competing with another cable time-shifted channel. I think the Internet's steadily going to win that competition. So the satellite people, who are launching at least downstream bandwidth all over the place, will bring major relief to Internet traffic.

1997 IEEE

Sematech

A recent article said that Sematech has played a pivotal role in the resurgence of the U.S. semiconductor market. My question to you is this: Do you think Sematech has any effect at all on the semiconductor market, and what does their experience tell us about things such as defense conversions, or the data superhighways?

Sematech was a fascinating case, because it was a negative force and retarded the advance of the U.S. semiconductor industry. Its chief focus was on photolithography, and its chief effort — where it invested the largest portion of all its funds — was in retrieving GCA Corporation, where the stepper was invented.

Sematech thought GCA Corporation had to be retrieved, because increasingly the American semiconductor industry was becoming dependent on Nikon, Canon and others. It happened that GCA was owned by General Signal Corporation, which also owned a company called Ultratech, which had a more innovative photolithography tool and which was being adopted quite rapidly by a number of entrepreneurial small companies and was actually making a profit.

But when Sematech endorsed GCA, which was trying to reproduce the same kind of steppers that Nikon and Canon were building, General Signal stopped investing in Ultratech and shifted its focus to GCA. GCA, however, was just playing catch-up-and-copy at this point. But the people in Washington representing the old industry had a sentimental attachment to GCA because it had launched the stepper, which was absolutely vital to their whole careers, so it was considered unacceptable to see GCA fall.

The result was that Sematech invested some $30 million in subsidizing GCA and promoting GCA steppers in competition with ASM and Ultratech. They actually hurt these other companies. The result of this principal effort of Sematech was to bring government competition to Ultratech and other photolithography companies. GCA still failed.

GCA has finally died, but it was the chief focus of Sematech; that was what they did. It was the only really novel important intervention that they pursued, and it was, by every measure, a failure. There was no way to explain it as a success. It had a destructive impact on other companies and it accomplished nothing.

You mean Sematech was not responsible for the resurgence of the semiconductor industry?

It was probably a negative. It compensated to some extent for its support for GCA by supporting the Perkin-Elmer spin-off, Microscan. Sematech subsidies for GCA created this problem, then created various solutions to this problem, which entailed more subsidies for other companies, and it distorted decisions in the private sector in a destructive way. It proceeded on the assumption that this is a national economy [and therefore] we can have all components and all capital equipment made in the United States, which is a futile and silly target to begin with.

They did everything wrong at Sematech. They did make some efforts to standardize technology, but these efforts were much less significant than the emergence of Applied Materials [using] clustered tools. This emergence established a new standard which was contrary to the standard which Sematech was promoting. During the course of this development, Applied Materials became the biggest semiconductor capital-equipment company in the world, and it's still growing. None of it has anything to do with Sematech.

It's incredible that the newspapers can even entertain bizarre claims of the successes of Sematech that are preposterous to anybody who was around.

1994 MARSHALL

What about the Sematech consortium's efforts to improve U.S. semiconductor chip-production technology? Isn't that an example of successful government funding of research?

No. Do you know about the photolithography disaster that happened? Sematech decided they had to retrieve GCA, which they viewed as the historic "American best hope" for photolithography. So they appropriated a substantial proportion of their money for photolithography and channeled some $20 million to GCA, the dominant U.S. stepper company. (Like a reversed slide-projector, steppers project chip designs inscribed on a photomask or reticle thru a series of reduction lenses and onto a chip.)

By keeping GCA alive beyond its natural span, they competed against Ultratech, which had an interesting 1-X stepper technology. (Ultratech simplified the stepper by moving the reduction optics away from each machine on the waferfab line back to the photomask maker.) And they competed against ASM Lithography, a company with mostly American customers and mostly American technology that happens to be headquartered in the Netherlands, which rendered them beyond the pale for Sematech.

Essentially what they did was to weaken all the forces that might otherwise have generated a successful photolithography alternative to Canon and Nikon, which themselves are competing intensely and supply American companies very satisfactorily. If there's a complaint that Canon and Nikon have too many links to Japanese semiconductor firms, then maybe ASM could be an alternative source — but ASM doesn't apply because they're foreign.

So instead of having a broad base of support for the industry, they balanced everything on one leg?

That's right. And the result was GCA was kept alive for a few more years, and Ultratech was weakened and didn't emerge as a real competitor. The combination of step-and-scan technology which originated with IBM and Perkin-Elmer was disadvantaged, because Perkin-Elmer essentially left the business when Sematech came in and decided GCA was their champion.

Really it had no good effect in photolithography, and that was the key area they chose to stress. They had already shifted from DRAM (dynamic random access memory) to SRAM (static RAM) to photolithography. And, after they screwed up photolithography, they moved to functioning as a kind of standards body for interoperability of other technologies and other cluster tools. Their chief function was to compete with Applied Materials, which was establishing a standard for cluster tools.

And so because of Sematech there were two standards: Applied Materials' standard, which really was the leading U.S. standard being extended around the world, and the MESA standard, which was the Sematech contrivance.

You know, they're still trying to find out what to do, and yet they have the temerity to claim they somehow were responsible for the recapture of the semiconductor industry that we never lost to Japan in the first place. There was a blip caused chiefly by the changing relationship between the dollar and the yen. Of course, if the yen suddenly doubles against the dollar, all Japanese production doubles in value in relation to U.S. production. But this was a transient.

I think the whole Sematech story is dishonest, and it's what happens when government launches a program.

1997 IEEE

Set-Top Boxes

First of all, they begin with the assumption that the set-top box will have to meet the form factors and price points of consumer electronics: It's got to be a $200 or $300 box. That means it's got to be hard-wired and only marginally programmable.

It's going to be hard to get even the limited functions people want — which include a lot of interactivity, superimposing graphic materials on existing programming, reproduction of VCR capabilities, and a lot of windowing. It's a difficult set of targets this little $200 or $300 machine has to hit. And it's unlikely they [the manufacturers] will target those functions just right.

Or they may be defined just right for the moment the

thing's launched. But within six months or so [emerges] some other function that becomes real important that they had not planned on...

The PC buyer is accustomed to paying $1,500 or so for the machine and another $1,500 worth of software and peripherals. There is no restriction to a $200 or $300 price point. And the capability of the machine is increasing enormously... The computer will be able to embody a set-top box in the course of its routine functions...

You have to project all these vectors at once. The vector of increasing PC capability, the vector of hugely increasing PC communications capability, the increasing capability of the users of PCs.

When you compare all that with this effort to put everything into a set-top box for $200 or $300 over the next few years, it looks pretty insignificant.

1994 UPSIDE

At the 1995 Western Cable Show, they finally gave up completely on television set-top boxes, and eagerly and ubiquitously embraced the cable modem and the Internet as the cable industry's great hope for the future. This is a wonderful hope, and I think cable companies are great buys right now, because they should play an important role in providing Internet services.

1996 HERRING

Software: As Bottleneck

Hardware progress proceeded about 48% a year for 30 years, while software progress — as measured by Ted Lewis (probably controversially) of *IEEE* computer magazine — has risen about 4.5% a year. And so you have this extraordinary explosion of hardware progress that hasn't been duplicated to [anywhere near] the same extent in software.

So [now we confront] an opportunity for a real breakthru in software. I think this breakthru in software has occurred, and it is the Internet. The Internet is imposing common standards on the entire world of information technology, and yielding the kind of multiplication of capabilities that previously was accessible only in hardware technology, where the Law of the Microcosm, combined with Moore's Law, yielded these tremendous gains.

Now the Telecosm — which makes all the resources of the Net, including all the software resources of the Net, globally accessible to a single person at a workstation — can yield these kind of exponential advances in software. You can have a situation where a single person at a workstation commands the creative power of a factory tycoon of the Industrial Era [along with] the communications power of a broadcast tycoon of the television era.

But I think it does depend in consummating this revolution in software, and really creating platform-independent systems, and component software systems — software <u>chips</u> — that can achieve the kind of exponential advances in effectiveness that microchips achieved in the previous era.

1996 DISCOVERY

Sony Corp.

I think Sony is doing it mostly wrong. Trying to perpetuate the age of consumer electronics into the visual arena, they're creating all these specialized, proprietary, incompatible appliances. They may be based in digital electronics components, but they break all the rules of the digital age.

Not to mention the rules of the age of networks, because none of them can interconnect with anything — they're all onanistic technologies.

[Sony is also] branding the content. They're trying to control both ends and it limits their output rather than expanding it...

[T]he whole point is that all these different forms can be merged in digital systems and you can address them in different ways and you can interconnect them. And that's the mistake Sony is making: They don't understand the Law of the Telecosm that, when you interconnect the computers together, their value increases exponentially. They're keeping everything separated.

1994 REPORTER

Spectrum Purchases

If we're moving as rapidly as you suggest towards bandwidth-abundance, why do you feel that companies and other entities are being so myopic in paying large sums of money for narrow regions of bandwidth? Is there a transitional phase here in which that is not such a poor investment? Or how do you see that transition occurring?

The problem, I guess, is the fear that the FCC will prohibit you from using other frequencies.

AT&T, for example, holds a lot of microwave frequencies around six gigahertz. They've been experimenting with these frequencies and they've found that they can conduct PCN at six gigahertz just as well as at 900 megahertz or two gigahertz. But, if they do this, they fear — and people there have actually told me — this would be regarded as a very aggressive act by the FCC, if they should start using these microwave frequencies for personal communications rather than just point-to-point long-distance communications, which is where they got it.

I think there's that fear — they want certainty. And if you actually have a license, you gain assurance that your control of the frequency won't be overthrown by some congressional panic or something. [But] there are just all sorts of ways to use spectrum beyond what is imagined at the FCC — and, as time passes, this abundance will be increasingly recognized.

1993 BIONOMICS

Teleconferencing

When I lecture, I am often at some little podium, with a huge screen above me on which the entire audience is focused. They don't even notice me at the bottom. Within the next few years, I will be able to meet a good part of my speaking schedule without leaving my home.

Teleconferencing is already a booming business. But the reason teleconferencing is still somewhat unattractive is that the computer is crippled by slow telephone connections. Overcome that barrier, and the computer can readily perform anything that television can: Not only receive digital video but store, shape, edit and even transmit it, as well as perform hundreds of other functions.

1994 PUBLIC

Toffler, Alvin

Although Toffler is an idiot on social issues, he is some kind of genius at explaining long-run technological change.

1992 GREGORSKY

Turing Test

The Turing Test assumes that if a computer can fool a human being into mistaking it for a human, it proves it can think like a human — [this was] Alan Turing's dumbest idea, short of his suicide.

1992 HILLIS

Tyson, Laura

The Clinton Administration really has some fundamental misconceptions of how the economy works. Laura Tyson spent a lot of her career studying semiconductors, and she has evidently learned virtually nothing. And here we're initiating a possible trade war to allow Motorola to impose some analog cellular system on Tokyo. In 1994, you're putting a new analog cellular system in Tokyo? If anyone tried that in Los Angeles, it would be a complete outrage. It is just amazing that these people, who think they are sophisticated and have some understanding of something, can go over there and try to do that to the Japanese.

1994 UPSIDE

Utilities: And Fiber-Optics

Power companies can lay fiber down [their] ground lines [because fiber] is not affected by electrical current.

The fourth biggest fiber network is owned by Williams Natural Gas Company of Tulsa. Williams was created when the oil and gas industry collapsed in Tulsa early in the 1980s. Everybody was mystified when Williams began buying up obsolete natural-gas pipelines that were the wrong gauge and seemed worthless to everybody. It bought them up for virtually nothing and now has the fourth largest fiber network — running thru natural-gas pipes.

1993 ACTUARIES

WebTV

WebTV is now in a few more than one-tenth of 1% of America's homes. Pushed by Microsoft hype, perhaps the machines can penetrate the 1% mark by 1999. By that time, an ordinary PC will run at 500 megahertz with full three-dimensional capabilities and video-conferencing powers, with a CMOS digital cameras, and will link to satellite downstream digital video at some 20 megabits a second and upstream at perhaps 500 kilobits.

By contrast, WebTV is in essence a dancing dog. As Boswell's Doctor Johnson explained, you are amazed not by how well it dances, you are amazed that it dances at all. But you are unlikely to choose it for your partner at the prom.

WebTV can display Web pages — but its resolution is inferior to a PC's super VGA.

It offers Internet access — but without the most exciting visual effects and at a premium price.

It can present text in a readable form — but not in as readable form as a PC, which in turn remains far inferior to paper.

It can supply mail, if you buy a keyboard — but it lacks the features of Eudora or other e-mail programs.

It is adopting a Java run-time engine — but it is limited to the more primitive applets.

Offering the form factor of HTML, web pages frozen into the form factor of television, the system is obsolete even before it reaches its one hundred-thousandth customer. The few score thousand buyers are mostly retired people, who find it a simple way to sample the Net. They are not the wave of the future.

1997 NEWSLETTER

WorldCom

From origins in 1983 in a Hattiesburg (MS) coffee shop as LDDS, WorldCom currently commands the backbone fiber network of WilTel, installed in [the latter's] abandoned mazes of natural-gas pipelines. To this foundation, it has added the MFS [Metropolitan Fiber Systems] bypass network linked to key office buildings in 23 states and running the Internet National Access Points MAE East and West. Further keys to the kingdom include UUNet, ANS and Compuserve internet access; IP fax and phone technology; and the optic lines of Brooks Fiber (BFPT) in 34 cities.

Now Ebbers is reaching out for MCI without a serious glitch in the ascent of his stock... With MCI in tow, WorldCom will be poised to usher in robust service for a broadband Internet. Starting now as the leader in cross-Atlantic IP FAX and Internet phones, the company will expand to global IP business services and video conferencing.

Think of WorldCom as the Standard Oil of the information era and [CEO] Bernie Ebbers as the new John D. Rockefeller. Think of all the oil-based industries unleashed by the collapse of oil prices under the Rockefeller aegis and you can get an idea of the forthcoming fruits of the WorldCom moment.

1997 NEWSLETTER

God's Way Of Business

Gilder at The Bible Speaks
— Spring 1985, Lenox (MA)

I'm really delighted to be speaking in this auditorium. It is full of memories for me, because I went to Lenox School for Boys here — [back when] this was Lenox Academy. And Bible Speaks has performed all sorts of miracles in Lenox, I can tell you — but none is quite so astonishing as the transformation of this building into a church.

I attended this building as a basketball player, and as a basketball fan. This building was also used for dances. At Lenox School, we never saw a girl for months on end. And then we'd have something called a "dance," on this floor, and we'd all clutch at some visiting group of victims [laughter] from some prep school around [here]...

But one of the things I've noticed about this building, since its use has been transformed, is that people emerge from it with a much greater glow of happiness and joy than they ever did from those dances [laughter] where people were specifically seeking pleasure.

This is the paradox of hedonism: When you seek pleasure directly, you don't get it.

Instead, you find pleasure by sharing love and seeking God — and this is what happens in this building, and that's why this building is so much more valuable today than it was in the time when it was used for dances and basketball games. Are you gonna transform the hockey rink into a church as well? [Laughter]

It's worth considering this [former] basketball court as an enterprise. Ideas in the head of Pastor Stevens, and the people at Bible Speaks, turned it into a miraculous enterprise. By considering it as an enterprise, you get another vision of how economies work, and why economists can't anticipate growth and creativity.

The demand-side economists would've come to Lenox and asked: "What do we need in Lenox? Do we need another church?" [Laughter] Nobody would've thought Lenox needed another church; there was no "demand" for another church in Lenox. No survey would have found any demand for another church in Lenox.

The second thing the demand-siders would say is, "If you do produce another church in Lenox, it'll be terrible for all the other churches." This is the zero-sum theory of economics: You have a limited market, and one person can gain only at the expense of other people. Socialists [especially] believe in a limited "pie" consisting of material goods, therefore they think capitalists can gain only by taking from others. They can't envision the expanding circles of gain that come from sharing and giving and love and the miracles of Biblical economics.

That's why this session is called "God's Way of Business."

So demand-side economics would've seen no need for another church here. "Lenox already has 20 churches, and they aren't filled up all the time [laughter]. It's clear we don't need another" — that's the first point.

The second point would be [how terrible the new church will be] for the existing churches. And if you speculate that the new church [will have] room for 900 people, and be filled to the gills every Sunday (and Wednesday night as well), they would say it would be a complete disaster for the other churches [laughter].

Yet there's no evidence that the emergence of Bible Speaks has had any damaging effect at all on the rest of the churches. As a matter of fact, it may have stimulated some of 'em to more vigorous and spiritually inspiring activities [laughter]. I notice that Hope Church down the road, which is the one closest by, is building new wings all the time.

This is the essence of supply-side economics: We don't have a zero-sum economy of a limited amount of resources. Because economists don't understand that, they predict depression, all the time, often right before the greatest booms in the history of the world.

All the economists said the Industrial Revolution would lead to the emisseration of workers. After the Second World War, there was a consensus that we faced a new kind of depression and decline. Particularly in Japan, all the economists saw Japan as a totally hopeless case: No resources, a little island out there, too many people. Edwin Reischauer of Harvard predicted Japan would be a burden on the world economy for decades to come [laughter].

This was just before Japan unleashed the fastest rate of economic growth, probably, in the history of the human race.

Established economists, in their models and everywhere else, all ignore the entrepreneur — and thank the Lord the entrepreneurs all ignore the established economists [laughter], so therefore we can have some economic growth. Otherwise it would be impossible. Imagine if all the entrepreneurs read these prophecies of depression all the time; nobody would ever accomplish anything.

Software is what changes a computer from a deaf and dumb machine into a workable piece of equipment to enhance productivity and growth. But software expenditures aren't included as "investment" in the national accounts.

As a matter of fact, in most countries, they haven't had this upsurge of software, and it's the lack of software that explains, for example, why Japan is applying high-technology goods much more sluggishly than we are. They're producing 'em at a great pace, but they can't <u>use</u> 'em. So we buy [those goods from Japan], and we actually put 'em to use.

Now, how did this tremendous surge of high-technology investment happen? How did the computer spread throughout American industry? It happened thru a completely unexpected development, which wasn't planned by the government and wasn't anticipated by any of the governments that <u>did</u> depend on planning to have economic growth.

What happened was the emergence of some 5,000 software companies. Some were started by high-school students, many by college dropouts — by nerds and hackers of every description [laughter]. Truly, you meet 'em and you know they're the lowly of the Earth — not the people who were judged "most likely to succeed" in high school.

But they started some 5,000 software companies — about 20 times more than there are in Japan. It was this completely unexpected surge of entrepreneurship that made possible the unprecedented upsurge of investment in high-technology goods, which in turn drove the growth of the American economy in recent years.

None of this was even glimpsed by any major economist. To them, "investment" is money and buildings — it's another form of "demand." They think the economy grows because of dollars in people's pockets. It doesn't grow because of dollars in people's pockets, it grows because of ideas in people's heads.

Most of these software entrepreneurs didn't have any money to speak of; they didn't have any "capital" in the usual sense of "capitalism." But they had ideas — ideas of how to make these computers do real work in the world rather than just manipulate figures.

And it's the ideas in people's heads that make the economy grow.

All its opponents dismiss capitalism as a mere expression of greed — a "deal with the devil" where [society gets] money and goods thru giving in to greed and avarice. Business is simply the pursuit of self-interest, the elaboration of greed — that's the essential belief about how capitalism works.

Even its <u>advocates</u> often maintain capitalism is motivated by greed. They might put it in smoother terms: "Self-interest" or "calculations of personal advantage." But everywhere it's believed capitalism is generated chiefly by greed.

Why do so many people believe this? Because, when you look at a capitalist economy, you do see a lot of people getting rich who aren't good — and you think: "There must be something wrong with the system. And what's wrong is that it rewards greed."

But imagine a system where everybody really <u>is</u> greedy. If capitalism really did consist of taking rather than giving, the system would quickly break down into a war of each man against his brother. No trust or faith could emerge. No contracts could be upheld. No long-term commitments could be made.

And the whole system would collapse. It would not produce ever-increasing spirals of prosperity and opportunity. Life would be "solitary, poor, nasty, brutish and short."

So the whole theory that greed can produce prosperity is fundamentally wrong. Some people can get rich by stealing. Some people can get rich by selling pornography or drugs. But, if everybody did it, obviously the whole system would collapse.

In other words, the source of the prosperity is not the stealing and the greed, it's something else. In fact, the stealing and the greed actually subvert the values of discipline and work and self-sacrifice and love and family which are indispensable to a successful economy.

Because conservatives have produced so few positive images of capitalism, you find somebody like the Pope — when he tries to summon inspirational rhetoric — turning to the Left. And this badly damages capitalism — it is very bad that the Pope can't understand capitalism. And conservatives who say, "It's an amoral system, that's just the way it is," not only betray the system they'd like to support, they also can't understand the system. What they end up with is Adam Smith's view of the "invisible hand."

Adam Smith was an aristocratic intellectual in England, and aristocratic intellectuals tend to disdain "men in trade." They really disdain businessmen. So intellectuals needed some theory of capitalism that praised the free market — because [free markets] seemed to produce wealth — but allowed them to continue to attack the actual capitalists! That's what they came up with: "The magic of the marketplace," the invisible hand, all these theories of economic growth which [amounted to] a new form of idolatry.

Markets are necessary, but it's not markets alone that produce wealth, it's men who produce wealth — men and women of enterprise. The spirit of enterprise transcends self-interest and drives economic growth.

So the crucial case for capitalism is a case for capitalists and entrepreneurs — how they behave, what they do — and their moral values. The value of a nation's goods ultimately depends on the values of its people. Goods don't have any value outside their use and the ideas that people bring to them.

Like this building is a kind of not too beautiful building — I won't go into an architectural critique of it. But, as a building, it's not very valuable. The ideas that entrepreneurs bring to it make it valuable. In the same way, the value of a country's goods depends on the values of its people.

All the leading texts of American history talk about the "robber barons" who built the wealth of America — these predatory, vicious creatures [who brought progress by] stealing from the people. This widespread myth is widely believed. But when you actually look at what the robber barons did, it becomes easier to defend them. They built the railroad, steel and oil industries on which American prosperity still heavily relies.

The real test of a "robber baron," or of an entrepreneur in an economy, is whether he rapidly reduces the price and improves the quality of his goods. This is what the capitalist should do; it's the real source of the expanding spirals of growth.

A robber baron, you would assume from most of the theories, would <u>raise</u> the prices and gouge for profit. [By this standard] we <u>do</u> have some robber barons now in America.

Lee Iacocca has not reduced the price of his cars. He has not really increased their quality. But, as a politician, he's been extraordinarily successful in Washington — getting a lot of special protections and benefits, for his firm and for his industry. In other words, he has been "making it by taking it." Although he has a certain entrepreneurial inspiration, and hasn't been a complete failure, he could be termed a <u>real</u> robber baron.

By contrast, Standard Oil — known to be the <u>worst</u> of the predatory monopolies led by the robber-baron Rockefeller — launched a whole series of technologies crucial for the production of oil. During its heyday, between 1870 and 1885, when it briefly gained 90% of the market, it rapidly expanded production all this time — and reduced the price of its principal product, refined kerosene, by 70%. This made it available to lots more people. By 1897, it had also reduced the price of refined oil, by more than 70%.

Its critics objected not chiefly to its "exploitation" of consumers, but to its superbly competitive <u>service</u> of them. Its behavior wouldn't pass muster at the Federal Trade Commission today. But Standard Oil's contribution to the nation's growth was vastly greater than the costs of some of its somewhat predatory activity.

As people make more of something, they do it better and cheaper. A worker learns to take shortcuts and improves operations. He improves the product, he learns to substitute better materials. The more accumulated experience you have in doing something, the better you do it. This means, in a successful capitalist system, that prices have a tendency not to go up; in general, they go down. The essence of this process is called The Learning Curve.

With computers, the government has completely missed this process. The Bureau of Economic Analysis in Washington assumes computers have been slightly increasing in cost for 25 years. They've missed the Learning Curve [as it's shown] in the cost-effectiveness of computers.

In fact, under capitalist competition, the highest <u>quality</u> goods have a tendency to be the <u>cheapest</u> goods, and the cheapest products have a tendency to be the best. The items that best fulfill the needs of the consumer can be produced in the greatest volume, which means all the materials <u>used</u> in their production also emerge at greater volume, so you have all sorts of intersecting Learning Curves — in a successful capitalist system.

And the computer is probably the most important new "good." The old expensive computers — the ones that would take up half this building — aren't made anymore. The process of learning, to produce ever greater volumes of computer power, has finally reduced the process to the inscribing of [integrated] circuits on grains of sand — the very symbol of worthlessness in poetry or literature. You don't get any cheaper than a grain of sand.

Gilder has never bought the Main Street homily that

government should be run "just like a business," but here is the one business/government analogy he likes: Like a firm slashing prices with the faith that its "loss" will be more than made up by a rising volume of sales, the government that cuts tax rates encourages more economic growth, and thus more government revenues — not as share of GNP, but in absolute terms...

It's futile to raise tax rates. I sort of learned it the hard way when I first made some money from *Wealth And Poverty*. It was widely publicized that I might have some money, and so I was besieged on every side by people trying to sell me tax shelters. Almost nobody came to me with an idea for a productive investment — as a matter of fact, I can say that nobody did. But I received scores of appeals and letters and phone calls [about] tax shelters.

The one I remember best is a guy who wanted to sell me a tax shelter in coal. The good news was that I could write off between five and seven times my initial investment in the first year. The bad news was that I would probably have to mine the coal myself [laughter]. But there was more good news: There probably wasn't any coal. Also, the guy was on his way to jail [laughter].

But this is what happens to everybody who makes any money in America: He's immediately beset by people who want to stop him from doing what he knows how to do — producing the product he has invented or launched; continuing down the Learning Curve to reduce its cost and increase its quality — and instead defer to the learning of tax planners and shelter accountants.

Caymen Island trusts, butterfly straddles, race horses, porno films and weeping-fig partnerships — the variety and array of tax shelters generated across the country are just incredible... That's why, when you cut the rates, the rich pay much more — and they always do pay more at lower rates — always.

In business, you've got to give to succeed. "Give and you'll be given unto" is the essential proposition of business success. Henry Ford didn't succeed by raising the Model T's price and gouging his customers for all he could get. He succeeded by two loops. One was by steadily reducing the price of the Model T while other cars were going up in price — reduced it by something like 80%.

He was always reducing the price to a rate <u>below</u> profitable operation. That meant he could succeed only if the lower price generated so much more value, and so much more learning and experience, that his costs dropped even faster. And his costs always did drop faster. So [even] as his margins went down, his profits went up. Because his volume expanded, he ended up dominating the entire market [during the 1920s].

Not only did he give to customers, without any assured return, he also gave to his workers. He created the $5 day, which was about triple the usual pay in those days. The *Wall Street Journal* attacked him [for] "applying Biblical principles where they don't belong" [laughter].

This is what a lot of people believe — that Biblical principles don't belong in business. And they're wrong. Without Biblical principles, business is just an empty pursuit of money, which ends up in an economy of failure and decline.

"God's Way of Business" is capitalism; it's the only way of business. This is the way wealth is created in the world. And groups like The Bible Speaks are crucial on the forefront of the creation of the real wealth of the world. Thank you very much.

Because the auditorium had no mike for the audience, this 1985 tape does not render the questions clearly. So the following bold passages convey the general inquiry and are partly the editor's inference.

How does the traditional strategy of investing institutionally stand up against the Reagan Era tax trend of giving the household and the small enterprise much more capital to invest?

When tax rates drop, there's more advantage in retaining disposable personal savings. And it's disposable personal savings that really fuel entrepreneurial progress — not surrendering your funds to an insurance company or a money-market fund or Treasury bills or even some mutual fund of stocks. It's having disposable personal savings that you can invest in...an area that you understand yourself, better than anybody else in the world — which is your own business. Or a new business you may want to start. Or the improved skills you may want to acquire.

Lower tax rates make more funds available for starting new businesses — more money available for the productive gifts of capitalism, which are investments in an expanding economy in response to the needs of others.

One question is completely inaudible, but it triggers the most Gilderized of responses.

That's why I think self-interest leads — as by an invisible hand — to an ever growing welfare state, not to prosperity but to socialism. Somebody who is really self-interested wants comfort and security first — and he'll turn to the government to give it to him. That's another reason self-interest is an inadequate guide to capitalist activity...

Unless [policymakers] address the whole array of retirement schemes and Medicare, and all these programs growing faster than the economy is growing, government spending is a problem. This spending can grow as fast as the economy — that's perfectly legitimate. But it can't grow faster than the economy without impairing the future growth of the economy and thus reducing the money available to support it.

The British spend less than half as much per capita on medical care than we do. They have nationalized medicine and they attempt to give [health care] free to everybody. All their intentions are to lavish funds on medical care. But they end up spending less, far less, and offering much less care, than we do in the United States. And the reason is that they have allowed their welfare state to grow three or four times as fast as their economy.

They retain these tax rates designed to redistribute incomes, but they end up just redistributing taxpayers — out of Britain and onto offshore islands and to the United States and into tax shelters and onto yachts and golf courses and into limousines and out of productive investment in the economy at-large...

What's crucial is to keep growth expanding and keep tax shelters dissolving. When people project growth rates and say we can't lower the deficit by growth alone, it's true: You can't lower the deficit by growth alone, you gotta have growth plus an expanding tax base — which you get by lowering rates. That's why we've got to continue lowering rates.

You sound like you're bashing real estate.

There's nothing wrong with real estate, particularly buildings and housing, as a crucial need of the public. So there's nothing wrong with investing in real estate, if the purpose is to produce better houses at a lower cost for the public. That's the goal.

If the goal is to accumulate some land somewhere and allow it to appreciate until it appreciates vastly because of some other development somewhere else, or a surge of inflation — that kind of investment may be legitimate, but it doesn't make any very important contribution to the economy.

Yet the tax system favors that kind of investment, and has for some time.

One of the reasons I want a flat tax [is that it will en-courage] more interest in the real-estate business in build-ing solid, valuable structures that accommodate people, and less interest in just erecting some apartment to gain an investment tax credit and 10 years of depreciation [but the owner doesn't] care if you rent it or it falls down.

Will deregulating phone service lead to a Tower of Babel?

I don't agree that will happen. The companies will have to collaborate and create standards and systems, which happen in all sort of businesses without conferring on one firm a monopoly. It's not necessary to give Bell a monopoly in order to have standards and systems that work. Standards will arise because all the firms have an interest in having them. Without standards, you can't have large volumes, and without large volumes you can't have low costs and you can't have a successful enterprise.

Gilderism On Demand

Art and Literature

It's true that, once upon a time, art and literature represented the pinnacle of creative achievement. That was before "art" meant Andy Warhol's soup cans and Jean-Paul Sartre's scribblings about the meaningless of life. If there is a Shakespeare alive now, he designs software or leads a corporation.

The average computer chip today contains more creativity and art than the average book featured in *The New York Review Of Books,* a journal few creative people have time to read before retirement.

1988 SUCCESS

Balanced-Budget Amendment

You get a national balanced-budget amendment, and there'll be so many exceptions and "investments." You know, the Democrats have 90% of the lawyers, and they'll get around any sort of legal barrier that supposedly restricts the expansion of government. The policy of "starving the monster" is really the only route we have to regain power.

1993 DUDLEY

Bars

A good bar is a good service. I don't acknowledge that alcohol is necessarily a terrible thing; if it's abused, then it's bad. But a good, exciting bar that fosters happiness and talk — why not?

1984 KING

Biological Engineering

The advances in the computer area were crucial to the advances in the genetic area. But it's obviously an area of fundamental importance to all health care — bioscience and the future and your extension of life, for example (although there are limits in that area). So I think it is of vital importance.

But it's a different kind of importance from electronics and communications. Electronics and communications have a more pervasive <u>systemic</u> effect, while bioengineering will have a tremendous impact on certain key <u>areas</u>. Maybe it will be even greater and more important in the long run, but it doesn't have the same sort of systemic, structural effect that computer technology does.

1993 ACTUARIES

The most socially disruptive use would be to manipulate sex choices. This probably should not be allowed, but it will occur sometime. It could be disruptive of the whole social order. Attacking the biological constitution of humanity itself poses a much greater threat than does creating "computer brains"...

Privacy invasion, or dehumanization thru computers, or the fragmentation of the culture — [they] are all fantasies, not significant threats. Access of terrorists to nuclear explosives and biological poisons is a <u>real</u> threat. An attack on the genetic constitution of humanity thru bio-engineering, which C.S. Lewis defined decades ago in *The Abolition Of Man,* is a real threat. The religion dimension of human life cannot be eclipsed.

Of course, computer technology makes bio-engineering possible, but it's always possible to use technologies in destructive ways. It's possible to use the old bacterial technologies to promote plagues.

1994 PUBLIC

Bionomics

This focus of bionomics on learning addresses both the

moral and efficiency issues of capitalism in a brilliant way. And I won't even get into the tapeworms and parasites, which — if you haven't read *Bionomics* [by Michael Rothschild] you should read it, because it gives the most vivid and sordid and inspiring view of the nature of government you will find in any book ever written.

1993 BIONOMICS

Cable-TV Reregulation

The chief significance of the [Democratic Congress's] victory today is a feast for lawyers. This was legislation made by lawyers and for lawyers, and its only result will be a huge outbreak of litigation. Cable companies will have to turn into law firms. This enormously complicated legislation transforms a market process of setting prices into a litigious process.

If you want to lower prices, it's simple to do: All you do is let the phone companies compete, as President Bush wants. Instead, the Congress refused to let more competitors in the race and created this regulatory monster, where the FCC in Washington is trying to control the price of every piece of equipment used in the cable industry — every converter, every service call, has to be supervised by remote bureaucrats.

This is just a ludicrous new advance of socialism in an era when technology is an enormously liberating and thrilling force of progress and opportunity.

1992 NIGHTLINE

Campaign Financing

What you need is to allow rich people to support politicians. That's where the money is. They're people, they're citizens, and they should be allowed to spend it, supporting politicians — so that you can run for Congress if you have five fervent friends with money who will support you.

Today, you can't have five fervent friends. The rich man himself can run for office; he can spend money on himself. But he isn't allowed to spend money on some candidate he wants to support. That's the key problem if they banish rich people from politics. (Most of 'em are delighted, by the way — they have the perfect excuse why they don't have to give a substantial sum of money to their buddy who's running for the Senate.)

Rich people come left, right, center. But the one thing about them is they're not, usually, monomaniacally committed to a particular issue the way a PAC is. A rich person is a citizen; he has a family, much of the time; he's got a community; he has a variety of loyalties.

But a PAC is a machine — a vote-buying machine. So, when you shift financial support from individual people with money to PACs, you've turned the system into a vote-buying machine. That's the problem today. And all these other restrictions [on] money — people just can go around all these other restrictions.

1993 DUDLEY

Castro's Cuba

Castro, in taking over all these stores and buildings and capital equipment in Cuba, thought he was taking over the crucial capital from the capitalists. And he allowed 5,000 folks to go to Miami. But he thought he was taking over what was important — the <u>physical</u> capital. What was really important was the <u>meta</u>physical capital — the ideas in the heads of the people who left Cuba who came to Miami.

Castro thought he could make a great Cuban city in the western hemisphere by dint of socialist planning. He did create a great Cuban city in the western hemisphere — unfortunately [for him], it was in Miami.

These people started with nothing. Sixty percent had been menial laborers in Cuba. One of 'em was an obscure chemist in the Havana Coca-Cola plant: His name was Roberto Goizueta. He came to Atlanta, worked thru the Coca-Cola hierarchy, and became head of Coca-Cola International...

One guy came and started peddling second-hand Cuban records on the street. After awhile he got enough money together to rent a little storefront. And it became Ultra Records, and now Ultra Records has about 20 different outlets in Miami and is importing records from all over

Latin America...

In general, the Cubans not only transformed Miami [but] the irony was that, throughout the '60s and '70s, Miami grew much faster...than all the parts of the country from which it was soliciting aid [to deal with the much-feared] terrible burden on the social programs [and higher unemployment from the new arrivals]. The solution was the Cubans themselves.

1984 KING

People imagine that Cuba is an island "90 miles south of Florida." But Cuba, in essence, is no longer <u>on</u> that island. Cuba — the enterprise of its citizens, the Cuban culture, the Cuban economy, everything <u>important</u> about Cuba — has moved to Miami, and to other parts of the United States. [Laughter]

And Castro thought he was capturing the essential wealth of Cuba when he expropriated the means of production, but the real means of production were in the heads of the people of Cuba — and they left.

We don't live any more in geographical time and space. We live in real time and space. And the nations that prevail in this new environment will be the nations that earn it, by liberating their people to create new knowledge, and thus new power for the world.

1986 BOSTON

Clintonomics

[President Clinton will be] the beneficiary of just the most explosive advance in technology in the history of the human race. It's the one thing that could completely save Clinton — it could engulf his Administration with prosperity in a way that would render many of his adverse policies almost irrelevant. That's their big hope, and they are trying to associate themselves with technology on all sides, although all their policies are hostile to technological progress. A boom is most likely.

1993 DUDLEY

Clinton/Gore: Technology

NEE: The FCC and the FTC and the Justice Department's Antitrust Division all seem to be more active. What do you think we'll end up seeing during the Clinton Administration?

In general, innovation gravitates to the least regulated arena. So, if they overregulate computer communications, it's going to be destructive.

Do you think this will happen?

In the end, I really see a "cock-a-doodle-do" strategy. The Administration wants to claim credit for all the technologies rising on the horizon during the next decade. As they arise, Al Gore will run out to a fencepost and say "cock-a-doodle-do."

It's amazing. Sematech, which actually damaged the American semiconductor industry despite spending hundreds of millions of dollars a year in the name of helping it, now claims credit for the American lead in semiconductors. If Sematech can claim credit for the American lead in semiconductors, anything can happen.

1994 UPSIDE

Colleges

Unlike American high schools...the colleges have to compete. Because they have to compete, and because of a huge number of small and private institutions, the number of computer scientists in the United States increased 46% a year, throughout the 1980s. The rise was from just over 11,000 in 1980 to 41,800 in 1986 to an estimated 100,000 [plus] in 1989.

It was just an explosive expansion of the colleges — responding immediately to this new market demand for computer scientists. A phenomenon that didn't happen anywhere else in the world.

Half of our Ph.D. students are immigrants. And it's not American "culture" that makes possible the U.S. success in high-technology, it's American <u>freedom</u> — the values that are propounded by schools like Hillsdale and which are embodied in our Constitution and political system — it's <u>freedom</u> that attracts people from around the world who want to work on the new frontiers of technology in the United States.

Education is a key "service export" of the United States that people don't talk about when they consider the totally obsolete and misleading figures of "the balance of payments" [and] "trade deficit."

1990 HILLSDALE

What advice would you give to the president of a college or university?

I think a kind of organizing principle, such as St. John's Great Books program or St. Thomas Aquinas's orientation toward the Catholic worldview, can animate an educational experience, whereas trying to be an educational smorgasbord of secular social theory is going to result in both a bad experience for students and failure as an educational institution.

You've got to be willing to teach some specific thing. You can't adopt some relativistic posture, because that will mean that fanatics will dominate the institution, and most of these institutions are dominated by propagandists rather than teachers.

And what would you advise college and university presidents to do with regard to information technology?

They should digitize their libraries and make them available from student rooms over computer networks. They should in general not restrict the resources of the college to the classrooms in it, but reach out from their own classrooms to students around the world who want to take courses with the excellent teachers available, while at the same time allowing the students on campus to reach out around the world.

In other words, make your educational institution one that summons the best from universities everywhere, rather than focusing on the faculty and students that happen to be assembled at your particular location...

I think there's greater diversity in higher education — quite a lot of diversity — and that the schools people think are good are mostly bad, and some of the schools people think are bad are in fact quite good.

For example, I think about 70% of the courses at Harvard are useless: You know less when you finish than when you started. All those endless sociology courses and social-science courses, and social psychology and political-science courses, and the endless efforts to retrieve some inkling of truth from Marxism!

You know, it's as though they were still teaching some pre-Copernican astronomy; they're really obscurantists in those institutions. It reflects the collapse of the elite culture in the United States.

But I think there are a lot of other cultures out there, and a lot of schools that people don't pay attention to are in fact a lot better: Schools like Hillsdale, schools like Thomas Aquinas. There are also schools like Caltech and Harvey Mudd — schools that are excellent in science and technology. These are the best schools in the country, because the only thing this culture does well is science and technology.

One of the real jokes is when you find MIT increasingly trying to teach students the humanities. I think the humanities as taught in existing universities are mostly perverse: Nihilist, relativist, feminist and Marxist. Marxism is just a completely worthless mode of study, and yet it's pursued intently at a great many elite universities as though there's something still in it.

1994 EDUCOM

Contrary Indicator

What is scarce in an Information Era? Is it energy? No, energy is more abundant than ever. Food? *Business Week* recently had a cover on impending food shortages — which is an unfailing signal that food is more abundant than ever. As indeed it is: Up 40% in the last 30 years per capita — food-production in the world...

1997 CATO

Deficit-Reduction: Versus Asset-Expansion

If you get rid of the deficit, haven't you freed up a pool of anywhere from $150 billion to $300 billion that doesn't have to be borrowed by government and, as such, won't money be in greater supply? Therefore, supply-and-demand would dictate interest rates would come down?

That's an accounting view of the economy. There's another view, which focuses on asset values. As John Rutledge at the Claremont Institute in California explains, we have something like $40 trillion of assets in the American economy. Those numbers you're using, relating to the flow of funds into the federal government, are picayune compared to the immense changes in asset-values that go on in response to different government policies.

If you cut tax rates, asset-values in general increase. And they increase not by a few hundred billion dollars but by trillions of dollars.

Money is relevant only as a symbol of productive services that somebody has offered. This idea that somehow you can unleash new money which will automatically expand the economy is the fallacy of demand-side economics (and I know you oppose that). But the balanced-budget illusion is largely based on demand-side calculations.

What about the theories, as advanced by Pete Peterson and others, that if we don't get a handle on it now the national tax rate is going to be 84% for a child born in 1990? That Social Security and all of these things that actually should be calculated as part of the deficit but aren't [will] bleed the economy dry, with taxation on fewer numbers of productive people? They say balancing the budget and paying for what you spend is crucial to keeping solvent all these various contracts we've made with the generations.

Several analysts have questioned the basic accounting functions Peterson and [Warren] Rudman and that group have been adducing. But, to Peterson, the whole Reagan

Administration was an absolutely catastrophic failure. He's one of these one-handed economists. "On the one hand," he can see liabilities. But he can't count assets — the other hand. So he sees the liabilities of the federal government growing. But he can't see the tens of trillions of dollars of new assets emerging from these new industries that have been generated and are now the spearheads of global economic growth.

American companies now earn some 47% of all the profits in the world economy. Except [for the extreme imbalances] immediately surrounding a war triumph, American dominance today — industrially — is probably as great as ever before. This is much more important than these numbers Peterson talks about...

The last time we had a balanced budget was 1979. It was an all-governmental balanced budget [meaning you also count the net surplus of the state and local levels], and we [also] had a trade surplus. Yet the whole private economy was in the red. With the Reagan years, America's assets have risen, since then, from about $17 trillion to $40 trillion.

1996 LIMBAUGH

The only real threat from [federal budget] deficits is that they will be financed by the government creating money, thus producing inflation — [or] that they will provoke politicians into tax hikes or protectionism.

1988 E-FORUM

Discrimination

Discrimination has been one of the great evils of American history, and I don't have any intention to downplay it or disparage it. However, in recent years discrimination has radically declined. During the course of my career, I spent a lot of time in the American Establishment...and I've yet to meet a bigot in a position of power in America. And I don't think bigotry is a very important force in the American economy... It is not a controlling force.

But the idea that it is [a controlling force] is very demoralizing and destructive. People who look for bigots under every bed, or turn to bigotry to explain every problem in their lives, become neurotic about it, and it makes them less effective in meeting the real difficulties and challenges of life in our economy.

1981 RATHER

Dumping

I keep hearing about dumping. Someday I'll get a story of real dumping. I've yet to see it. Whenever they impose anti-dumping penalties, it's always wrong. The test of dumping is whether the product's price, a price that went down during the dumping, goes up afterward. That's the clincher, they all maintain: Driving out the American producer, then jacking up the prices to exploit our consumers.

I've challenged protectionists to name one case of that.

They don't have any case. The one they speak about most is color-television sets — and their prices just constantly went down. All the prices went down. Yet everybody believes in anti-dumping laws — laws that have already inflicted more damage on the U.S. computer industry than all of Clinton's likely industrial policies put together.

1992 GREGORSKY

These dumping rules are just very destructive. Any time the currencies sift, you can always prove dumping because dumping is defined rigidly in the law as selling products more cheaply here than in Japan.

1994 UPSIDE

Earnings and Effort

I have an assignment from Phyllis [Schlafly]. She wants me to talk about the 59-cents movement — the differential in earnings between men and women...

The Institute for Research on Poverty, at the University of Wisconsin, is probably the major body studying poverty in America. It's financed by [HHS] and it assembles all the leading liberal economists devoted to the study of poverty.

In the course of examining earnings-discrimination against blacks, they recently did a study of what they call Earnings-Capacity Utilization Rates. What [that term] means, essentially, is how hard you work outside the home — how intensely you're devoted to your career. They measure, first, how many hours you work and, secondly, how much you earn. The combination of hours worked and earnings, together, signify the use of your earnings-capacity, as is measured by your education, credentials, age and a number of other factors in the study.

Now they skew the statistics quite heavily to begin with, because they start by saying there's massive discrimination against women. So, in order to say that women work as hard as men, they allow women to earn a lot less than men. In other words, women have to earn less to be ascribed the same amount of work effort... Second, they correct for child-care responsibilities. Again, women aren't expected to earn as much as men or work as many hours in order to get the same credit for work-effort outside the home.

Well, with all these adjustments, what did they find out?

They found out that married men work between two-and-a-third and four times as hard, outside the home, as married women do — of the same age and credentials. And married men work twice as hard, outside the home, with all these corrections, as do female family-heads.

This work-effort measure — which registers the "spirit" in which people enter the work force, how much they're willing to sacrifice to gain more wages and salary — shows just a massive difference between the sexes. Far greater than the difference between their actual earnings — the difference between 59 cents and a dollar.

So this liberal think tank really confirms that it's quite possible that there's discrimination in favor of women in the workforce. At least judging from the degree of engagement in it, and the yield gained, it would seem that women earn about at least what would be reasonable.

Now this difference is further exacerbated by another consideration they found. While men — as they gain more education, more age, more experience, and more children — work continually harder and more intensely, and exploit their opportunities more, and exploit their educational capacities more, women, as they get more education, work <u>less</u> hard, spend <u>fewer</u> hours outside the home.

This means their devotion to long-term careers is unlikely to achieve the highest salaries — if the very women who are most <u>capable</u> of earning high salaries have a lower engagement in the workforce. This proposition seems somewhat contrary to what people might expect...

But perhaps the most striking evidence against the proposition that the labor market is dominated by discrimination...is that single <u>men</u> only earn <u>57</u> cents for every dollar that <u>married</u> men earn. (I suppose single men could go around with a "57¢" label on.) As a matter of fact, single men and single women, of the same age and credentials, earn the same amount of money. Thru their lifetimes, single women actually earn more than single men do — because they're healthier and stay in the workforce more.

If discrimination is so massive, if sexism is so dominant in the work force, how come it doesn't help single men?

Women between the ages of 25 and 59, the prime earning years, are <u>11</u> times more likely to leave the workforce voluntarily... You just can't expect people who are 11 times more likely to leave the workforce to earn as much, because earnings are obtained thru real commitment to careers, increasing experience, increasing skills, increasing reliability. And, if you're 11 times more likely to leave voluntarily, it's unlikely you're gonna earn as much...

Single women on college campuses are supposedly a great arena of sexism — judging from the amount of discrimination suits that arise [there]. Well, single women with Ph.D.s, who stay in universities — who got their Ph.D.s in the forties and fifties, now earn more than men of the same credentials, age and qualifications, on campuses. This does not stop a tremendous number of suits alleging discrimination against women on campuses...

There's just nothing to the [59-cents] statistic — it's just meaningless, a figment of intellectuals. It doesn't have any reality in the real world. In the real world, it's chiefly married men who work hard to support their families — that's the chief fact [applause]. And they share their earnings with the woman — actually the woman spends more than 50% of the earnings [laughter]. And she contributes very heavily to his success — as you can tell by examining the statistics of single men...

Women enter the workforce in a radically different way than men do... Women have better things to do than pursue the dollar as their prime goal in life; they have crucial experiences and crucial responsibilities in civilized society. And I think it's important to know that liberal think tanks — the best analysts of this particular problem, who compile all this data — have massively confirmed this proposition.

1981 EAGLE

Economic Growth

What matters is growth. And growth is inhibited by excessive regulation, taxation, and mandates imposed on small businesses, litigation — all these Democratic activities; they all, almost, define the special-interest groups of the Democratic Party. They're all hostile to growth — private-sector growth.

1993 DUDLEY

Economic Growth: And Technology

[T]he only meaningful economic growth comes from the launching of innovations, new technologies. And that's why I think, as the central source of new technologies in America, Silicon Valley has been absolutely central to the American economy for the last 30 years. During the 1980s, Silicon Valley became absolutely dominant in the world economy. Yet you can read a hundred books on economics with scarcely a mention of this explosive process, which has caused a 10,000-fold total rise in the cost-effectiveness of computing over a decade. This central process of economic growth is ignored by most economists.

1990 UPSIDE

Education: Overhead

There is no correlation — period — between spending per student and performance per student, adjusted for education and income of parents. But there is a very significant negative correlation between the amount of bureaucracy per student and the performance of the student. So it's clear the middlemen in education are not merely dead wood, they are also a destructive force, and they actually prevent education. It's teachers that are needed, and teachers don't need much supervision.

1994 EDUCOM

Energy Crisis

Most of the companies which played a decisive role in overcoming the trials of the 1970s and early 1980s hardly existed when the era began; they were merely ideas in the heads of entrepreneurs, or tiny firms amidst the throng of millions.

The energy crisis, for example, was not resolved chiefly by the large oil companies or by leviathan vendors of nuclear power and subsidized synfuels. Rather, it was overcome by thousands of wildcatters around the world and by a few entrepreneurs who recognized — against all the geological expertise in the Department of Energy — that the fuel of the future would be natural gas, and that it is virtually inexhaustible.

Additionally, thousands of firms, and millions of individuals, increased the fuel-efficiency of virtually every mechanical process in the economy, conserving energy at a pace far exceeding the prognosis of those urging an era of draconian controls...

In retrospect, energy scarcity has given way to a glut that, barring a major war or price controls, will likely grow for the rest of the century, imparting a new impulse to growth.

1988 E-FORUM

Environmentalists

The essential proposition of the environmental movement — that we should protect our environment — is positive. But it has been delivered over to an almost entirely dishonest, deceitful and scientifically discreditable movement. It is amazing how any group could perpetrate so many preposterous howlers in a row and retain the respect and attention of the country and the press.

And it really has become a kind of pseudo-religion, a new kind of paganism. It is accepted as the only religion in our public and most of our "prestige" private schools — they all worship nature in this perverted way. Environmentalism is part of this multicultural vision which denies that any one culture is better than any other. Indian culture didn't fail because it was virtuous, it failed because it was a corrupt and unsuccessful culture. These tribal cultures they are trying to import from Africa are tragic failures, too.

To uphold these destructive cultures that have been virtual social suicide for the people who live in them is a terrible perversion. That is what multiculturalism is. And environmentalism is a kind of religious rite of the multiculturalists.

1994 ACTON

On the radio this morning, everybody wanted to tell me about the environment. Well, these new technologies mostly subsist on the human mind and, as they spread, they almost inherently overcome all the environmental crises alleged by these opponents of economic growth who go by the name of the "environmental movement."

1994 RECAP

Europe

For decades, in every political campaign there, the major issue was jobs — preserving jobs, creating jobs. But after 40 years of "preserving and creating jobs," the Europeans today have unemployment rates that resemble the United States during the Great Depression. Today Europe has long-term unemployment (unemployment for longer then six months) six times higher than U.S. rates. The Europeans have levels of overall employment decidedly lower than in the United States.

This is the result of government "solving problems." They have been solving the unemployment problem in Europe for 30 years, and the result is an unemployment disaster — a real crisis, which again derives from this overall problem of excessive government.

1994 RECAP

Fatherhood: Versus Feminism

I had been a fatherless child — my father was killed in World War Two — and I felt that loss very deeply. I think it contributed to the psychological instability that caused me to flunk out of Harvard and to have a totally chaotic school career. Yet the chief effect of many of the programs of the women's movement, it seemed to me, was to make it easier for fathers to split. They talked about liberating women, but what they were really doing was liberating men: Freeing men to relinquish their family responsibilities.

1981 RV-CHRON

The women's movement tragically reduces female sexuality to the terms of male sexuality. When this happens, she reduces herself to the male level of recreational sex. Paradoxically, when that happens, the woman loses all her power over men — the reverence and respect toward the procreative potential of woman is lost. And this really destroys the family.

But, when the power of "choice" is given up, the woman actually ascends to a higher level of sexuality, and her body attains an almost mystical power over men.

1994 ACTON

Fathers: As "Deadbeats"

Chasing "deadbeat dads" is just another attack on marriage. I mean, a woman can't have the access to the income of a man unless she marries him — this is the crucial rule of social regeneration. And to further reduce the need to marry the father of your children is just to further contribute to the breakdown.

So this "deadbeat dad" obsession makes everything worse. It makes it still more perilous to take a productive job, because you might have your wages garnisheed as a result of some child you didn't know and can scarcely remember...

[I]t's just another example of the constant focus on increasing the power of the women in relation to the fathers. And the fathers are going to be absolutely critical to overcoming any of these problems. Single-parent families will never do it.

1997 RETREAT

Fifties: No Golden Age

This idea that somehow we were way ahead in the 1950s but then fell behind in later years is exactly contrary to the facts. During the 1950s, the U.S. steadily lost ground [and] didn't even keep pace in defense. In electronics, the Japanese essentially caught up... Sony was producing transistors — particularly high-frequency transistor radios — more efficiently than [Texas Instruments] at that point...

It wasn't until after a general lowering in taxation in the 1960s that the whole Silicon Valley ignited and launched this renaissance in electronics that I think continues.

1990 UPSIDE

Futurist — Not

People accuse me of being a futurist, but I am <u>not</u> a futurist. I look at what's out there right now, and determine the implications. I really think there is going to be so much change by the year 2000 — you know, chips with a billion transistors and the equivalent power of 16 of today's supercomputers. How can you project beyond that?!

1996 HERRING

Harvard: Legacy

I had trouble all thru Harvard — just struggled. My one

success was a paper on arms races for Professor Henry Kissinger. It was supposed to be 30 pages or something. I wrote 125... It was a major paper, a real breakthru for me. Although it was focused on arms races, it articulated my emerging economic beliefs [as to why] the <u>dynamics</u> of a process are incomparably more important than the "equilibrium science" of it. Economists constantly begin with the equilibrium and just laboriously incorporate a few dynamic functions. But, in an economy, the dynamic is all there is. There is no equilibrium.

1990 UPSIDE

Homelessness

The more socialized housing is, the more homelessness you have. More than half of all public housing is in New York — that's why New York has no homelessness problem. Rent controls all over New York City assure rents won't be too high, and having half of all the public housing in the country accommodates everyone who needs housing. By this means, I understand New York [grinning] has completely eliminated homelessness and vagrancy.

1992 GREGORSKY

Hong Kong

When I was at Harvard, everybody was saying that the wonderful Maoist experiment would inspire Chinese all around the world; the Communist experiment would exert this great magnetism on all these little barren islands around the coast of China which had suffered so deeply from their lack of material resources. (And Japan was believed to be among these victim nations after the Second World War that couldn't possibly generate economic growth because of the lack of resources.)

Well, I've been saying for some time what will happen in 1997 — Hong Kong takes over China.

1993 BIONOMICS

Kennedy, John F.

I now think Kennedy's Administration was the best of the postwar era. It really established the grounds for everything that's happened since. It did [the intellectual spadework for] the big tax cut [passed in March 1964, which then] demonstrated that tax cuts could generate more revenue and growth. It passed the immigration bill, a major Kennedy project that allowed all the Asians to come in and stimulate our technology.

The civil-rights bill was launched [by JFK] and then passed under Johnson — critical in bringing blacks into the economy and the South into the country. The whole South was as segregated by its segregation as were blacks — the South was segregated from the rest of the country. Kennedy wanted the trade negotiations [i.e. "the Kennedy Round," begun in 1963 to reduce tariffs worldwide]. Then the space program really galvanized a lot of technology.

So you had those five key things. One was tax cuts [and], without Kennedy's tax cuts [to serve as a modern example], Reagan's program would have been a lot less likely. Then four other key accomplishments: Civil rights, immigration, free trade and space. For a thousand days, under any Administration, I don't think anybody has exceeded that. I think Kennedy's was the best Administration.

1990 UPSIDE

Lawyers and Litigiousness

Free enterprise is based on trust. That's why I call the spread of lawyers and litigation the cancer of capitalism. Capitalism is based on trust. But [when you fear being] sued by your workers and by your collaborators and by your customers and by your shareholders, then the essential environment of trust and honesty necessary to nurture productive companies dissolves.

That's why the law should be the framework in which capitalist activity proceeds. It should be a stable framework within which entrepreneurship occurs. When entrepreneurship begins to be directed to the manipulation of the law itself to the benefit of the manipulators, it's a kind of cancer. Every success creates a new need for more legal defense and more opportunities for legal manipulation... Litigation introduces conservatism into what should be a creative process, and this is terribly bad news for America.

1990 UPSIDE

Everyone hates "Congress" like they hate "lawyers." Yet, when they need a lawyer, as when their own Member finds a lost Social Security check, "I'm glad they fought for me." So how do you make the case against lawyers?

You don't make the case against lawyers, you make it against laws that provide field days for mischievous litigation — what's called *champerty*. ["A sharing in the proceeds of litigation by one who agrees with either the plaintiff or defendant to help promote it or carry it on" — *The Random House Dictionary* Unabridged 1987, p. 344.] Enterprise requires a structure of stable law, and entrepreneurship flourishes when the legal structure is secure. But when entrepreneurship is devoted to manipulation of the legal structure itself, it becomes the cancer of capitalism, attacking the system's very cell structure. That's the distinction.

That makes American society the most malignant of the democracies right now.

Yes. It really faces cancer. I'm on the boards of several companies. Our board meetings are constantly preoccupied with totally baseless litigation. I've never seen a case which had any grounds. Literally: After 10 or 15 years on boards, I've never seen a suit with <u>any</u> grounds —

Not one? Out of dozens?

Out of dozens. Never seen one that had any justification. Anyone who scrutinizes them closely, who knows the case, finds a completely mischievous suit: Someone has been fired for stealing — and they sue. For sex harassment. If they can claim some kind of disability. Whatever pretext is available.

So the [1991] Civil Rights law, and the Disabilities Act, were absolute godsends to this cancer?

Pure carcinogenic bills. The courts have a hard enough time dealing with murders, and muggings, and other obviously vicious crimes.

1992 GREGORSKY

Microcosm: Versus Old Right

In the *Chronicles of Culture* [sometime in 1990], Charlotte Low Allen reviewed *Microcosm*. She said it was poorly edited and "useless as business history." Then she discussed the way you profile the folks who invented semiconductors, detecting "a Tom Wolfe-like passion for describing colorful personalities." But — and this is what I'd like your comment on — "Gilder lacks Wolfe's imagination and, more important, Wolfe's interest in the people he writes about — except insofar as they serve to make a point."

I think that's right. I'm not a Tom Wolfe, and I'm not a biographer. But that part about *Microcosm* being worthless as [business] history? She showed in that review she didn't comprehend the book. It was a bestseller in Silicon Valley. I still get [asked to give] some 25 highly paid speeches a year based on it.

Everything it predicted — such as the death of analog TV and the triumph of the U.S. chip and computer industries — was dismissed at the time as Pollyanna. But it is all coming true. People interested in these subjects find the book definitive. A reviewer who didn't appreciate the history of the microchip, or never heard one until *Microcosm*, can't possibly judge it.

Allen's summary, to be fair to her, is not bad; it does show some understanding of the book's themes. But do you see a general problem with what is called the Old Right — the Russell Kirk, "Tory" conservatives — when it comes to understanding how technology can play out for the good of society?

Yes. They're inclined to believe that technology is the machine. Agrarian conservatives resisted the Industrial

Revolution. [But] blanket skepticism about technology is totally ignorant — particularly about <u>this</u> technology, history's first fully humane technology. It enhances the mind, which is human, rather than physical strength, which is animal.

I think, for example, that contemporary technology is a lot better than contemporary art. Technology is far superior in its representation of...America's essence, its achievement, its spirit, its discipline and inspiration, than today's art, movies or books — in general. So I really don't have enough respect for that [Old Right] position, and she sensed that. I probably should've answered it.

But I think Charlotte Allen is terrific in most of her stuff. And I like Russell Kirk, and Sam Francis, and all these people. But I don't think they have a clue about technology. They just don't get it.

Technology is part of the modern age, which the traditionalists prefer to be at war with.

That's right. They don't distinguish between computers and assembly lines. The obtuseness is so great that it's very hard to even have a discussion with them. They constantly focus on the earliest versions of all technologies, which are always cumbersome and klutzy, and don't really respond to human needs.

But maybe *Microcosm* was harder to read than it should've been.

1992 GREGORSKY

National Debt

We have $35 trillion of total American assets. A $4 trillion debt is not a problem if the economy is growing. If the private sector is growing and expanding, it can sustain that debt. No matter <u>what</u> the debt is, if the private sector's opportunities are extinguished, the country will be stagnant and troubled... The debt doesn't eat up the capital. The key thing is opportunity. If opportunities for growth are available, capital can be created. You can collateralize all kinds [of things with] $35 trillion worth of assets. They can be collateralized in one way or another to finance business ventures exploiting opportunities. But if you close off the opportunities, it doesn't matter how much you reduce the debt — it will not help the economy.

1993 DUDLEY

Why do all politicians, from left to right, bemoan interest payments on the national debt? Do they believe it's money sent out into space or burned in a trash heap? They don't see the $200 billion [in interest payments] cycling right back into the private sector to banks and bondholders.

Debt interest is the most positive part of all government spending; no other part is so valuable — because the payments can flow back into investment, and to investors. During the 1980s, the U.S. actually [climbed out of a] deep hole of <u>real</u> debt — chiefly in government pension funds and Social Security, both awash in red ink — into a surplus at both the state and federal levels. Check it out.

1992 GREGORSKY

National Security

It is crucial that the NSA [National Security Agency] and the various constabularies stay awake on the job. We need to remember that we're still in an arms race and we've got to win it! Our concern should not be focused on people stealing money from the Net, but on how small teams of terrorists, saboteurs and violent enemies might use the technologies against the creators of technology... Using various pattern-matching algorithms will make it possible to identify terrorists in crowds and follow their tracks around the world.

1996 HERRING

Parochial Schools

Unless a culture is aspiring toward the good, the true and the beautiful, and wants the good and the true [and] really worships God, it readily worships Satan. If we turn away from God, our culture becomes dominated by "real crime stories" and rap music and other spew. This is the most fundamental point. When the culture becomes corrupt, then the businesses that serve the culture also become corrupt.

You have called parochial education a "precious national treasure." Why do you say this?

Secular culture is in general corrupt, and degraded, and depraved. Because I don't believe in secular culture, I think parochial schools are the only real schools.

1994 ACTON

Planning

Human creativeness seems to flower best in our society but could easily be destroyed by government attempts at what you call the oxymoron of innovation planning.

If you could plan for innovation, you wouldn't need it. The very plan itself would constitute the innovation.

1994 MARSHALL

Rand, Ayn

I haven't read *Atlas Shrugged* [but] I've read a lot of Ayn Rand's essays. Ayn Rand devoted her last speech, at Fordhall Forum I believe, in Harvard, to an attack on *Wealth And Poverty*. She didn't like my stress on the altruistic dimension of capitalism. She celebrates "selfishness" in a special way; she makes selfishness into a sort of religious and noble experience.

I agree with lots of Ayn Rand, and I think she was a wonderful writer and an inspired thinker. But her atheism blinded her to the spiritual dimensions of capitalism.

1984 KING

Regulation

If all federal regulations on business were enforced, the U.S. economy would collapse.

1988 SUCCESS

Roaring Eighties

The present productivity gains of the U.S. economy were born 10 years ago, exactly when conventional economists were prophesying doom... [T]he Roaring Eighties came. We had the longest peacetime recovery, as we all know. We had a 200-fold rise in venture capital over [what had been the average level] during the overtaxed first seven years of the 1970s, and a tenfold rise in initial public offerings. We had the fastest manufacturing productivity growth of any period of the postwar era.

An entrepreneurial explosion, in fact, impelled the Roaring Eighties. Indeed, the convergence of low tax rates and high technology was the centerpiece of this exciting era...

Entrepreneurs are always concerned with capital gains, the increase in value of their companies, and their power to attract investment or secure loans as they launch new goods and services. After the capital-gains tax cut of 1978, all the indices of the entrepreneurial economy moved massively up, as a long backlog of innovations at last found significant funding. By the end of the year, new commitments to venture-capital funds had risen almost 15-fold, from $39 million in 1977 to $570 million in 1978. By 1981, actual venture outlays had tripled to some $1.4 billion and the total venture-capital pool had doubled to $5.8 billion.

The tax cut of 1981, dropping the maximum rate on long-term capital gains to 20%, spurred a new surge of investment... The number of major venture-capital partnerships soared...from 25 in 1973 to more than 200 10 years later.

Entrepreneurs and investors need a flourishing stock market to get their money back, and indeed it was the entrepreneurs (not the leviathans), followed by the smaller firms, that led the stock-market resurgence... From 1978 to

1980, the number of companies listed over-the-counter surged 60%...from 2,600 to 4,000. The total yearly amount raised in new public issues catapulted from $300 million in the mid-1970s to an average of more than $15 billion in the mid-1980s.

1988 E-FORUM

Salary Gaps

There is no big difference between men and women with equal drive and ambition, but there are far fewer hard-driving women.

1981 RV-CHRON

We now have women who, by any plausible measure, are the most fortunate of Americans being covered by this extraordinary panoply of federal programs designed to eliminate bigotry.

But they're mostly based on false propositions. Women get paid less than men in the American economy because they're 11 times more likely to leave their jobs voluntarily than men are. They have less than half the time in jobs that men do, and they tend to be less aggressive in pursuing advancement than men are. This is the reason why women earn less money; it's not because of discrimination.

You're not suggesting that you think that women, as a whole, are not discriminated against in jobs?

No, I don't think they are.

You do <u>not</u> think they are?

I do not. I don't think there is any evidence that, in general, equally qualified women...willing to undertake the same training and compete with the same persistence and aggressive as a comparable man, will not be rewarded by much. Indeed, single women earn just as much as single men in America — of the same age and qualifications.

It's a great myth that women are now subject to great bigotry in the marketplace... Men <u>work</u> for women: The average man, you ask him why he works, why he submits to the struggle and drudgery of daily labor, and he'll take out his wallet and show you a picture of his wife and kids.

1981 RATHER

Smart Highways

I'm interested in your thoughts on government's ability to use technologies to regulate further — [in this case, with] "smart highways." Government transportation planners, who are now picking up the notion that cars never pay their full cost, [could] seize on these technologies as a means of extracting that supposed full cost from people who drive cars. In effect, the whole notion of personal mobility would be turned into nostalgia.

That is a frightening prospect. The first part of your question, the idea of government as a purchaser, is very important. It is eminently desirable that government does purchase advanced technologies to perform its own roles more cost-effectively.

But I really oppose the shift of DARPA to the Department of Commerce. With defense, you can actually test the equipment against some clear function. With "competitiveness," anything goes. So to the extent that the Commerce Department takes over the role that DARPA has played, it will debauch it, it will become politicized, and they'll have to have a project in every Congressional district.

That's happened some with Defense, but it will be far worse with the Commerce Department. They're going to have "smart highway" technology everywhere, and they're going to be constantly collecting tolls on every car that runs by. That's a big tax hike, and I hope people are alert to it.

But, all the same, it would be nice to have the tolls collected more efficiently, rather than having everybody line up in a big jam every time you have to go thru a booth.

1994 MARSHALL

Stocks: A Buyer In 1981

We're going to see a booming period. The current technologies will create an enormous upsurge in productivity. The stock market will start to move — I think it is a candy store right now.

1981 RV-CHRON

Strategic Defense Initiative

On the larger strategic domain, you have the Strategic Defense Initiative, which has its much celebrated flaws. But nonetheless, SDI does capture the essence of our new opportunity, which is to substitute information for heavy missiles and explosives. SDI applies information technology to our crucial strategic predicament. It gets our defenses on this learning curve of the information economy...

To the extent we do get our defenses on this electronic-industry learning curve, we will necessarily prevail in the arms race. To the extent we want to compete with Russia in mobilizing manpower and large missiles, we will tend to fail...

The point of SDI isn't that it seals off the sky, but that it defends against war by accident or miscalculation or, you know, some [pause] — it's a fairly effective system with regard to those most likely dangers and third-world desperadoes... It's the only anti-<u>proliferation</u> policy we have, because it increases the threshold for acquiring some kind of meaningful missile capability in a third-world country...

I'm not a great expert on this, but I think the importance of it is that it is a more favorable direction to invest in the arms race, and it does get us on that learning curve that Carver [Mead] was describing. And if our defense technology gets securely tied to that learning curve, the yield will just be tremendous: It really might, in the course of time, make nuclear weapons obsolete. This was considered to be a wild exaggeration when Reagan made it, and it is a wild exaggeration of the near-term possibility. But the <u>long</u>-term possibility of getting on that learning curve is really to radically change the whole nature of national defense.

1987 CALTECH

[T]hese technologies will have a great impact on society.

One thing they will do is completely vindicate the insight of the Marshall Institute that strategic defense systems will be feasible, and will grow more feasible day after day.

I remember some argued that it would be impossible to have an SDI system, because the complexity of the software would be too great, and huge supercomputers would be needed in order to run the system; such supercomputers would not be feasible with the software programs that would be needed to run them. They said you'd need a hundred Crays and hundreds of billions of lines of code, and that you couldn't produce a system that complex that would work. This was one of the most trenchant attacks on the whole concept of SDI.

But if you can have that kind of supercomputer power in each interceptor, you don't need any coordinating overall software program. Suddenly, programs like SDI become much more feasible. They respond to the Law of the Microcosm which imparts this exponential increase in performance.

If you don't understand these trajectories, you really will make dreadful public-policy mistakes.

1994 MARSHALL

Sweden

For 20 years, Sweden has done virtually everything the feminist movement would like: Day-care centers on every block, contraceptives in every bathroom, abortions on demand, sex education from kindergarten thru high school, in every school. They have paternity leaves for fathers. They've done absolutely everything they could to create the supposedly blissful kind of society the feminists envisage for us [here in the U.S.].

And what is the result? With all this contraception and sex education, they would have low levels of legitimacy, right? Nearly a third of all Swedish children are illegitimate — a third. This is three times worse than in the United States. Moreover, this represents a radical degeneration, beginning at the point [when they] adopted the "sexual suicide" society.

[But] it's wonderful that the kids are being born. With a

third of all the children born illegitimate, it's clear that [Sweden] couldn't have very many abortions — who's gonna have 'em? As a matter of fact, that [assumption] would be wrong as well: For young women in Sweden, half of all pregnancies end in abortion...

A further point: America's divorce rate is very distressing to us. But Sweden's divorce rate is 60% higher than ours.

So the programs have been tested. It's not some speculative question of whether they work or not. Here you have — in a white, middle-class, rich European cosmopolitan society — the perfect arena for experimentation, everything you might want.

And they have worse statistics than the center of Harlem.

And they do it by enacting the very agenda which the feminists [in America] present as a way to <u>overcome</u> illegitimacy. They say it reduces illegitimacy, they say it makes for happier marriages. All their claims are not even worth confronting: They've been completely disproven in the most careful and extensive social experiment you could have had...

The real problem of Swedish society is the dominance of a secular humanist creed — the rejection of God, essentially, in human life... This creed very rapidly degenerates into animalism. What it really is is secular animalism [laughter], when people no longer have standards and aspirations above themselves; when they believe that "our bodies, our selves" are all there is, you find that human life rapidly degenerates into an uncivilized mess.

1981 EAGLE

Taxation and Deficit

Whenever we mention the deficit, as a test, or a symbol of conservatism, or as a goal to close, we lose — because it implies that taxation is somehow a reasonable response to the deficit... Talking about the deficit is a loser for Republicans. It just guarantees more government spending and taxes. That's why the Democrats won this time. It was because Perot defined the deficit as the key problem. Bush just had no response but to talk about how he was gonna cut away all this government spending, which mobilizes all the interest groups against the Republicans. Taxes taxes taxes — as far as I'm concerned, <u>forget</u> anything else.

1993 DUDLEY

The Republicans are essentially saying, "We're going to tax you just as much, but we're going to give you less." And I think this formula will not work. It is desperately hard to eliminate government programs, or even to cut them back. Well, the same people who will fight to the death to preserve their little government benefit will also desire lower tax rates. And it so happens — although I know you don't want to believe it — that cutting tax rates precipitates a virtuous cycle of all sorts of other changes that, in the end, can create an environment where government will shrink as a share of total GNP and national assets.

1997 RETREAT

If we cut spending 20%, we could finance the whole government with bonds — this would be fine, it would be beneficial to the economy. There's nothing bad, in principle, about issuing bonds to voluntary purchasers to support government spending. It's the amount of resources that the government actually extracts from the economy that's the problem. It's not whether the government taxes to extract those resources, or issues <u>bonds</u> to extract those resources — that doesn't matter. What matters is how much power the government brings to itself. Whenever you start talking about the deficit as the chief problem, then you imply that some sort of compromise — where you raise taxes here, and pretend to lower spending there — actually makes a difference. It makes no difference. What makes a difference is whether the private sector is growing faster than the government sector; that's all that matters.

1993 DUDLEY

Government now takes 40% of GNP at all levels and people sometimes divert themselves by saying that certain foreign countries have even higher levels of government spending. But, if you examine it closely, you see that the countries with higher levels of government spending all have nationalized health care. In other words, health care is all included as "government spending."

In the United States, we spend more on health care than anywhere else, and we have heavily government-regulated and restructured and subsidized health care. But, if you exclude health care from all these numbers, you find that the U.S. has levels of government spending comparable to any of the major competitors in the world. We are not laggards in government spending.

1993 ACTUARIES

[Y]ou say the current Republican fervor to balance the budget is "Hooverian," and that they've wasted a year on this premise.

When you [make] a balanced budget your goal, you play into the hands of the Democrats. You immediately put the focus on cutting government spending.

So your whole campaign is perceived by the people — who get their information largely from the media megaphones — as negative. The Republicans are somehow going to cut spending drastically, and this terrifies the 33% of Americans who are dependent one way or another on government jobs and subsidies.

So you end up terrorizing millions of people, but you don't achieve anything of value. Because Democrats succeed: As a result of this threat, they succeed in mobilizing sufficient political force to stop major cuts.

Meanwhile, the things worth doing, the things people will really enjoy — tax-rate reductions, privatization, deregulation, all these positive programs Republicans should push and you've been pushing for years — get lost.

So we end up just talking about balanced budgets seven years from now. Who the hell cares?...

But is it an error of substance they've made? Or an error of strategy? Because obviously what they're trying to do

is not just balance the budget. They're trying to end the welfare stare. They're trying to reduce the size of government so as to make more prosperous the individual. You would agree with that, wouldn't you?

I agree with their visions. I don't agree with their tactics — and their tactics have now, in my judgment, largely subsumed their vision. So they end up essentially attempting to achieve something called "balanced budget" by cutting various government programs. That is a completely negative formula, and it's political poison. Moreover, it doesn't achieve any good results...

I think you have to start by cutting tax rates. Big tax-rate reductions would be entirely positive. They would pay for themselves. They would enrich the country. They would make Republicans popular — despite what the polls happen to say.

The Democrats would do the same thing, though. They would call them tax cuts for the rich, and you'd still have the same arguments that are taking place now. Because Democrats are not going to lay down and let happen what the true objective is, which is to reduce government, regardless of how the Republicans characterize it.

To the extent the goal is defined as cutting back government programs, the Democrats win. To the extent the goal is defined as unleashing the American economy, creating huge numbers of new jobs and opportunities, reducing tax rates, deregulating bureaucracy, we win.

The focus on the balanced budget is a mistake, and this mistake was imposed on the party by a pollster. Politicians who follow public-opinion polls earn the contempt of the public. And that is the big danger today, because Republicans on television most of the time are saying something about a balanced budget that isn't true.

Such as?

Such as, that it will greatly lower interest rates and produce all these marvelous benefits. This could be

achieved by tax cuts, but [not] by the balanced-budget
process — because you have to begin by saying tax cuts cost
revenue, which is nonsense. Republicans from the beginning agreed to accept the static budgeting method, [which
assumes] that tax cuts don't affect economic behavior. Tax
cuts increase revenue, as you've explained endlessly,
though this still hasn't penetrated beyond your audience...

The Gingrich error [after he became Speaker of the
House] was to start by cutting — by threatening — existing
programs, rather than by starting with the flat tax. That
should have been what they came into office with. Let
Clinton make all the arguments about why we shouldn't
have a tax return on a post card.

1996 LIMBAUGH

Tax Reform: 1986

The new "American Challenge" is the new tax reform,
which attracts and emancipates entrepreneurs. This 28% top
rate may not seem too significant to some Americans. But if
you go around the world, as I've been doing recently, they
are <u>riveted</u> by that 28% top rate. If you think capital and
immigrants and knowledge are flowing toward the United
States now, wait until this new tax reform is fully in place.
Entrepreneurs from Europe and Asia and around the world
will send capital, and often follow themselves. Of course, if
we have a big capital surplus, we'll necessarily have a trade
deficit — but it will reflect the strength of the U.S. economy,
not its weakness.

1987 CALTECH

**Yay or nay, up or down, the whole '86 bill — given
what's happened to venture capital [in the six years]
since, did we miss something back there?**

The bill was good. At the time, most of us assumed that
the states would compete to lower their capital-gains taxes
— a <u>major</u> miscalculation; was I ever wrong about that! The
states eagerly jumped on the bandwagon of higher federal
capital-gains tax rates.

I also took for granted that Congress would lower them, and they <u>would</u> have. But [in October 1989, President] Bush capitulated to [Senate Majority Leader George] Mitchell and completely blew it. White House management of that issue was incredibly maladroit.

So, I was wrong about predicting the results. But I would support it [the '86 tax reform] again — to get lower marginal rates [on individual incomes]. As for the capital-gains fiasco, it didn't have to happen.

1992 GREGORSKY

Television: The Exceptions

Compare two serious approaches to television: PBS and C-SPAN. Some people have said that C-SPAN is what public television ought to be. What do you think?

C-SPAN now exists without the aid of public TV, and PBS works at all only because of the garbage that's on all the other channels. Just by being explicitly elitist, PBS can shine luminously in the darkness.

But, beyond that, I just don't really believe any of these channels or networks have a future. And, particularly, I don't think TV news has a future at all.

So I believe that, within the existing regime of 30 channels or whatever, C-SPAN and PBS are better than the others — [yet] it's all still a vast wasteland. A channel like C-SPAN will still have a place in a world where you have one channel and it's yours. But enterprises like PBS and CNN are resources only for a world in which there are few channels and no control over them.

Why is there no future for TV news?

Because TV news is all governed by the two-minute rule, which says that you can't devote more than two minutes to a story unless it's a war or something. But the reason for this is not that people have any particular desire for two-minute stories. To the contrary, people want much <u>more</u> than two minutes, on any story that actually interests them.

TV's two-minute rule exists because people will zap any story longer than two minutes that <u>doesn't</u> interest them.

And so network [and local] news is guided entirely by this negative constraint and, within the two-minute limit, it necessarily has to go for sensational images and crashes and fires and murders and whatever.

1994 EDUCOM

Television: Tyranny

Television really is a tool for tyrants. In all totalitarian regimes, they have many more televisions than telephones. In the Soviet Union, they have six times as many television sets as they do telephones or two-way media. This is almost a test of the democratic character of a country. If it's a totalitarian country, it has overwhelmingly more TV sets than telephones. If it's a democratic country, it has as many telephones and computers together — two-way systems — as it does top-down systems like television.

1990 LONGBOAT

Trade Secret

The three leading Latin American countries — Brazil, Argentina and Mexico — are now running a trade surplus of about $15 billion. They also have very weak economies, which might raise some question about the linkage between strong economies and trade surpluses, which so many people erroneously entertain. The weakest economies in the world tend to have trade surpluses.

1988 HILLSDALE

Urban Poverty

The chief problem of black poverty in America comes thru the welfare system. It comes among poor people who are demoralized by the destruction of their family thru the extension of benefits that far exceed what they can earn themselves in the work force.

So a man who sees that the government can support the family better than he can is in a way cuckolded by the welfare state; he's having his role, his crucial masculine function, usurped by a bunch of government bureaucrats...issuing checks. This was a very bad deal for the poor — because broken families are incapable of escaping poverty...

To the extent that, by increasing the incomes of the poor, we reduce their family stability, we don't fight poverty, we intensify and perpetuate poverty — and that is the strange fruit of the Great Society. It focused on the black and inner-city poor and, after 15 years of it, these inner-city poor are its chief victims.

1981 RATHER

Essentially, welfare benefits are far better than low-wage, entry-level jobs. Welfare gives benefits far superior to entry-level jobs because they yield valuable leisure-time for the recipient. Thus it usurps the male role as chief provider and undermines the foundation of families. His provider role is absolutely central to the family: If the state replaces the male provider, you don't have families. The welfare state cuckolds the man. That is why we have 80% illegitimacy rates in the inner cities. The welfare state has been far more destructive to the black family than slavery was.

Is there a difference between black and white poor families?

No, the poor whites have the same kind of patterns as poor blacks. They aren't concentrated in the urban centers in the same way. Because they are dispersed throughout the country, it is not as pathological a culture as is emerging in the inner cities. [But] the illegitimacy rate among white welfare-recipients is close to black rates — around 60%.

1994 ACTON

Urban Renewal

It really only can come from religion. And it's happening to a considerable extent in the black community. At first it was the Black Muslims; they have a patriarchal, structured, religious order, oriented around families and male responsibility for families. And the Black Muslims actually generated lots of small businesses and actually quite a lot of upward mobility. [Or] this guy Youngblood, in Brooklyn;

who was recently celebrated on television and in a book by Thomas Friedman — he also emphasizes patriarchal religion. This is necessary to support families. Secular hedonism cannot support families. So that's what has to happen and it has to be pretty much a bottom-up thing...

1993 DUDLEY

What the poor really need is morals. The welfare state destroys the morals of the poor. Poor people in America live better [in material terms] than the middle class in most other countries in the world. The official poor in America have higher incomes and purchasing power than the middle class in the United States in 1955 or [than] the middle class in Japan today. The so-called "poor" are ruined by the overflow of American prosperity. What they need is Christian teaching from the churches. But these same churches are mostly inept at actually preaching to the poor. Instead, they support the welfare state as a sort of proxy.

Why is the poverty line, in your words, a "virtually useless measure" of real poverty?

Because poverty is not a matter of income but a matter of prospects. College students are regarded as impoverished, as are all sorts of single people who live with their families. The poverty line in a rich country like the United States is a meaningless standard. Strictly speaking, we have no "poverty problem," we have a desperate problem of family breakdown and moral decay.

1994 ACTON

What the inner-city needs is emancipation from this socialist regime that exists within our own borders. Everybody gets their check from the government. They get their education from government schools. Their housing is mostly either government-run or rent-controlled, regulated and coded. So there is essentially a socialist regime in the middle of a capitalist country...

I spent time in the inner city and wrote about it. One of the first things that strikes you is the television. Television sets are everywhere. They all have television sets and they're always on, all the time. They virtually live in this TV world. It's the cheapest form of entertainment in history.

But it also is a form of cultural transmission that is very destructive. All the messages it sends argue for immediate gratification, immediate goals, and it's hostile to the kind of deferred gratification and long-term goals that are necessary to succeed.

I think the telecomputer will be cheap and powerful and will allow people in the inner cities to educate themselves — it will improve their opportunities more than [those of] anybody else... It won't solve all the problems. You do have to have families — I mean, that is a rule of human life. The nuclear family is not an optional kind of system, which means you will have to reconstruct the welfare system and other things. I can talk about this later, but there is a positive impact from computer technology on even this problem.

1993 ACTUARIES

Urban Violence

His programs had virtually nothing to do with [his appeal to blacks], as far as I was concerned. The key thing [Jack] Kemp [as HUD Secretary] did was to gain lots of black support for Republicans by going around the country arguing for <u>opportunities</u> rather than offering alibis. The Democrats all offer alibis to blacks. Kemp stressed opportunity — the critical need.

You know, stop lying to blacks. The Rodney King case is a perfect example. Most of the press lies to blacks — by implying there was something wrong with what the police did. There was nothing at all wrong with what the police did. King was lucky not to be shot. If I charged the police after leading 'em on a chase thru the city, I'd expect to be shot — literally, [or] I'd expect my son to be shot.

The fact they had to keep beating him was 'cause they didn't hit him on the head. If they had belted him on the head, once, with one of those nightsticks, he would have been out. But they carefully didn't beat him on the head, they hit him on the sides and in the legs...

You can't have effective policing in the inner city unless the police can use force... You're gonna have to have a revulsion against liberalism on the part of the communities themselves... Religion is essential to support families, particularly in poor communities [fighting] all sorts of corrosive forces. I don't think you can have a prosperous or productive society without a foundation of secure families.

1993 DUDLEY

Vietnam War: The Victor

Vietnam is no longer in Vietnam. The essence of Vietnam is in the United States today. We got everything of value out of that country. The value in Vietnam was in those boats.

1987 CALTECH

Welfare Policy

I believe you have to have welfare benefits, because capitalism is founded on <u>voluntary</u> participation. And, without a welfare system, you're forcing people to work at pain of starvation — and that is coercive, and inimical to the spirit of freedom of voluntarism, which makes Capitalism so creative and productive. So I'm not for abolishing welfare, I'm for reforming and making the system work rather than just destroy jobs and families, as it does today.

1984 KING

You know, Charles Murray's contribution was brilliant and indispensable. But I really think he made a mistake talking about "abolishing welfare." That immediately turns off anyone who might've listened to his ideas as a political possibility. We're not going to allow people to die on the streets, no matter what the situation. Nor will we recreate the community fabric you might have known growing up in rural Iowa or Massachusetts.

Or Harlem in the 1920s.

Or in the 1930s. So "abolishing welfare" is quixotic and

foolish; it's probably even wrong. It's technically true that we'd be better off today, by far, if we'd never had any welfare system — but it's also irrelevant. Those mistakes have been made; people have changed their lives.

1992 GREGORSKY

The program I prefer...is child allowances, which go to all families with children regardless of their income. I'm for a program of child allowances, which could be instituted thru eliminating the child-deduction and replacing it with child allowances. [The idea is to] make a system in which welfare isn't the source of income that expands as the family grows. Today, almost all big families can do better [economically] going on welfare than staying at work, and that is a disaster — and it's had a <u>catastrophic</u> impact on poor families.

1984 KING

Welfare State

I believe in a limited welfare state. I think you do need to have certain welfare programs. The government has all sorts of crucial roles to play. And I agree with Alfred Marshall, the great economist, who said, "Government is so precious that we have to be terribly careful to use it intelligently."

1984 KING

I agree that welfare and insurance systems are indispensable to any compassionate economy, and I don't oppose them. I oppose them when they go beyond the point of moral hazard — when they begin to promote poverty rather than relieve it.

1981 RATHER

Welfare: Thru Workfare

"Workfare" is a real menace; in order to do it, you need day care, which means more special benefits. And when recipients go to work, it tends to be at make-work, CETA-style, public-sector jobs — which means not having to do anything, so they don't learn what work is. If "workfare" makes being on welfare nicer, it will be a real catastrophe.

1992 GREGORSKY

Even conservatives who want workfare want to further enrich the welfare state. To them, it's not enough to give mothers of illegitimate children all sorts of supports and special pregnancy services, housing, special educational and training programs. You now have to give them jobs and day-care centers on top of it.

This constant enrichment of the welfare state ignores the victims of the real problem, who are not on welfare. They are unmarried men and they have rendered many of our big cities unlivable. They have reduced the real-estate values in American cities by trillions of dollars. It is single men who commit the violent crimes.

1994 ACTON

Welfare: Versus Immigration

[T]he great problem with immigration is that it responds to the incentives you offer in the receiving country. Today, the incentives are increasingly for people who don't want to come to work, but who want to come to loaf.

And that is the problem [applause] — the problem is not immigration. The problem is the fundamental paradox of the welfare state, which is [how] compassion for the non-poor, in the United States, forces complete callousness toward the wretched of the earth — the poor in the rest of the world. That's what it does.

The so-called poor in the United States have higher incomes than the average American [did] in 1955. They have more purchasing power than the average Japanese person today. The problem of the poor in the United States is not money, it's moral collapse [applause].

And this welfare state can destroy immigrants as it can destroy Americans — and that's the problem [as opposed to] any fundamental change in immigration.

1993 CON-SUM

Immigration is undermined when the welfare state grows too generous. Under such conditions, you effectively spurn the real poor in order to support special-interest groups.

The United States is approaching this point, particularly in California, which has some of the most generous welfare "benefits" on the face of the earth. Immigration is becoming impossible there because the state actually lures in immigrants with welfare programs while punishing businessmen who employ them. So, if you are an illegal alien, it's legal in California to go on welfare, but it's not legal to work.

We are creating this nightmarish, and really vicious, welfare system that not only destroys American families but now is "reaching out" to destroy immigrants as well.

1994 ACTON

Why The Trade Gap Is Great News

Gilder at Hillsdale College — Summer 1988

I am honored to be introduced by George Roche, who himself — although he recently published a really splendid book called *A World Without Heroes* — is a hero of all of us, for leading Hillsdale as one of those pioneering institutions which has asserted the key values of America in the face of an establishment of universities that have attempted to repress and debauch those values.

I come from Harvard, as George revealed to you — and I admit it. Harvard is said to be a great repository of learning. And I say it <u>must</u> be a great repository of learning, because the students come there knowing so much, and leave there knowing so little [laughter].

In my case, I came there believing in family, capitalism, freedom, God — and I left believing in some amazing materialist amalgam of agnostic ideas. It took me several years to recover my education that I had brought, from my own family, to that great institution.

We're now discussing trade [and] why the trade gap is good. My daughter told my one reason why the trade gap is good this morning: She informed me that most of the great <u>horse</u> lines in Kentucky, which sustain Kentucky as the horse capital of the world, were imported from overseas.

It's this kind of "import" that built America during its period of most rapid growth. We had 100 years of trade gaps as America emerged as the world's leading economy

— [and] we never "paid it back."

The idea that somehow a trade gap is some huge debt that we'll eventually have to defray — some debt that my poor daughter and her sisters will eventually have to defray — is just false. Countries all over the world have run trade gaps for <u>decades</u> — scores of years, even — without ever, in any sense, contracting their standard of living in order to "generate a surplus" to repay the foreigners to whom they supposedly owe money.

To understand how this works — why the trade gap is good — we have to understand our recent history.

It's often supposed that American competitiveness collapsed during the 1980s, which led us on a binge of imports. Since we could no longer produce cars and other equipment as efficiently as foreign countries, chiefly Japan, we increasingly imported these goods. It's somehow a failure of American competitiveness that led to the trade gap...

What <u>really</u> happened in the early 1980s is that the United States began growing much faster than it had in the '70s, and much faster than its trading partners were growing. Now if you're an exporter from the United States, and you are exporting to a stagnant global market, you won't able to expand your exports as fast as an exporter from a foreign country that faces a <u>booming</u> American market. The reason for the trade gap is that, throughout the 1980s, the United States was growing between two and three times faster than most of our trading partners.

One of our key trading partners, during the '70s and previous decades, was Latin America. Suddenly Latin America...faced a major debt crisis and no longer could import from the United States. As a matter of fact, the World Bank and the United States tended to impose austerity programs on these countries, which prohibited them from continuing to import at the same rate. So Latin America, one of our main markets, essentially collapsed.

Africa's economy lost some 20% of its GNP. The European economy, which grew faster than ours during most of the postwar era, suddenly went into a prolonged and desperate slump, signified by the loss of almost 2% of its employment, while the United States was increasing its employment by some 16 million jobs.

So our markets — the countries to which we sell products — collapsed. The U.S. market ignited. Therefore, the chief reason for the trade gap, from the point of view of the United States exporter, is that [he] had the unique disadvantage of being the only exporter in the world who could not export to the United States. That was his basic problem, and that's why American exports stopped growing during the 1980s, or didn't grow fast...

However, our economy was growing much faster than foreign economies. Indeed, we are the only economy [among] the major industrial countries that either increased investment, as a share of GNP, or reduced unemployment after 1981. It was this performance — this extraordinary competitiveness of the U.S. economy — that caused the trade gap everyone is bemoaning today.

[Watch out for] single-entry bookkeepers [and the way they misrepresent] the world economy: They count debts, but ignore assets. During this period when our debts were increasing, our assets were increasing much more rapidly. As a matter of fact, our assets rose from about 180% of GNP in 1980 to 244% just before the Crash [of 1987], and they're now about 240% of GNP.

In other words, our asset position greatly improved throughout the 1980s, because of the rise in the stock market, the rise of real-estate values, the emergence of new technologies.

Meanwhile a very different kind of experience was undergone by Japan. After 20 years of running a trade gap — during its fastest period of growth — the Japanese economy began growing much more slowly, toward the end of the 1970s. At the same time, most of the Japanese population were hitting significant marginal tax rates. This made their savings exemptions — all these savings benefits and [tax] exemptions — much more valuable.

So what the Japanese experienced was a steady increase in savings despite a decline in investment opportunities [in their own country]. They piled up a huge horde of savings — which has bid up the real estate of Japan to a value greater than all the real estate in the United States.

In 1981, the Bank Of Japan allowed Japanese in general to invest all around the world. There had been many restrictions on the outflow of Japanese capital, until 1981. The result was a tenfold rise in the net foreign investment of the Japanese. This <u>huge</u> outflow of capital has dominated all these "balances of trade" over the past decade.

When the Japanese decided to invest abroad, they looked all over the world. Where was the best place to put their money? What nation was most competitive? Latin America? The Middle East? Africa? Europe? All these [places] received <u>some</u> Japanese investment, but the bulk of it came to the United States.

Not only did the Japanese decide we were the most competitive economy in the world, Americans also realized we were the most competitive. During the 1970s, we had been a "net lender." We lent money all over Latin America; we lent money to totalitarian despots [and sent it down] Communist ratholes — which made people with a single-entry bookkeeping view of the U.S. economy feel good.

After sending their money [to such places] during the 1970s, the Americans suddenly stopped — [and the result was] an 80% drop in American investment overseas. With Americans investing in the United States again, and with Japanese investing in the United States, and Europeans and Latin Americans [doing the same], it was absolutely necessary, mathematically, for us to run a large trade gap: If you have a dollar, you can buy American goods, or you can buy American assets. Unless you want to just eat it, you have to do one or the other.

So "capital flight" — from countries all around the world [into the U.S.] — necessarily meant that we would run a trade gap. The drive of foreign investment, rather than any lack of competitiveness of American production, caused this trade gap...

While the trade gap grew, more important things were happening. We had a fundamental transformation of the world economy...originating with the new science, which has resulted in a series of new technologies [bringing] the entire world economy together for the first time in human history. Entrepreneurs have created a global ganglion of capital markets and information technologies that allow entrepreneurs to send their capital anywhere in the world in microseconds...

This has changed the very character of "goods and services." Fiber-optic cables and telecommunications satellites don't merely transmit funds in real time, they also transmit goods. This global network can transmit a far greater value of goods than whole flotillas of supertankers.

And the key "goods" of the Information Age are software packages, microchip schematics, VCR programs — a whole array of goods that are the fastest growing [sectors] in the world economy. And they aren't transported any more across national boundaries, they are transmitted by the global telecom network.

In the past, nations really did "trade" with one another: They sent widgets across borders thru arduous processes [and sent] clipper ships across treacherous seas. Today you send the products with the greatest value-added down fiber-optic cables, and bounce 'em off satellites around the globe, in microseconds. This totally transforms the nature of the world economy.

To give you an idea of just what an information technology is, and why the usual concerns people voice about the "hollowing out" of the American economy are misconceived, I'd like to show you an information technology: It's a book.

I was debating the author of another book on the issue of manufacturing. His thesis was that U.S. manufacturing capability had collapsed and was dooming America's standard of living. I held up his book and I asked him: "Where was it manufactured?" He didn't know.

A book is not chemical and paper technology, a book is a technology of ideas. A book costs between 80 cents and a buck to manufacture in volume. But it sells for the value of the ideas it contains; it sells for between 10 and 50 times more than the cost of production. And this is typical of all the products of the Information Age.

I could just as well have held up a CD-ROM, which can hold some 600 books. (A megabyte is essentially a big book [and] a CD-ROM holds 600 megabytes.) I could've held up a videocassette. A videocassette is an information tool that costs between 60 cents and a buck to manufacture in volume — and sells for the value of the movie. You don't worry about where the videocassette was manufactured. All the added value is in the information it contains, and in the retailing and marketing and creative work of the artists who lent it its value...

Some people say, "Yeah sure, that's true of software and obvious information vessels like books, CD-ROMs or videocassettes. But the real <u>heart</u> of the Information Economy is computers and telecommunication switches — all these vast networks which comprise and require some of the most exacting manufacturing processes in the history of the human race."

Yet, interestingly enough, the key value in a computer is embodied in a few microchips, and these microchips are essentially inscribed on grains of sand. The value of these microchips comes from the content of the design — it comes not from their "substance," but from their contents.

And the design is a technology of ideas. It's produced, often by a single person, at a workstation costing $20,000 or less. And each of those microchips — like a book, like a CD-ROM, like a videocassette — costs between 80 cents and a couple dollars to produce in volume.

Yet, depending upon the quality of the design <u>on</u> that microchip, its value is between 10 and a <u>hundred</u> times as great.

This global ganglion of telecommunications represents the great new <u>transportation</u> facility of the current age. It is comprised chiefly of giant switching systems, 80% of the value of which comes in the software. Eighty percent of a telecommunications facility derives from the software. All the chip-designs that go into the telecom switch are also based on ideas; they're based on software.

So to say that the United States is about to be "hollowed out" — is about to lose the crucial sources of value in the Information Age because we may be less efficient at producing certain dynamic random-access memory chips, or because we have less pure silicon, or less clean industrial gasses — is like predicting that the Canadians will dominate world literature because they have the tallest trees [laughter]. Or predicting that Kodak will dominate the movie industry because it manufactures the film...

The real [threat to] American competitiveness is moral, not economic. Apart from the legal domain — the collapse of Law resulting from the glut of laws, and perhaps from lawyers — our economic policies [are sound]. The real crisis is moral, and the answer to it is a religious revival.

And I believe a religious revival is underway in the United States. It's not led mostly by the old established churches, it's led by new churches. But it's spreading thru the old churches, and improving them as well. And it's the real hope for the future success of the American economy.

The old fundamental morals — upheld by the great religions, and by the Christian religion above all — are still absolutely indispensable to a prosperous society. To the extent this moral order collapses, the economic efforts are futile...

And this is the reason why the movement of new colleges, new conservative institutions across the country, is really retrieving the U.S. economy. It's far more important to the competitiveness of America than anything going on today at Harvard or in Washington.

Hillsdale, and [its] Shavano [Institute], and Bellarmine, and all these small colleges that are renewing the American moral fiber, are critical to the future competitiveness of the country. Because ideas come from individuals, and what determines the effectiveness of individuals is their morality and character, not their power in Washington or their ability to issue orders to other people...

In the modern age, even slaves are worthless — [because] they bind you to obsolete means of production. In the olden times, if you had a huge industrial plant of some sort, to which you could dispatch thousands of regimented workers, you gained economic power. But regimented workers are increasingly worthless. What you need is individual creators... Ideas always originate in human minds, and they ultimately repose there...

In this new global economy, trade gaps between nations are totally irrelevant. They make no more difference than the trade gap between California and New York. California runs the biggest trade gap in America — the trade gap of the state of California is bigger than the trade gap of all the rest of America. Get rid of California, and we could probably have a trade surplus again [laughter] — and we probably would, because California happens to be one of the most creative state economies.

Just as during the first hundred years of our history, when we were opening the western frontiers, the United States ran a trade gap every year and it was very good for America, so — in the next decades — we probably will keep running a trade gap, if we continue to grow as fast as we've been growing. Because we are now opening the new frontiers of information technology.

People will tell you the United States is falling behind in these areas. I've devoted the past 10 years of my life to exploring these technologies and understanding them and writing [*Microcosm*], and I can guarantee you we are not falling behind. All the statistics you hear that imply we are falling behind in the new technologies are false — they're just misinterpretations of the data.

We dominate four times as much of the computer industry as Japan. We produce four times as much telecommunications equipment. We have four times as much computer software.

And, at a time when information technology is increasingly moving to small computers, we have 11 times the distribution of small computers as Japan does. Small computers are now 90 times more cost-effective than the great mainframes of the past, and any of us can have one.

With a single small computer, one engineer can command more creative power than the ruler of a giant steel mill of the industrial [era]. One creative man at a workstation can design a microchip more <u>complex</u> than a steel mill, and more <u>potent</u> in its ultimate impact on the future creation of value.

As Michael Novak has said, "capitalism" comes from the Latin word *caput*, for head — the chief source of capital in the new economy. And the effectiveness of learning comes from the moral foundations of the society. The value of a nation's goods derive from the values of its people, and that's why Shavano and Hillsdale are on the forefront of creating new value and competitiveness for the U.S. economy.

Thank you very much.

The World On A Turnpike

Driving Across Massachusetts — June 6 and 8, 1997

Bruce Chapman, who wrote the introduction for this book, was behind the wheel during these sessions, and makes his presence known by taking issue with George. Both of these treks occurred in the aftermath of their 35th Harvard Reunion.

When Technologists Should Get Political

FRANK GREGORSKY: Two polarized views exist of what the computer and high-tech sectors ought to do regarding politics. One was articulated in the March 4, 1997, *Wall Street Journal* by Tim Draper, founder of a venture-capital firm in Redwood City.

GEORGE GILDER: And Rich Karlgaard's first sponsor; he helped fund *Upside* —

FG: Okay. Among other things, he said: "Teaching the folks inside the Beltway too much about our business is a dumb idea... We ought to count our blessings that most of our industry is 2,500 miles from Washington and that most bureaucrats either fear, don't care about, or don't understand technology." Look what diligent lobbying did for the phone companies, the utilities and the broadcasters, he adds derisively.

Then, in the May issue of *Upside,* is George Sollman, chairman of the American Electronics Association. He points to "four defining events" in technology policy since

1994 — defeat of the FASB stock-option plan; overturning Clinton's veto of securities-litigation reform; defeat of the 1996 immigration bill; followed by defeat of Prop 211 in California — and he concludes: "We learned that involvement is not a liability but an asset — to the engaged individual, his or her company and the industry at large... When we work together, we can make a measurable and visible difference."

I know you are in the middle of these extremes, but — closer to which one? (Also worth noting: You are probably the only technology authority in America who, in an earlier professional life, worked the public-policy process for 15 years.)

GILDER: I think there are two points here. One is that all these successes Sollman cites consist of blocking some intrusive and destructive kind of invasion of the technology sector. And that is crucial: You gotta defend the space.

But you don't want the government "solving your problems" in technology. You don't want our technology CEOs petitioning government for special supports on the basis of the crucial benefits which technology offers.

FG: Sollman doesn't —

GILDER: The government can't <u>possibly</u> move at the pace that technology is moving. In recent years, government's chief goal has been to promote something they call "competition." And competition is usually defined as a "level playing field," where everybody reaches the arena with exactly the same capabilities and rights and [profit] margin. But it's really an arena where nobody can make any money and nobody wins, including the customer.

FG: If Sollman were here he'd say, "I'm not for special favors. But, if we got more involved with these elected officials, we wouldn't have so many bad things coming at us." Is this at all —

GILDER: Well — you know, politics is obviously vital. If the United States adopts a Buchananite protectionist

stance, excluding immigrants and fomenting war with
China, and generally adopting some Embattled America
posture, technology will move to other countries, and all
the benefits will be lost.

Yet many of the technology entrepreneurs will continue
to prosper — [because] they will <u>move</u>. That's what [Pat
Buchanan's program] will do. It'll just drive them to other
countries and other ways of accomplishing their goals, and
it'll be destructive to the United States.

And I'm a patriot! I want the United States to succeed.
If the United States doesn't succeed, it's likely that the
world, in the end, will be a much grimmer place, with all
kinds of terrible terrorist eruptions using biological and
chemical weapons of fearsome effect. So it's crucial that the
U.S. does remain dominant, and does win the "arms race"
against evil, which persists in the world.

But we won't win without maintaining the world's
leading economy and remaining on the leading edge of
technology. And I think maintaining that economy and
[keeping] that edge does depend on a <u>lot</u> of immigration.
Today, U.S. technology is heavily dependent on immigration for critical skills and inventions and patents. This has
been true ever since the Manhattan Project — even before,
going back to the rise of the automobile industry, which
was fueled heavily by immigrant inventors, technologists
and engineers.

So national policy, and the politics behind it, are of vital
importance. At the same time, I don't think technology
entrepreneurs should spend a lot of time in politics. You
know, they should —

FG: Because it ends up being industrial policy?

GILDER: They end up getting distracted, and their
lobbyists all end up urging industrial policy. They become
another interest group, to be traded off against the other
interest groups. In other words, "you can have a little
money for Sematech in exchange for more money for
condoms in the schools" — you know, whatever it is.

FG: Give me an example of a CEO who shows a nice

balance right now between making [the occasional] policy-oriented push and sticking to the knitting. Andy Grove?

GILDER: Yes — except that Andy Grove in the past has been too [inclined toward protectionism]. I think Gates [has the balance], although I don't like his politics — actually, because I don't like his politics, I think it's great that he stays <u>out</u> of politics. But I'm absolutely confident that his position on charity is correct: Currently, most of his money gets invested very productively. He could be giving it to all kinds of destructive causes, so I'm delighted he's not giving his money away.

FG: [*School's Out* author] Lew Perelman says that the profits from the first edition of *The Road Ahead* were given to the NEA. You haven't heard that?

GILDER: No I haven't. But it's the kind of thing that happens.
Here's the problem: To really <u>run</u> one of these companies is a completely exhausting kind of activity. Staying up with these technologies takes all your time and energy and knowledge. And most of these people don't have <u>time</u> to learn about politics. So, when they enter politics, in most cases, it's perverse, or contrary to their real interests.
The exceptions are cases where you get a direct attack on their livelihoods and ability to continue their entrepreneurial activity.

FG: FASB and 211 are the classic examples [of direct attack]. Immigration is a little bit more subtle, except for software.

GILDER: And hardware! Software is full of immigrants, but hardware is <u>really</u> even more based on foreign engineers. I would suspect that, in semiconductors, about half of the key hardware engineers in America are immigrants. A third of <u>all</u> of 'em are immigrants in Silicon Valley and, of the key ones, about half are immigrants. The immigrants tend to be of very high quality; that's why they've been lured to come to America.

Grown-Up ISPs and Smart Radios

FG: Give me an A thru F grade on the Reed Hundt administration of the FCC, and any kind of strong plus or minus about his tenure.

GILDER: I think he's [five-second pause]. You know for awhile he was [another five-second pause].

He's <u>positive</u> in as much as he understands that he shouldn't micromanage technology. He <u>does</u> comprehend that he shouldn't take over the Internet. There's certain pressure on him to attempt to take over the Internet; he understands he can't do that, and for him to do it would be destructive. So that's a positive feature of his career. I can't be entirely negative about him, because he has been quite positive, at various junctures, in protecting the Internet — and that's a crucial issue. If we subject the Internet to telecom regulation, it will wither and die.

FG: [Skeptically] Really?

GILDER: Or it'll become just another part of the telecom infrastructure, which gets renovated about one-fiftieth the speed of computer networks.

The whole Law of the Telecosm asserts the likelihood of network bandwidth expanding 10 times faster than Moore's Law, which [itself] doubles [the productivity of the micro-chip] every 18 months. So this is a <u>tremendous</u> kind of dynamic being depicted — an exponential dynamic — and, if the government moves in and tries to regulate it, it'll necessarily be years behind when it actually imposes its "solution." Whatever solution it imposes will be totally irrelevant.

FG: Should we keep treating the ISPs [Internet Service Providers] as the infant industry?

GILDER: [Five-second pause] They <u>are</u> an infant industry, but I don't — I think it might be a coup to — you know, if they have to pay more to the RBOCs for access, it may be beneficial to the emergence of bypass systems. So I'm not one who believes it's the end of the world if the ISPs have to pay some kind of access charges to the RBOCs — [though] I'm afraid this example will be followed by all sorts of regulations and by other gouges imposed at the state and city levels. You know, it'll be a —

FG: That [Internet companies will] get sucked into the universal-access tax?

GILDER: And other stuff. But what I really oppose on the part of federal policy is the effort to create a "level playing field." That just requires constant and permanent regulation — because there's no way you can ever create a level playing field without reducing everybody to essentially a tame instrument of government policy, with all their markets allocated and supervised.

FG: All of the other free-market think tanks call for the abolition or phaseout of the FCC. Since entities like CATO are anti-government by nature, they are driven to tailor their analysis so it opposes government, which of course includes the FCC. You, on the other hand, are listening to the technology — as opposed to the ideology — so maybe here we could sketch a "correct future" for the FCC.

Three years ago in *Upside,* you told Eric Nee "I did have a role for the FCC — sometimes I forget it, but there is one [laughter]. Among other things, you don't want people [who use] big interfering technologies like TDMA violating the rules. The transition is going to be quite awkward, with all kinds of incumbent users, so I'm sure the regulators will find something to do [in that zone]."

And then he says, "What about things like ensuring reliability and availability of 911 services? Or can that be left to the market?"

You respond: "I don't think the government has much of a role there. If you are doing kiddie porn or really vicious stuff, lots of laws allow you to be prosecuted, and you should be. Otherwise, all this regulation assumes scarce spectrum" — and then you make your familiar argument about bandwidth-abundance.

GILDER: Yep. What it can do? I'll tell you what I think
it can do. You know the new model: Rather than issuing
spectrum licenses, they issue driver's licenses. Anybody can
use spectrum as long as they don't interfere with other
users, or they don't exceed the speed limit — [in this case],
use too much power, or pollute the environment by all sorts
of uncontrolled frequencies.

I think the FCC should promote the emergence of free
spectrum, in which the <u>user</u> of spectrum is responsible for
finding unoccupied frequencies. That role is increasingly
capable of being performed by "smart radios," which can
survey a span of spectrum and identify ways to use it,
unobtrusively. So, rather than clearing the whole Massachusetts Turnpike in order to accommodate one truck down its
length — which is controlled by the two ends — you have
thousands of people using the Mass Turnpike at the same
time, with each one responsible for driving their own ve-
hicle and not crashing into other vehicles or [otherwise]
interfering with the flow of traffic, or using excessive power
or polluting the environment.

That's the kind of regulation that makes sense and
would allow a real efflorescence of creativity in the industry.

FG: Not building roads, not even [playing] traffic cop,
but certification of driving skills.

GILDER: That's right — the roads are already there. But
we're really going to rue the day we established the principle that spectrum was scarce and should be husbanded
and taxed and regulated and auctioned and parceled out in
exclusive spans to favored companies.

Spectrum is in no sense a "natural resource." It's created
by the incredible ingenuity of the radio-engineering community, which has created all these new devices that make
it possible to generate microwaves and manipulate them
and receive them and process them — gyristors, flystrons,
ferractor diodes — a whole stream of gallium-arsenide and
hetero junctions, a very demanding set of gun diodes,
photoreceptors, and every kind of converter and mixer.

These are amazing technologies, and they <u>create</u> spectrum. Spectrum is not something that's just "there," it's created by these technologies. And most of the technologies are American.

Yet here we are establishing the principle that, all around the world, people can start taxing the emissions of these valuable American products. I'm afraid that at some point the UN will get involved: Because so many regions aren't owned by any particular country, the UN will start to extract taxes — and, as time passes, they'll want more and more.

So it was a terrible principle for conservatives and liberals to agree that spectrum is a natural resource. "Precious beachfront property" is the analogy. That's really [what's behind] the auction model today, in the United States, and it favors old technologies. If you can give people exclusive spectrum, then analog technology works pretty well. That's what broadcasters really would like, but —

Who Will Firewall the Broadcasters?

FG: Let me get back to this issue of regulation of one of the old technologies — and don't try to get off the point by giving me the *Life After Television* speech. I want to believe that but, in the meantime, whether it's five years or 20, we still have these broadcasters, we still have TV that any family can see by clicking [the switch on a $50 set]. If you abolish the FCC, what is there to stop Larry Flynt or anyone else from buying a TV station or a whole network and running anything at 4:00 in the afternoon?

GILDER: I think pornography — most kinds — is illegal today.

FG: But the FCC keeps the major broadcasters, to some extent, from slipping further and further into the middle of the day and [televising] more and more blatant things. If the FCC isn't there, who does that?

GILDER: I think the courts do it. I mean — but I don't think people should be allowed to broadcast using conventional frequencies anyway.

FG: Okay.

GILDER: I think broadcast is an intrusive activity. And, if you are going to be broadcasting ubiquitously across the landscape to dumb terminals that can be just switched on by any child, then you have to accept the responsibility not to transmit pornography!

FG: Thank you, that's good! But you can't hear anything like that from [several libertarian and conservative think tanks who glibly say] "get rid of the FCC." They haven't addressed the practical question of where the [public decency] firewall will come from.

GILDER: No. I just don't think porn is free speech. I don't think it can be abolished, but kiddie porn has to be confined and quarantined and restricted.

FG: Everybody agrees there, so that's not the real issue.

GILDER: Well, hard-core porn — you know, constant depictions of sexual activity — is an offense to civilization.

FG: So someone would have to sue the Larry Flynt Network after they tried it at 4:00 in the afternoon.

GILDER: Yeah.

FG: And then?

GILDER: And throw 'em in jail. "This is not legitimate."

FG: Well, if you're going to keep the FCC for licensing in effect, you might be able to keep [their ban] on the "seven dirty words" and a few other things.

GILDER: Yeah, well. See, I honestly believe that this point is moot. The key thing that worries me today is the entire political order, together with the FCC, is determined to preserve broadcast television. This is a mistake, and it probably will fail — as a matter of fact, I think it inevitably will fail, in time. But they may be able to subsidize it enough, and nationalize it enough, that it persists longer — thus making this problem you're describing to me more acute.

FG: We do have a transition issue, though, and there is some censorship — always has been.

GILDER: Well, I'm not against censorship. You don't have a right to put a billboard of a sex act along the highway.

FG: Exactly.

GILDER: And that's what a TV station, as you describe, would be doing. I just think it's a public mischief — you know, it falls under lots of [prohibitions] — it's a "pollutant," whatever you want to —

FG: So you think there are legal, regulatory and other weapons that could be used, even in the absence of an FCC?

GILDER: Yes, right.

FG: Against renegade broadcasters.

GILDER: Yeah. Even so, abolishing the FCC, and transferring its powers to some other government unit, doesn't especially gratify me. I am a minimal-government advocate — I mean, I agree with the libertarians in theory.
However, today government accounts for about a third of the economy, and takes 40% of personal income, and finances between 50 and 80% of industrially-relevant science and engineering in our universities.
So to talk about "abolishing the government" is just a complete distraction. It's philosophically interesting, and I'm glad the libertarians have these philosophical debates and arguments, since they exert pressure for restricting and limiting government.
But the idea of its being abolished is ridiculous. That's the tragedy of government — that it can't be abolished. It's

almost impossible politically, because [you would threaten] all these interest groups —

FG: So the good guys have to outgrow those bad guys.

GILDER: You gotta outgrow 'em. This idea that a direct attack on government is a promising strategy was proven false [during 1995-96]. Now there are these cases where considerable progress has been made once government gets over 50% or so, and you have a national crisis, where the whole economy is collapsing and the welfare state crashes. But it's not worth getting to that point in order to then launch a whole set of reforms that get us back to where we are today. That's essentially what the New Zealanders have accomplished.

FG: Right, right.

GILDER: But it is encouraging that a small country of six million people, which was once virtually socialist —

FG: Chopped its top tax rate from 66% down to 28%.

GILDER: Is that what it is now?

FG: Yep.

Network Computer, Durable Microsoft

FG: Gary Miller is founder and president of the Aragon Consulting Group. He agrees with your indictment of WebTV. He calls it, instead of "niche" marketing, nick marketing — by which he means "a technology ahead of the market that manages to reach a few people by glancing off a niche. It's not an opportunity, it's an accident."

However, when it comes to the so-called NC, or Network Computer, he splits the difference between you and Microsoft.

Using NCs, he told *Investor's Business Daily*, "corporations can get most of the advantage of [centralized] mainframe computing and still cut their costs and stay at the leading edge." (I would add: That scenario delivers the 10-to-one Drucker standard for changing a whole company's equipment paradigm. Some medium-sized chemical company can buy 10, instead of 500, copies of the latest software upgrade.)

Then Miller says this: "But if you look at the 45% of U.S. households that have computers — which is the market targeted by NC-makers — 85% of those have children, and those kids want the same level of computing at home that they have in school — the ability to run different applications and to store data, for example. The cost factor [for these families] is diminished when you consider you can buy a used Pentium running at 75 megahertz for about the same price as an NC."

"So why would you want to buy a low-grade home appliance?"

GILDER: I don't see the network computer as a "low-grade home appliance." I see it as a new and more powerful architecture. So I reject the assumption that his [used] 75 MHz Pentium — with its Windows95 and its constant crashes and its glitches, and interplay among the various programs, and its labored access to the Internet — [is better than an NC]. All those are problems I wouldn't solve. I'd pursue the opportunity of creating a new architecture.

There are a number of ways to create a radically different and better architecture that would yield a device which is optimized to operate on the Internet — for homes, companies, schools, libraries, kiosks, or wherever you need a robust machine with most of the complexity integrated on a few chips.

FG: Okay.

GILDER: And so the kinds of memory conflicts and other problems afflicting the typical PC, in all its increasing complexity, can be transcended in new single-chip machines that integrate a lot of memory on the chip with the processor, and thus overcome the "speed of light" that has the average Pentium 233 spending 70 to 80% of time in "wait" states.

We have a chance today to define a powerful new architecture as a network computer, based on Java, that will outperform the typical Pentium.

Now, many people will want to plug in a <u>disk drive</u> to this machine, and disk drives will be attachable. There'll be new forms of storage, such as DVD, allowing these machines to enact movies, for example, which will be an important resource for them.

FG: So a combination of functions on the chips, and software downloaded just in time off the Net —

GILDER: — and a system optimized to reach the Internet, so that it really can be left on all the time, and be constantly connected.

After all, what's more sensitive than people's money? People are willing to leave their money in a bank. Why wouldn't they be willing to leave their data in a very safe server that's constantly backed-up rather than in their own disk drive that may very well crash? (Unless they back it up all the time, which most people don't do.)

So I see a lot of opportunity for a network computer that's not a thin client, as Andy Kessler puts it, but a muscular client — a client based on a new architecture, optimized for the Internet.

FG: Why are so many companies having a hard time <u>building</u> this $500 device?

GILDER: Because the systems chips are not being produced in volume yet. Until you move down the learning curve with these systems on a chip, you don't get economies of scale. The best architecture has probably not been developed yet. And Java, for all its tremendous gains — in two years, <u>unbelievable</u> momentum and incredible dominance of the attention-space of developers — still is not entirely robust and perfected for this kind of system I'm describing.

So we just haven't got there yet. But it's a very desirable paradigm-shift, and I think it's going to happen. It will start in libraries and schools and hotel rooms and (maybe) airplane seats — all these different places — and it's not an inferior appliance.

But I think PCs [will remain] very prevalent.

FG: The PC paradigm is not being overthrown, it's just sort of being "built over"?

GILDER: That's right.

FG: If this is America's War for Independence — [in terms of computer platforms] — are we at [March] 1775, with the first shots being fired, but still a year away from the Declaration of Independence?

GILDER: No, we have the Declaration of Independence: Netscape and Java. Netscape was really crucial to get us onto the Net, and the development and announcement and propagation of Java was crucial to establishing a truly new paradigm on the Net. And so the two are together.

But, without Netscape, Java could not have reached its critical mass nearly as fast. It was the adoption of Java by Netscape, end of 1995, that made the explosive deployment of it possible.

Suddenly — within weeks — the Java run-time engine was on 50% of the world's computers (or something like that — all of them that had Netscape Navigators). Soon Java was incorporated in Microsoft Explorer as well; and, in new computers, I think Java is almost universal.

But still the programs haven't all been written; the tools haven't all been developed; the markets haven't been established; the details haven't been worked out. So — it's not surprising that the prices haven't plummeted to the crucial point of mass acceptance.

FG: You're not a detached commentator watching Microsoft battle Netscape and Java; you have a favorite in the race. You also try to hedge your bets occasionally [by giving] Microsoft tactical advice.

GILDER: Microsoft will do better in an information economy that moves rapidly to the Java paradigm of platform-independence than it will do in a smaller information economy that it dominates.

What's happening today is that Gates made the mistake — or the redemptive decision, depending on your point of view — of bringing 300 Java programmers (and now more) into Microsoft. Those Java programmers <u>love</u> Java, and they're five times as productive as any of the other Microsoft programmers! Even Microsoft's own V.P. for Internet Marketing has declared them to be three or four times as productive. And they are rapidly gaining influence in the company.

So Microsoft is going to change — yet it remains to some degree the enemy of the new paradigm.

FG: How is it the "enemy" as opposed to slowing things down?

GILDER: I find Gates a more appealing figure, more interesting, than (say) Lew Gerstner of IBM. But IBM has adopted Java, while Microsoft has adopted it only with many reservations, and with much hostility, and with much effort to extend its proprietary ways that reduce the possibility of a fully platform-independent world. IBM is this huge company. Would I normally have an emotional attachment to IBM? I don't. I <u>think</u> I'm appraising these companies in proportion as they adopt the paradigm. IBM has adopted it, and Microsoft still resists it as much as it can.

FG: You're talking about sentiment, attitude, maybe ego, here. But in terms of all its <u>activities</u>, is now Microsoft *de facto,* on <u>balance</u>, advancing the new paradigm?

GILDER: Could be. Maybe just —

FG: 51-49 [laughter].

GILDER: Yeah, it's pretty close. And you worry just what kind of strategy they really have — because when you talk to them, they really declare the new paradigm can't work. You worry when the leading intellects at Microsoft still tell you it can't work. You wonder how truly wholehearted is their embrace of the technology. They may want to hug it to death [smiling].

FG: What if all those new programmers, in June of 1998, are being rated by Gates as <u>eight</u> times more productive? I mean, he respects results.

GILDER: Yes he does. And I think he's changed a lot. At least he's been willing to recognize the market demand for Java. So he's committed himself to satisfying that market demand — by assigning superb programmers to the task. You know, the single fastest Java run-time engine-implementation comes from Microsoft. But it may be displaced by the Hot Spot, which is an ingenious new form of just-in-time compilation that supposedly will make Java just as fast as C programmers.

FG: You're in effect saying, "There'll always be a Microsoft."

GILDER: Oh yeah, yeah.

FG: And five years from now it'll surely be as big, and perhaps two or three times as big, as it is now — in terms of revenues, let's say.

GILDER: Oh I think it will be at least twice as big five years from now.

FG: You're pulling your recommendation to short the stock?

GILDER: The problem is a Microsoft stock price [with a P/E that assumes the company will keep growing at 50% per year].

FG: Which would make for much <u>more</u> than a doubling.

GILDER: Right — though I'm not gonna short. As Jim Rogers says, it's perilous to short Microsoft. But I wouldn't <u>buy</u> it today. And, if I held the stock, I would think this an opportune time to take some profits. Gates certainly believes that [laughter].

FG: Well, he's been doin' that since [right after the IPO], so —

GILDER: I know, I know.

Electronic Commerce: Arrested By Meters?

FG: Long question. The May 10th "survey" in *The Economist* — titled "In Search of the Perfect Market" — is all about electronic commerce. And it notes how, in early 1996, the combined market value of Wave Systems, First Virtual and CyberCash was $1.4 billion. Those same three companies now have a market cap of only $200 million, or a loss of 86%.

The magazine goes on to conclude that these firms are trying to answer the wrong question — and here is <u>my</u> inference of that wrong question, not theirs: "How can we use electronic currency in small sums to facilitate microtransactions in information goods and services, so that consumers can pick and choose from the global marketplace" — not to mention produce their own text for it — "without committing themselves to expensive subscriptions?"

But — the magazine counters — "the psychology of microtransactions is all wrong. Individual consumers... dislike paying for information and positively hate meters. Witness the poor reception of pay-per-view television and the enthusiasm for flat-fee Internet access." Bottom line: "Consumers choose well-known brands to avoid disappointment, and are attracted by package deals that promise no hidden costs."

Nathan Myhrvold of Microsoft adds that hardly anyone will want to pay for stuff on the Net when most of what's there is free. And he recommends to all peddlers of electronic information: Drop the price to zero and get your revenue from advertising. *The Economist* then slamdunks: "To the dismay of the digital-cash companies, that indeed is what most on-line publications have done" — i.e. followed

Mhyrvold's strategy.

_Is_ the industry trying to answer the wrong question?

GILDER: It's _very_ premature to give up on transactions on the Internet before any standard has been established or anybody's adopted very robust and simple technology to conduct transactions.

And [Mhyrvold's advice] is very discouraging because it's evidence of Microsoft continuing down the wrong path. They don't accept the idea of the Internet emerging as a broadband "universal mall" on which all kinds of transactions and purchases and activities, and advertisements of all sorts, will have their full expression. Rather [they speak in tones of] some clever exploitation of the limits of the existing system — which is, nonetheless, accommodating ever greater commerce.

Of course, there will be a mixture of broadcast features, targeted personal advertisements, push, pull — just as commerce itself is extraordinarily diverse and entrepreneurial insights are very diverse, all kinds of things will be at play in this vast new field of activity. But to dismiss transactions at this point —

FG: _The Economist_ doesn't do that.

GILDER: — just because there's no way to conduct them efficiently.

FG: They're not [dismissing transactions].

GILDER: I think Wave Systems actually _does_ have an array of very efficient ways to do it. But it requires a large commitment from some major player before it can happen.

FG: More than [the commitment by] IBM [in November of '96].

GILDER: IBM endorsed the technology, but it has not implemented it widely as yet.

FG: _The Economist_ [concurs], and has charts saying that, yes, Net commerce and transactions are rising. Rather than pouring water on the general growth of that, they're making a different point. They're saying that the model of metering and microtransactions is contrary to what consumers in all previous ways have shown tolerable. That's what I'm trying to get at [in asking you whether the wrong question is being tackled by these new companies].

GILDER: I make fairly "micro" transactions all the time — as I walk thru the airport.

FG: Not metered.

GILDER: Not metered, but I pay. I'm constantly paying for small discrete services.

FG: One-shot.

GILDER: Packages of information, foodstuffs, entertainments, whatever. Las Vegas [laughter] is a vast arena of people constantly conducting transactions. I really think they are focusing on a phenomenon that is true — it exists.

FG: The resistance to metering.

GILDER: The resistance to metering. But business is a whole set of pricing problems. Software pricing, for example, is askew. Because people have no way to purchase small, software programs (or "applets") today, software gets widely stolen. As I've said before, you don't worry when thieves steal software — thieves always steal things — it's when honest people steal software [that you should worry].

FG: Which tells you the system is poorly designed.

GILDER: And also that defensible property rights have not been defined and established. Until they are, you either have to overprice for materials — [knowing that] people will rebel — or you give 'em away free, and hope that secondary benefits will accrue.

But, at that point where a good, refined, robust market

emerges, you can then price appropriately. Many things will have flat-rate prices, other activities will have detailed micro-payments — but the combination will be more profitable and creative than today's marketplaces, which by comparison are very limited.

FG: Some people say push technology will end the golden age of the Net — [the original mix of] individualism and non-commercialism — by yanking us in the direction of TV, dumbing down, [thrusting] overly branded and simplistic things at us, and narrowing the choices of those who are now confused enough to welcome the narrowing. Do you share that fear?

GILDER: Not really. I mean, I don't think push is gonna be a big hit. This whole idea of their being able to reproduce a billboard-advertising mode on the Internet is misconceived. There will be some of that — a sort of "TV dimension" to the Internet — and portions of TV will be incorporated into the overall smorgasbord of <u>choices</u> the Internet affords.

FG: As part of the coming victory of the Internet over TV, you need a little bit of accommodation —

GILDER: You have to accommodate the best of TV, or [at least] the most <u>desired</u> [features] of TV — and you actually improve upon it by making it available at the moment of choice, without regard to geography or time. That is a big gain, and it will make TV compete with thousands of other diversions and options and courseware and hobbyware and games — all kinds of attractions. Only some TV will survive this discipline. TV <u>news</u> will be an early victim — we'll see if I'm right about that. But I think TV news gets worse and worse and worse.

Death By Equilibrium

FG: Kevin Kelly has given the best [pitch on the reality] that technology is really income-redistribution: Rich people pay for the high R&D costs; they buy the $200 calculators and then, five years later, poor people and middle-class kids can get 'em for $12.

GILDER: Sure, and I say that all the time too. That's why it's crucial when families with more than $40,000 of annual income [adopt certain behaviors and buying strategies]. This makes for a large body of purchasers who are paying to eliminate the bugs and glitches and paying for movement "down the learning curve" in the semiconductor industry — specifically, toward creation of the network computer, which will really be robust and simple to use in classrooms and the inner-city.

FG: That's a good "global" rebuttal to the Thurows of this world.

GILDER: It's more national. A global argument would point out how the spread of this technology is leveling the playing field of the global economy.

FG: Okay — I meant "global" intellectually.

GILDER: The key event of the past 30 years is that a billion Asians, among the "wretched of the earth" as recently as the 1960s, are now enjoying middle-class lifestyles.

FG: Is there another good-quality, wide-ranging rebuttal like Kevin Kelly's on this matter of technology and poverty? Something you could say and a whole middle-class audience will say, "Oh, that's right." Any other good quality arguments like that?

GILDER: [Five-second pause] Human beings are technological creatures. We're *homo faber*. We're made in the image of our Creator to be creative. To speak against technology, or to say it's somehow inegalitarian or bad for poor people, contradicts the whole history of the world.
It's so obtuse that the question almost takes my breath away.
Technology is the only thing that makes it possible to overcome poverty. Without technology, we have to com-

pletely give up on the billions of people in the world who are still desperately poor.

And poverty does not need an explanation, poverty is the usual human condition. What needs an explanation is wealth, and the explanation for wealth is human creativity — manifested, very importantly, in technology, <u>vitally</u> in technology. It's technology that endows new work. It's technology that makes workers more productive, and thus more employable.

Technology is the remedy for its own job-displacement, because it generates investable capital that in turn endows new work. It's just central to the human adventure in the world.

Throughout history, all the leading economists have envisaged some exhaustion of the creative impulse and the [subsequent] adoption of some kind of "steady-state economy."

FG: The Patent Office guy in 1899 saying we've invented everything we need.

GILDER: Yep. From Adam Smith to Schumpeter to Sismondi to John Stuart Mill, all these great capitalist economists [seemed to] envisage the <u>end</u> of capitalism. At some point we would have everything we needed and we could subside into some sort of leisure environment — which Marx also envisaged. As a matter of fact, from that point of view, the distance between Marx and Schumpeter is not that great.

FG: That's the first time I've heard you criticize Joseph Schumpeter.

GILDER: Well, I <u>have</u> criticized Schumpeter for his end-of-life prophecies of the death of capitalism — as if capitalism is optional, as if some other kind of system could create wealth.

FG: So you give him credit for understanding creative destruction — describing it — but his pessimism is the problem.

GILDER: Oh, he's great. He was the greatest economist. But <u>all</u> the great economists have had this flaw. They did not —

FG: They think there's an equilibrium.

GILDER: They think there's an equilibrium, right — that's very good. But equilibrium is death — that's what equilibrium is.

FG: There's your title for the next book [laughter].

GILDER: Capitalism is constantly creating new Creative Disequilibrium, and thus creating new opportunities for poor people to become rich.

Home-Schooling in the Berkshires

FG: The number of home-schooled children in the U.S., according to the *New York Times,* climbed from 350,000 in 1990 to 500,000 [in '96]. In New York State, during the same period, the count climbed from 5,000 to 12,000. You and your wife Nini, as parents, were ahead on this trend as on many others.

GILDER: All three of our daughters — [Louisa, Mellie and Nannina] — have had at least one year of home-schooling. And Richard will have his starting this Fall.

FG: So tell us what <u>you</u> have learned — about home-schooling, the related technology, and this Berkshire community?

GILDER: What you learn is that direct home-schooling, besides being beneficial for the "students," is a wonderful boon for the parents. You get closer to your children — you actually see them every day, spend attentive time with them — and can respond exactly to the pace of their learning.

Mellie was phenomenally good with me. We could move thru lots of material at just tremendous speed. I mean, she actually moved ahead of me during a lot of it.

What we did was try to combine math and physics by teaching electrical engineering, essentially. What we taught Mellie was really engineering math — which was something I hadn't studied enough, meaning that I'd be learning at the same time she was. This was very edifying for me, and Mellie went on to jump a grade of math after she finished.

FG: This started when she was 12? What age was she?

GILDER: Seventh grade — age 12, right. She also did some ham-radio stuff, which gave it a sort of physical correlation. I think this is a much better way to teach math. Teaching math chiefly as an abstraction — or even as a series of so-called word problems — is a great mistake. It's much more effective to set forth a systematic body of math with constant confirmation by physical experience, with real relevance to amazing electronic equipment and electrical machines.

Not only is this the best way to teach math, it's the best way to teach physics. It constantly reminds you that physics is largely a mathematical science [and] that physics and mathematics are an integrated field of study.

FG: And what topics did Nini handle?

GILDER: Nini taught history and art and architecture — all these subjects [in a form that combined to make] Cultural History. We also did some [Francis] Schaeffer — his interesting set of cultural commentaries called "How Should We Then Live?" It's an excellent, kind of Christian, history.

Some of the English was taught by Nini, and my <u>mother</u> did the rest of it. We're very fortunate to have her [living] down the street — she's an enormously cultivated literary and religious teacher. She's been teaching our other kids too.

FG: Physically, where did the lessons take place?

GILDER: With Mellie and with Nannina, our youngest daughter, they took place mostly [at] my mother's, down the road, at Four Brooks. With Louisa, [who] was the first one, we [home-schooled] with three people. That was a little different kind of phenomenon, more of a classroom type —

FG: This was on the second floor of a barn or something?

GILDER: Yeah, that's right — more like a little school. But Mellie and Nannina were both alone, and we did it in the house, in the living room, and also at the computer. We used the computer quite a lot, and we'll be able to do that more, I think, with Richard, next year — because he's very interested in computers.

One thing we did, in teaching algebra, was make constant correspondence between equations and graphs. In other words, not teach graphs first [and equations later], but have constant [overlap], so you'd immediately know what kind of equation yielded a circle and what kind a hyperbola or parabola. This provided a constant sense of how mathematical forms have physical manifestations, or graphical <u>images</u>.

The point is: You <u>really</u> can innovate in home-schooling. And you can respond to the needs of the individual pupil. You can also strengthen your family by strengthening the connections to your children. Also, because it's a collective family experience — I did the math and physics, Nini did all the history — we would be talking about [the subject matter in a variety of ways and settings].

It also teaches me. Because, in order to teach any of these subjects you gotta know 'em a lot better than you do when you just sort of, as an adult, casually think you remember your math and English from high school. You really don't.

FG: I think it was Drucker who said, "The only way to really learn something is to teach it."

GILDER: Well he's right, as usual. I go around quoting Drucker all over the place: "Don't solve problems, pursue opportunities" — how often have you heard me say that one? To solve problems is to end up subsidizing your weaknesses, starving your strengths, and achieving costly mediocrity, which in a global economy eventually runs out of business. Outsource problems, sell them off — but don't "solve" them.

The key way to <u>identify</u> opportunities is also offered by Drucker: The opportunity signal is the upside surprise.

FG: The good news you were not looking for or expecting.

GILDER: The unexpected good news, that's right; the unexpected bonanza — this is the opportunity signal. Then my speech can plug in all the upside surprises, as a way to bring in the news — I take advantage of the *Technology Report* and the charts done by Ken [Ehrhart, GTG Research Director] to present the latest <u>news</u>.

For example, in the first quarter of 1997, PCs outsold TVs by 36%! [laughter] Also, 60% of the families with incomes over $40,000 now have PCs, and they use those PCs twice as long as they use their TVs. The PC isn't a complete substitute yet, but you already have this phenomenon with the top group of families.

FG: One final thing on home-schooling. Doesn't the state mandate a "balanced curriculum"? Don't you have to prove to somebody [that the kids] are getting so much of this subject [and so much of that one]?

GILDER: It's just like books, where the strategy is to please the people who run the school. So every Fall we do a curriculum that, you know, fulfills the requirements — and then we vastly overrun what we committed to in the curriculum. I mean, the curriculum is a minimum set of goals —

FG: So by presenting [the book list] to the local school administrators, you're saying, "Yes, we have this balanced ticket, and you don't need to worry about us for a while."

GILDER: That's right. It's probably a little easier for us

— although Sorina Kulberg is part of a whole family in Lenox that did home-schooling from beginning to end, from first grade to 12th. She did extraordinarily well in all her SATs [and] has won all kinds of prizes. It's just been a tremendous success [for her].

Home-schooling is a good thing — even if you're sending the kids, most of the time, off to school. The great secret of Asian academic achievement in America is that the parents are deeply involved, day after day, in teaching their children. These are children who go to ordinary schools every day — but they also [spend time with their] parents.

FG: Any thoughts about what age tends to be best to start this?

GILDER: Well, part of my goal is to inoculate the kids against the dominant culture (to put it crudely). The dominant culture, governed by TV and [other] lowest-common-denominator entertainment of sorts, is depraved. Because of that, it's destructive to education [and] destructive to socialization — which should be chiefly vertical rather than horizontal. Whenever anybody asks about "socialization," they always think the key is socializing horizontally with the other kids. My purpose is to socialize vertically with responsible adults. That's what home-schooling does, and it's the more important socialization — what education's about.

FG: Role models, good examples —

GILDER: Transforming people into responsible adults. By socializing with adults, you achieve this goal faster than by socializing with kids.

To a great extent, the schools are an extension of TV culture and, as such, responsible parents should attempt to inoculate their kids against this culture, which pervades the schools. And to do that you need some home-schooling. We probably don't do enough. We've done one year for each child, and it's usually [during the junior-high years]. It was ninth grade with Louisa, seventh grade with Mellie, it's gonna be eighth grade with Richard — but it was fifth grade with Nannina.

FG: Why so young for Nannina?

GILDER: She was getting bored at the Catholic school we sent all the other kids to. Louisa and Mellie did quite well at this same Catholic school, an excellent school with a good moral atmosphere and discipline. It had lots of benefits, among them the yearly oratorical contest, which had the kids compose a somewhat polemical speech, and deliver it over and over again at different levels of competition.

But somehow, by the time Nannina came along, the key teacher — Sister Eileen — got sick. She had been the key champion for that [oratorical endeavor]. In any case, Nannina was not flourishing the way the others had; she was bored. We felt we had to do something different, so we chose —

FG: Was that because Nannina had a greater attention-span early on? Or less of an attention-span?

GILDER: She has a very good attention-span. But she had digital coordination problems — writing was physically hard for her. She could do a lot of things, but anything that involved writing went very slow, maybe because she hurt her arm falling off a jungle gym. She's also a very petite little creature, and we felt that was a good year to [try home-schooling] her.

And it was a great year — she liked it from the beginning. She was pleased to get out of school. Richard is [also] pleased to get out of school [laughter] — but he's gonna learn a lot more than he expects, I think [laughter]. I feel quite challenged.

FG: No great regulatory or legal problems in Massachusetts?

GILDER: Luckily, none — certainly not in our town. We have a school board and, each year, we just made a routine submission. The local high schools have a kind of positive attitude toward home-schooling. They get our money —

and they don't have to teach our kids! So they're kind of positive — and they still let the kids do some sports and stuff [at Lenox High]. In other words, the high schools have learned how to deal with home-schoolers, to actually let them participate. Mellie started skiing during her home-schooling year, doing it at a local day school. The past two years she's been third and seventh in the state.

Computers In Class, Languages At Bay

FG: Sticking with education, a question from Joe Marlow, an eighth-grade social-studies teacher in Kansas City who is also a Baptist minister. After downloading your stuff from the Discovery Institute web-site, he wrote us as follows: "I do want to go deeper" — and here he means with his students — "into the subject of technology and poverty. What resources — books and journals — do you recommend that directly address this issue? What professional associations deal with the topic?" He adds: "My teaching assignment for next year is computers for sixth-graders." And, because his primary specialty is social studies, Mr. Marlow "integrates a lot of history and social implications of technology" into his classes.

GILDER: What has been written about this? As far as I know, not a great deal. Mike Bookey [and his people at Digital Network Architects] do a lot [in and around Issaquah, Washington].

Educom is another resource — they offer a newsletter, and a magazine. They may be somewhat oriented toward college education, but I think they're good; they're constantly thinking about this issue — not especially with the emphasis on poor children, though that issue constantly comes up, so they are a good source. Educom has been publishing for several years now, and their magazine *Educom Review* has an article at least connected to that subject almost every issue.

FG: And how would you describe their worldview? Is it technocratic? Is it conservative?

GILDER: It's not conservative, it's just, it's just —

FG: "These are neat tools, how do we use 'em"?

GILDER: That's right. And I guess the key thing is: You don't use cathode-ray tubes to teach reading. This is a crucial point. Cathode-ray tubes involve a completely different ocular exercise from reading a book, which means it actually may <u>impede</u> the process of practical reading.

FG: Cathode-ray tubes mean you don't use TV screens to teach reading.

GILDER: Or PC screens. Most of the time, a PC is a cathode-ray tube, with only one pixel illuminated at any particular point in time. It's just a different way to use your eye: It depends upon that bright spot moving across the screen faster than your eye can resolve the whole image. And the impact of that light lingers in your eye, so you see a whole page of text, even though there's maybe only one character, or less, illuminated at any particular moment.

FG: Hmmn. I never heard that; that's interesting.

GILDER: So to learn to read on this bizarre sort of machine is probably counterproductive. That's why you don't like to read extended e-mails, even, or articles — not to mention <u>books</u> — on CRTs.

FG: Will this ever change?

GILDER: It will change with flicker-free liquid-crystal displays and more advanced similar displays that are flicker-free and offer resolution comparable to paper. Today, the resolution of a typical screen is equivalent to about 72 dots an inch — [while] a laser printer is 300 to 600 dots an inch. So you can see that we're still some distance from being competitive with paper.
The new field-emission displays — FEDs — are quite expensive, but they're quite bright, they're flicker-free, and they do close to 300 dots an inch. Both Xerox and Canon

have displays that are 270 to 320 dots per inch. So they're getting to the point where it's close to the resolution of paper.

Still, your notebook is a better place to read than your CRT — a notebook [computer] has flicker-free display, even though the resolution is fairly low.

Again, the key point: Don't use the CRT to teach. Don't imagine that the computer is a substitute for reading or a substitute for books — it isn't at all, today.

FG: Nobody of authority is walking around assuming that, are they?

GILDER: I don't think —

FG: But some well-meaning people might make that mistake absentmindedly.

GILDER: That's right, yeah. However, the computer is <u>very</u> good for teaching math. You can instantly move from graphics to equations at the pace of the learning process; it's already terrific for learning math.

Our [eldest] daughter Louisa had not had any Spanish — none at all. But she wanted to enter Spanish Five — the fifth year of Spanish at her high school (for whatever that's worth). To learn Spanish over the course of the summer, she used two computer Spanish programs. At the end of the summer, she took a test, and entered Spanish Five.

FG: Wow.

GILDER: So it's extraordinarily —

FG: Now was she about to go to Spain for two weeks? Must've been some super incentive —

GILDER: No, she [simply] wanted to be in Spanish Five with her classmates. But she'd gotten a little off schedule in languages. She'd done some Latin and maybe a little Greek — but no modern languages.

I don't think it's worthwhile to learn modern languages

— I'm opposed to learning modern languages, I think it's a waste of time. There are so many of 'em — hundreds of 'em — you'll never be sure you're learning the right one at any time. Unless you have some extraordinary aptitude (which some people do have — a kind of mimetic ability to learn foreign languages), you shouldn't take the time.

Learn basic languages — like Latin and Greek, which <u>are</u> valuable to study. They give you an <u>internal</u> understanding of words — that's the crucial point.

Most people learn English only by context; they don't know a word, except thru its context. So they never get inside it. Words are experienced only from the outside, and your mastery of language is always to some extent limited — because of this lack of experience of the <u>history</u> of each word. When you know the history, you get a kind of intuitive sense of how you can use all these different words — [of] what is a natural fulfillment of their meaning [versus] a twisting of their meaning or perversion of it.

So learn basic language; they are valuable to study. Modern languages aren't.

You know, my great moment in debate with Lester Thurow came when he declared we would have to learn all these modern languages. I said: "Yeah, I agree, you better learn modern languages — like C++." [Laughter] I would've said learn Java, but I didn't think anybody in that audience would know what Java was.

FG: Did Thurow know what C++ was?

GILDER: Yes he did.

FG: He's been so wrong on so many things, yet still he gets quoted. What a jerk.

BRUCE CHAPMAN: George, do you really want to be on record opposing people learning foreign languages?

GILDER: Yeah. It's a provocative thing I say that makes people think.

CHAPMAN: They'll think you're <u>wrong</u>.

GILDER: Well, fine.

CHAPMAN: The whole economic-development field [asserts that] when Americans don't speak the other nations' languages, they <u>lose</u> the edge in doing <u>business</u> with them. You can't expect everybody to do business with us in English.

FG: If someone's gonna go to Japan [for much of] the next 20 years, you wouldn't dissuade them from learning Japanese?

GILDER: Oh no! I'm for learning languages at the time [of need], *ad hoc*, for a given purpose. In probably two months of immersion, I learned enough Italian to speak it when I got to Italy — which was valuable back when I was 15, or 18, or whenever it was I ran off to Italy chasing Katy Motley.

CHAPMAN: It was more like 23, wasn't it?

GILDER: Maybe 25.

FG: He aged 10 years while he was over there chasing her.

GILDER: [Laughter] But anyway —

FG: Bruce is talking about an important intellectual exercise for younger people as opposed to something you may need at some point in [adult] life [professionally].

GILDER: If you go to the Monterey military school [Defense Language Institute], they teach you languages thru an immersion technique, and that's what —

CHAPMAN: Opportunity favors the prepared mind and, if you don't have some background, the chance of your being able to instantly acquire a language [is poor].

GILDER: But it's getting a lot easier to do instantaneous [translation].

CHAPMAN: Well, not really. Louisa got into a higher level of high-school Spanish. I don't know if that means she can speak and write Spanish.

GILDER: She can write it some; she can't really speak it yet. That's what so pathetic: All these people who take years and years of these languages —

CHAPMAN: I expected to hear you [advise using] the technology to learn the language better. Isn't that the real point?

GILDER: Bruce, I am adamant on this. It's something that brings the house down when I say it. People talk about it afterwards, and they strongly support me — it's a <u>big</u> winner.

CHAPMAN: Well, that doesn't mean it's <u>right</u>.

GILDER: Well, it <u>is</u> right.

FG: It's a great polarizer.

GILDER: It's right because it leads people to understand the crucial advantage we have, which is English. English is the *lingua franca* now, the global language. Lester Thurow is completely wrong about things happening so much faster overseas that we have to learn [their language]. The truth is that technology is happening so fast [here] they have to learn <u>English</u>.

CHAPMAN: All true. But what about when you're trying to <u>sell</u> something, as opposed to buying something? If you want to buy from a foreigner, they'll be happy to learn English, or to use English. If you want to <u>sell</u> them something, you better know how they think — inside their own language. It certainly is an advantage. Your chances are minimized when you don't know other languages. This country as a whole doesn't have a reservoir of people who can speak these other languages.

FG: And would you also say, Bruce, that it's a lot easier to start doing that at 17 than it is at 35?

CHAPMAN: Yes — <u>much</u>.

GILDER: I think it's easiest to do when you have a direct target. It's easiest to learn a language when there's a reason to know it. Without a reason to know it, you'll forget it, and it's <u>incredible</u> how fast.

I am partly voicing my own experience. I spent five years learning French [in school]; after that I did Berlitz to learn French. I've spent months in St. Barts and I still can't speak French — I start talking French in France and they're resentful. I mean, it's a <u>waste</u> of time to learn French, yet people all across America are learning French. But the French are still practicing Socialism — [if they keep that up] they aren't going to <u>matter</u> in 20 years. Their language will wither. Unless the French start to forget their socialist fantasies, their language will wither into nothing.

We really should get realistic about foreign languages — understand when we have to learn 'em, and when not.

First Glimpses of the Book After *Telecosm*

FG: A book on physics, religion and technology is said to be in your future. Some of us call it "the God Book," while "Secular Suicide" is a title used by others. Never mind the when and never mind the how. Could you [instead] explain to us the what, and [especially] the <u>why</u>, of this prospective book?

GILDER: I'm very hostile to sort of touchy-feely parapsychology — when people imply we'd all be better off in some primitive sort of world: "Technology's evil because it represses the primal being that's closer to God" — or whatever. In other words, New Age thinking, of which I've been accused —

FG: Who has accused you of that?

GILDER: Oh, Robert Wright did a big piece in *The New Republic* when *Microcosm* came out.

FG: Did he specifically go after the last chapter?

GILDER: He went after the last chapter. But he skipped the whole history of the semiconductor — you know, with its solid-state roots — and treated the book as if it were chiefly a mystical affirmation of new-wave spirituality. He also inveighed against the idea that computer technology represented anything new and was likely to change the economy and hugely increase productivity.

FG: Did his attack make you back off a little bit?

GILDER: No, I didn't. And I was quite pleased, because I was just <u>very</u> sure he was completely wrong on that.

FG: But you didn't want to go around being portrayed as a New Ager.

GILDER: I certainly did not want to be portrayed as a New Ager, but I was pleased that he plunged into the murk and denied the significance of cybernetics. It [suggested] that the Left was going to completely miss this radical change that would transform the global economy.

FG: They have! But keep up with the narrative [and describe the new book].

GILDER: What [certain public and personal events of 1970-74] gave me is the confidence that the current physical model of the brain is insufficient. The kind of naturalistic model of human intelligence — in other words, "biochemical reactions in the brain explain all of thought" — is false. Thus the idea of creating a computer model of the brain is inherently misconceived.

FG: Who tipped you off to Wilder Penfield?

GILDER: One of those books of essays on the brain.

Carver Mead got me interested in Max Delbruck, and the neuroscientists, and neural networks, and Warren McCullough, and collections of essays on the brain; and I think this was actually in a collection that may have been edited by somebody named Wilder. And it contained articles by Francis Crick (probably) and a whole bunch of scientists, one of whom quoted Wilder Penfield. So I ordered the book from the Princeton University Press — as I recall, it was a collection of essays.

FG: Was Penfield the most important [source] to allow that last chapter [of *Microcosm*] to be written? Or would you have written something like it anyway?

GILDER: I was gonna write something like it anyway. But Penfield was useful [pause]. You know, I'd written the last chapter <u>before</u> I read Penfield, and then I plugged him. Beforehand [in that zone], I'd probably quoted more the British physicist who was Einstein's chief popularizer — I can't remember his name now.

FG: So what is the next layer beyond that last chapter?

GILDER: I want to sort out all these mind-brain [differences and better explain] why human beings need religion. Why there is this hunger for God. And why it's indispensable to society.

The eclipse of God really destroys the foundations of (obviously) monotheism, and thus of a permanent reality in which one can have confidence as a scientist. In other words, the sources of science and religion are not in conflict, they are complementary — and they both depend on a belief and a foundation of reality that is unimpeachable.

So [the danger is coming from] all these kind of relative theories of truth, obscurantist theories of science — like Thomas Kuhn, who I think is a fraud, yet everybody reads him. A lot of religious people read Thomas Kuhn.

I want to attack the religious hostility to science. I believe science is another form of revelation. You have scriptural revelation, but you also have the revelation of nature itself, in which God is in some sense manifested. For religious people to adopt Thomas Kuhn, who doesn't believe in any reality at all —

FG: Why do they adopt him?

GILDER: Because he attacks science. "Science is just relativistic and truth is just really based on fashion, which crystallizes in a paradigm which is then overthrown by a subsequent paradigm and there's no cumulative truth — and certainly no absolute foundation for truth that's cumulatively exposed."

Karl Popper is really the key philosopher of science — and I'm Popperian rather than Kuhnian; that's an important distinction.

So I got a lot of ideas [for this book], but I haven't figured out what the formula is, or what the theme is.

FG: Is anyone close to a Carver Mead role for this next book?

GILDER: Not really. Not that I know, at the moment.

FG: Your view of science as a revelation of some of the works of God — wasn't that Sir Isaac Newton's view?

GILDER: Yes, it was.

FG: So, in terms of spirit and attitude, we're not "inventing" something new here.

GILDER: That's right. But currently there is this division between science and religion, which I think is destructive to both, and I would like to try to integrate them more. I don't know how successful I'll be; there are a lot of challenges. What I'm giving you is a set of propositions, or a set of ideas, looking for a book [laughter] — looking for a vessel to give 'em coherence.

FG: Who would you see the key audiences as being?

GILDER: Oh — everybody. Everybody who reads.

Whenever I write a book, I have the idea that it will be a popular book. I thought this about *Men And Marriage.*

Atheist Ayn, Bloodless Brits

FG: I know what your greatest disappointment is about *Wealth And Poverty* — that conservatives and Republicans didn't get the new vision of capitalism [as by far the best form of altruism].

GILDER: Yep.

FG: Do you have a similar-sized disappointment about *Microcosm?*

GILDER: [Five-second pause] I really don't. You know, the book wasn't a "big success." It was a commercial success. And it was something of a critical success, particularly as time passed. *Business Week* did a second review of *Microcosm,* after I started working for *Forbes.* They sort of recanted — in the guise of reviewing *Life After Television,* but essentially about *Microcosm.* And since they had done the first and most conspicuous review of *Microcosm* — which really destroyed its opportunity of taking off at the beginning — [coming back for another look] when I was a directly competitive writer was a very nice thing for them to do, and I'm very grateful for that.

FG: Who was that second reviewer?

GILDER: Peter Coy is his name — very smart guy. In Silicon Valley, the book's still read, and is generally regarded to have been "right." I guess it sold 60,000 copies, so far, and it's still in print.

FG: What's the count on *Wealth And Poverty?*

GILDER: Probably 700,000 altogether, all around the world.

FG: A ten-to-one gap?!

GILDER: About ten-to-one. But probably *Microcosm* has been more fully adopted by "the experts in the field" than *Wealth And Poverty* was. *Wealth And Poverty* was adopted more by the public than it was by experts in the field, most of whom disagreed with it. Conservatives mostly attacked its view of capitalism.

A guy named Arthur Selden, who is head of IEA [Institute of Economic Affairs], refused to publish a whole expansion and special article on the moral sources of capitalism — even though he had commissioned it, for the IEA magazine. As a libertarian, he didn't want to hear that capitalism wasn't based on greed.

Selden has a new book, on capitalism, and I should go look at it. But IEA, the libertarian establishment think tank in London, provided a lot of the people for the Thatcher Administration — [e.g.] Alan Waters. And it was the single most hostile audience I've encountered.

FG: There's a bloodlessness about the English Conservatives that's just chilling.

GILDER: I know. They were just <u>furious</u> about my belief that capitalism is based, in some fundamental way, on altruism — Christian responsiveness to the needs of others. The reason capitalism prevails is because it's consonant with religious truth. And this proposition was just considered by these people to be an outrage! It's partly because [of so much] Randian thought — and of course altruism is the ultimate evil in Randianism. Although when she actually wrote about capitalism, when she tried to <u>depict</u> these capitalist heroes —

FG: Very romantic, yeah.

GILDER: They were very romantic, and sacrificial, and quite altruistic creatures. Nonetheless, her philosophy completely excluded this model, which she associated with socialism.

I think my key insight in *Wealth And Poverty* is that greed leads, "as by an invisible hand," to an ever-expanding welfare state — because truly greedy people want to be

compensated beyond their own deserts, beyond their own
ability to create goods and services for others. Greed leads
as by an invisible hand to socialism — another proposition
not about to pass muster at the IEA.

FG: Steve Forbes advocated pretty much your whole
agenda [during his presidential campaign]. But — how
much altruism was he willing to put at the root of what you
would've thought was a good agenda?

GILDER: I think Steve has pretty much bought my
model.

FG: But he never talks about it.

GILDER: Some, he does [pause]. I think he's —

FG: But he passes out those Adam Smith ties.

GILDER: Right. Well, you know Adam Smith was a
great man, and he was the first to show the magic of capitalism. But it's chiefly an efficiency argument he made — he
missed the creativity at the foundation of capitalism. Creativity is different from efficiency.
Even libertarian theorists of enterprise — people like
Israel Kurzner — miss this. They assume a given set of
possibilities, a given "band" of resources [and] capital, and
then identify the entrepreneur as an "opportunity scout."
He sees ways to reorganize the existing resources and capital in a more productive way. Or they see him identifying
price-variations in different markets and reconciling these
thru arbitrage.

FG: A glorified calculating machine.

GILDER: That's right — he's really a glorified calculating machine. But the entrepreneur is a <u>creator</u> — more so
than even the artist, because he has a greater necessary
responsiveness to the real facts of the world. He creates in
just as inspirational ways as an artist does, and in a more
<u>altruistic</u> way, because the entrepreneur really is bound to

respond to the needs and wants of others, and to collaborate with others in the process of launching these creations. He has to <u>imaginatively</u> respond to the needs of others before they've been articulated — in many cases, before they are even fully manifested.

When all the information's in, the opportunity's gone.

Where Is The "Soul" Of Silicon?

From a speech at the Vatican — April 29, 1997

Work becomes ever more fruitful and productive to the extent that people become more knowledgeable of the productive potentialities of the earth and more profoundly cognizant of the needs of those for whom their work is done. In our time, in particular, there exists another form of ownership which is becoming no less important than land — the possession of know-how, technology and skill. The wealth of the industrialized nations is based much more on this kind of ownership than on natural resources.

> — *Centesimus Annus,* May 1, 1991 (on the
> Hundredth Anniversary of *Rerum Novarum)*

Published on May 1, 1991, *Centesimus Annus* returns to the themes of a lapidary encyclical of 100 years before, *Rerum Novarum,* which refuted Marxism long before it had refracted into a global plague of tyranny and murder. The critique of socialism in *Rerum Novarum,* however, did not signify an affirmation of capitalism, and the "new things" receiving the Pope's attention then were anything but positive or even new.

In 1891, *Rerum Novarum* had addressed "the terrible conditions to which the new and often violent form of [capitalist] industrialization had reduced great multitudes of people." What was really new was not the terrible conditions. It was the survival of unprecedented multitudes at ever increasing standards of living, together with a new intolerance toward the kind of poverty previously accepted as inevitable. The themes of this great encyclical, in fact, were immemorially old: The poverty which we always have with us, and the brutality of sinful men in power.

Within 10 years, however, came in Europe a profoundly new thing that would permanently change the dimensions of human life and vindicate once again the age-old revelations of scripture. That new thing was quantum physics. And, though quantum theory is an abstruse and formidable field, its philosophical and theological implications come down to one shattering effect: The overthrow of matter.

At the foundation of nature, claimed all previous physics, were the material particles — as Newton put it, "solid, massy, hard, impenetrable, movable particles...even so very hard as never to wear or break in pieces; no ordinary power being able to divide what God himself made one in the first creation [to] compose bodies of one and the same nature and texture in all ages." For some 200 years — excluding the part about God and creation — nearly all leading scientists shared these materialist assumptions, based on sensory models and deterministic logic.

At the foundations of the physical world, so it was believed, are physical solids — "building blocks of nature" — that resemble in some way the solids we see and link together in causal logic like a set of cogs and levers. These solids were deemed to comprise all matter, from atoms and billiard balls to the human brain.

Adam Smith, Newton's great 18th-century countryman, extended the materialist metaphor to society, contending that the economy itself is a clockwork, a "great machine." Later Karl Marx applied materialism to the very fabric of political and social ideas, which were deemed mere figments of ownership in physical capital (or of alienation from it). Darwin extended the materialist scheme to the *Origin Of Species* and the elaboration of social life. Sigmund Freud and his followers developed a psychological theory of forces and pressures, inhibited or released, built up or fed back, much like the classical mechanics of steam engines.

Only 10 years after the publication of *Rerum Novarum*, these materialist fantasies collapsed, when Max Planck showed that Newtonian theory does not apply at the heart of matter itself. The atom, once regarded to be a solid particle, emerged as a baffling convergence of fields and forces that, as Richard Feynman would later put it, "behave like nothing that you have any direct experience about...not like waves, [or] like particles...or like anything you have ever seen." As Planck saw, the new theory required us "to take the enormous step from the visible and directly controllable to the invisible sphere — from the macrocosm to the microcosm."

There is no longer anything solid or physically determined in the prevailing theory of the atom. At the root of all the cascading changes of modern economic life — devaluing material resources in technology, business, and geopolitics — is this original overthrow of material solidity in the science of matter itself.

In the past year, the anti-materialist cascade has overthrown the Darwinian theory of biology as well. Just as Newtonian materialism collapsed at the turn of the 20th century when physicists addressed the microcosm of the atom, so Darwinian materialism is collapsing on the eve of the 21st century as biologists address the microcosm of the cell.

Leading the charge is Michael Behe, a Catholic molecular biologist from Bethlehem (PA) and Discovery Institute Fellow, who stresses the "irreducible complexity" of cellular systems. Behe quotes Darwin: "If it could be demonstrated that any complex organ existed which could not possibly have been formed by numerous, successive, slight modifications, my theory would absolutely break down."

Similarly, the eminent incumbent Darwinian, Richard Dawkins, declares: "Evolution is very possibly not, in actual fact, always gradual. But it must be gradual when it is being used to explain the coming into existence of complicated, apparently designed objects, like eyes. For if it is not gradual in these cases, it ceases to have any explanatory power at all [and] we are back to miracle, which is a synonym for the total absence of [naturalistic] explanation."

Behe shows that the new findings of molecular biology

conclusively meet the test of Darwin and Dawkins. We are indeed back to miracle. "No one at Harvard University, no one at the National Institutes of Health, no member of the National Academy of Sciences, no Nobel Prize winner — no one at all can give a detailed account of how the cilium, or vision or blood-clotting or any complex biochemical process, might have developed in a Darwinian fashion."

But, Behe then asks, "All these things got here somehow; if not in a Darwinian fashion, then how?" The irreducible complexity of living cells — the fact that they function only with the simultaneous presence of all their parts — indeed signals the absolute failure of the Darwinian model.

As Behe writes, "Just as the pleasing shape of a jetliner belies the complexity of its internal organization, so the complexity of life mushrooms as one gets closer to its foundation. The shape of the eye, which Darwin tried to explain, pales in comparison with the interactions of rhodopsin, transducin, arrestin, rhodopsin kinase, and other proteins in the visual cascade. Explaining how the swimming behavior of a whale might be produced gradually...would be a walk in the park compared to explaining the bacterial swimming system — the flagellum, which requires more than 40 gene parts to function... Astonishingly, science's own journals contain no explanations... [Strictly speaking], Darwinism is not science."

Like the microcosm of physics unveiled by Max Planck and his followers, the biological microcosm is irreducibly complex. This means that its phenomena function only in the presence of all their mutually dependent parts and thus could not have evolved in a Darwinian materialist process.

Mind Over Matter

The overthrow of matter in physics and biology requires a return to the social issues treated in both *Rerum Novarum* and *Centesimus Annus*. All Catholic teaching insists on the inadequacy of materialism as an explanation of life. Today the collapse of materialism — in the very science of matter itself — vindicates the centrality of Catholic metaphysics. It opens the way to assert the primacy of spirit throughout the domains of human existence.

The Church stands as the one world institution that upholds the moral and spiritual foundations of scientific truth and extends them to the contentious issues of man in society. Nowhere is this forte of the Church more relevant than in the realm of political economy — the subject of *Centesimus Annus.* In technology, economics, and the politics of nations, wealth in the form of physical resources is steadily declining in value and significance. The powers of mind and spirit are everywhere ascendant over the brute force of things.

The true capital of the current capitalist economy is not material. It is moral, intellectual, and spiritual. It is produced less by factories than by families in collaboration with the Church.

This change marks a historic divide. Dominating previous human history was the movement and manipulation of massive objects against friction and gravity. In the classic image of humanity, Atlas bears the globe on stooped shoulders, or Sisyphus wrestles a huge rock up an endless slope. For long centuries, humans grew rich chiefly by winning control over territory and treasure, slaves and armies. Even the Industrial Revolution depended on regimented physical labor, natural resources, crude energy sources and massive transport facilities. Wealth and power came mainly to the possessor of material things or to the ruler of military forces capable of conquering the physical means of production — land, labor, and capital.

Today, however, the global network of telecommunications carries more valuable goods than all the world's supertankers. Whether in the air or in a wire, the electrons or photons themselves do not travel; they wiggle their charges, causing oscillations that pass thru the medium at close to the speed of light. As in waves of water, the wave moves — but the molecules of water stay in the same place. Quantum theory reveals that photonic waves do not move thru a discernible medium. Thus belied is the analogy to particles and bullets still used by some physics teachers.

The immaterial character of wealth is transforming the modes of production. Wealth now comes not to the rulers of slave labor but to the liberators of human creativity, not to the conquerors of land but to the emancipators of mind.

Remember, materialism no longer prevails <u>in the science of matter itself</u>. The atom at the heart of physics is as empty, in proportion to the size of its nucleus, as the solar system is empty in proportion to the size of the sun. The electrons at the heart of electronics cannot be defined at a particular time and location.

The exemplary technology of the era is the microchip — the computer inscribed on a tiny sliver of processed material. More than any other invention, this device epitomizes the overthrow of matter. Consider a parable of the microchip once told by Gordon Moore, a founding father of Intel Corporation and leader of Silicon Valley:

"We needed a substrate for our chip. So we looked at the substrate of the earth itself. It was mostly sand. So we used that."

"We needed a metal conductor for the wires and switches on the chip. We looked at all the metals in the earth and found aluminum was the most abundant. So we used that."

"We needed substances both to protect the chip chemically during manufacture and to insulate it electrically in use. We saw that the silicon in sand mixed with the oxygen in the air to form silicon dioxide — a kind of glass that both protected and insulated the chip at once. So we used that."

The result? A technology — metal oxide silicon — made of the three most common substances in the earth's crust. The most valuable substance in this fundamental product of the era is the *idea* for the design. The most important force of wealth-creation in modern capitalism is therefore the *caput*. As Michael Novak points out, capitalism is overwhelmingly a <u>mind</u>-centered system.

Thus, as a conservative advocate of capitalism, I applaud the Pope's critique of the materialist claims of free-market economics and the greed of capitalists. Christian truth must also apply to the economic sphere — to all the great ventures of enterprise and production to which most of us devote so much time and treasure.

Yet capitalism, for all its productivity and creativity, has foundered in its own materialist superstitions, and failed to produce or create a compelling argument for its own essential morality.

Capitalist Fools

The problem began with Adam Smith. Like many present-day intellectuals on the Right, he was charmed by the ways of free markets but disdainful of businessmen. Seldom did they gather but to "conspire against the public interest," wrote Smith in one of his most famous passages. "Not from benevolence," he insisted, should one expect one's bread from the baker. Rather, it's an alchemy of self-interest — guided by an invisible hand — that will bring us the benefits of capitalism. Later, the more mathematical advocates of capitalism would sing of *equilibrium*, a Newtonian dance of equations, as the source of our multiplying loaves.

To this day, most conservatives would rather celebrate free markets than applaud a private enterprise. They would rather laud individual freedom than praise the particular free individuals — the entrepreneurs — who make the system work. This is a vision of capitalism without capitalists. It sees the system as an interplay of interests lifted into "equilibrium" by an invisible hand and consisting chiefly of invisible men. It is an economics bereft of both man and God. No wonder the Pope finds it offensive.

In response to this free-market nirvana, the Left, by contrast, can offer seductive indictments of "monopoly capitalism," vivid catalogues of "crime in the suites" and grim recitations of "dark satanic mills." Leftist academics cap the critique with tales of predatory "robber barons" as the founding fathers of our economic system and lineal forebearers of its current multinational leaders.

Against this onslaught, the Right usually retorts only the evidence that capitalism works to create material wealth — "it delivers the goods" — and, by the way, its associated freedoms are congenial to the self-interest of intellectuals. To the Left's dramatic tapestry of capitalist criminals and monopolists, robber barons and oil sheiks, in counterpoint to the images of the exploited poor and homeless — to a Leftist repertory of "compassionate socialist leaders," militant protesters, and austere revolutionary heroes — the Right responds with apostrophes to abstract market processes and the sovereignty of consumers.

As the Pope has eloquently maintained, this will not do.

The case for capitalism is necessarily the case for capitalists. Why is this so difficult an argument to make? Even the so-called robber barons built the railroad, steel, and oil industries on which American prosperity still partly relies and on which the Third World still heavily subsists. For the first time, the robber barons made it possible for the masses of poor to hope for an escape from poverty and oppression — and even to dream of wealth. Luxuries once sold only to the rich became accessible to the majority of the citizens of the world. The monopolists grew by steadily lowering their prices. The robber barons ended by making automobiles and gasoline and telephones and hamburgers and television sets available to the poor in nearly all capitalist countries.

We have seen, however, that such practical and materialist arguments fail to persuade most Christians, including the Pope. Christianity is not chiefly a materialist faith and therefore does not respect a materialist test.

The most telling claim made against capitalism — a charge constantly echoed in Catholic writings, including *Centesimus Annus* — is that the system subsists on selfishness and greed. Accepted by most defenders as well as critics of free enterprise, this assertion — that material self-interest lies at the core of capitalism — implies the deadly idea that the system violates crucial religious and moral teachings. Our wealth implicitly springs from some "deal with the devil" by which we gain material benefits in exchange for succumbing to the sin of avarice. By their fruits, you shall know them. Originating in sin, the system bears the fruits of a corrupt and tawdry prosperity that feeds the body and starves the soul in a neon wilderness.

The Left even maintains that all too often, amid this glut of shoddy goods, millions of worthy poor go hungry and homeless, while God wanders with them, bearing the cross by crowds of complacent capitalists.

This is the critique that resonates in *Centesimus Annus* and informs the statements of the U.S. Catholic Bishops. This is the critique that the defenders of capitalism have so pathetically failed to answer.

The critique may be addressed chiefly to the abuses that the public mind associates with capitalism, and not to capitalism itself. But if this important distinction is over-looked or disregarded, the criticism leads churches to abandon their supreme role of moral and spiritual leadership in economic matters, and it makes workers and entrepreneurs ashamed of their labor in satisfying the material wants of mankind. It creates a wasteland in which ignorant armies of clerics and businessmen clash by night.

The clerics implicitly demand that the entrepreneurs give up the profits that sustain their businesses, while the businessmen, relegated beyond the bounds of the churches, gyrate between sieges of guilt and amoral defiance. Both sides implicitly accept what I have termed "the materialist superstition" — the idea that wealth comes chiefly from the self-interested manipulation, distribution and consumption of material goods.

The moral core of capitalism is the essential altruism of enterprise. The anthropological evidence shows that the system begins not with the greed that provokes tribal wars, but with the gifts that prevent them. Yes, capitalism begins not with taking but with giving.

The Gift's Link To Profit

The tribal capitalists were not warriors or predators; they were the feast-givers, the potlatchers, and the mumis — the so-called big men who transcended the constraints of barter by simply making offerings to their neighbors. Such gifts, ubiquitous in the anthropological literature, imposed implicit debts on their recipients, who tried to reciprocate with gifts in return. Thus were extended and accelerated the processes of exchange that had been stalled in the intricacies of predetermined trading or in the conflicts of a precapitalist zero-sum mentality.

In a "zero-sum" game, a gain for one player can only come at the expense of a loss for another: A +2 here caused a -2 there, leaving the sum stuck at zero. In voluntary capitalist exchanges, however, both participants tend to emerge better off than they were earlier, or else they would not have willingly made the exchange.

The most successful gifts are the most profitable — that is, gifts that are worth much more to the recipient than to the donor. The most successful givers, therefore, are the most altruistic — the most responsive to the desires of others. In the most rewarding and catalytic gifts, the giver fulfills an unknown, unepressed or even unconscious need, in a surprising way. The recipient is startled and gratified by the inspired and unexpected sympathy of the giver, and is thus eager to repay him. In order to repay him, however, the receiver must come to understand the giver. Thus, the contest of gifts can lead to a deepening of human sympathies.

The circle of giving (the profits of the economy) will grow as long as the gifts are consistently valued more by the receivers than by the givers. In deciding what new goods to assemble or create, the givers must therefore be willing to focus on the needs of others more than on their own. They must be willing to forgo their own immediate gratification in order to produce goods of value to others.

Capitalism today still thrives on the same principles of imaginative giving in conditions of freedom. A gift is defined not by the absence of <u>any</u> return, but by the absence of a <u>predetermined</u> return. Unlike socialist investments, investments under capitalism are analogous to gifts, in that the returns are not preordained and depend for success entirely on understanding the needs of others.

Just as successful gifts are normally valued more by their recipients than by their donors, investments succeed only if their resulting products are valued more by the potential purchasers than by the producers.

This difference — the increase in value imparted by the process of production and exchange — is the profit engendered by the system. Profit thus emerges as an index of the altruism of a product — a measure of the extent to which an investment reflects an accurate understanding of the needs of others and a suppression of the immediate needs and desires of the producer.

Egocentric producers, oriented more to self-expression than toward the service of others, often claim special virtue and demand public subsidies for their unwanted output — whether of alternative energy, excess butter, unintelligible poems and music, or undesired personal counseling services. They disdain businessmen for their "other-direction" (as American sociologist David Riesman put it 50 years ago). But it is these market-oriented entrepreneurs who are willing to sacrifice their own interests and self-expression in order to serve others.

Even then, profits reflect not a mere calculation of the demonstrated needs of others, but an inspired guess about their future. Profits are residual gains beyond the predictable gains. When gains are surely predictable, they are bid away — leaving the capitalist earning mere interest (which in many countries rarely exceeds inflation and taxes).

In fact, the owners of most of the large companies in Europe in recent years have — adjusting for inflation on their stockholding over most of the past two decades — gained no net profits at all. That is why labor unions almost uniformly oppose profit-sharing plans in the kinds of large companies most critics still imagine are representative of capitalism.

Large companies, however, often are the sclerotic face of capitalism in decline, seeking government favors to replace the profits they no longer can earn by serving others. When the heart of any economic system becomes taking, rather than giving, the body will run down and rot.

Generally, the spirit of enterprise is generous and optimistic about human nature. "Give and you will be given unto" is its fundamental theme, and altruism — an orientation toward the needs of others — its moral and commercial compass. Not only must the entrepreneur comprehend the wants of others; he must also collaborate with others in his business.

And, most of all, he must wish that others succeed. The businessman must be full of optimism and hope for his potential customers. He must want them to prosper. Above all, he must want the poor to prosper, if only because the poor always comprise the world's largest untapped market. He begins by saving — by forgoing personal consumption in order to serve others. And he is sustained by hope for, and celebration of, the successes of others.

The argument that capitalism is a valuable system chiefly because it recognizes and exploits human greed and rapacity is the opposite of the truth. Greed, in fact, impels people to seek first their own comfort and security. The truly self-interested man most often turns to government to give him the benefits he lacked the moral discipline to earn on his own by serving others. He follows his own hungers at the expense of his family and leaves them on the dole.

Consumer demands (whether avaricious or just) are impotent to impel growth in the absence of disciplined, creative, and essentially moral producers of new value. All effective demand ultimately derives from supply — because a society's income cannot exceed its output. And the output of valuable goods depends not on lechery, prurience, lust, and license but on thrift, sacrifice, altruism, creativity, trust, and faith.

Giving, beginning within the family and extending outward into the society, is the moral center of the system. It does not succeed by allowing the leading capitalists to revel in riches; if they hoard their wealth the system tends to fail. It succeeds by inducing the capitalist continually to give his wealth back to the system in the form of new gifts and investments.

Grateful For Waste And Irrationality

The Christian foundations of capitalism go still deeper — for, contrary to the usual notion, capitalism is profoundly antimaterialistic. Capitalists thrive largely to the extent that they partake of the gifts of the spirit, which come from the Church. An amoral and tawdry capitalism bespeaks a failure of the churches more than a failure in the economy.

Walter Lippmann, a columnist and a great American political philosopher, approached this truth in *The Good Society,* a book written during the Great Depression of the 1930s. Speaking of the rise of industrial capitalism, he wrote: "For the first time in human history," an economic system had emerged that gave men "a way of producing wealth in which the good fortune of others multiplied their own." At long last, he declared, "the golden rule was economically sound," and "for the first time men could conceive a social order in which the ancient moral aspiration of liberty, fraternity, and equality was consistent with the abolition of poverty and the increase of wealth."

Lippmann continued: "Until the division of labor had begun to make men dependent on the free collaboration of other men, the worldly policy was to be predatory. The

claims of the spirit were otherworldly. So it was not until
the industrial revolution had altered the traditional mode of
life that the vista was opened at the end of which men could
see the possibility of that Good society on this earth. At
long last the ancient schism between the world and the
spirit, between self-interest and disinterestedness, was
potentially closed."

The belief that the good fortune of others is also finally
one's own does not come easily or invariably to the human
mind. It is, however, the golden rule of economics, a key to
peace and prosperity, a source of the gifts of progress. It is
the absolutely crucial Christian source of wealth-creation.

The optimism of the entrepreneurial investor is always
in a sense irrational. In a free society, he has no way to force
a market for his goods, and people have every right to deem
them worthless. His investments therefore must spring not
only from a spirit of altruism or charity, but also from a
commitment of hope and faith.

Government planning assumes that the future can be
predicted and controlled. But, as the British economist
George Shackle has written, "What has a world where
knowledge is already complete and everything is known to
do with a world where choice is about the future but knowledge is only about the past?"

In the light of existing knowledge, the entrepreneur
usually appears a fool. Throughout history, most of his key
inventions have been scorned by the experts in the field.

In fact, the vast majority of new investments in unex-
plored fields or untried products do fail. Of all the plausible
new inventions, fewer than 1% are brought into production;
of all the books that are written, only a small proportion is
published, and perhaps only 10% of these would be said to
compensate the writer for his time and effort.

Yet such "irrational" investments, such waste of creative
energies, are the secret of capitalist success and the source
of human triumph, against all Malthusian odds, over the
centuries.

A rationalist intellectual may be reluctant to depend on
a fundamentally irrational process like capitalism, which
subsists on optimism and faith, for the very survival of
human civilization. He instead will prefer to rely on plan-

ning and control and physical collateral.

Above all, the rationalist intellectual will fear the multiplication of human lives on this earth, for he will see the earth as a limited material system and he will see each new baby as a mouth to feed rather than as a mind to think. He will see "population" as a problem to be solved or overcome, instead of treating people as opportunities for love and creativity. He will count up the numbers, compare them with the material reserves and resources, and predict the decline and fall of the race. He will advocate the hoarding of material wealth and its forced redistribution, rather than the emancipation of people on the frontiers of new creation.

The secular intellectual is a man of little faith, and his lack of faith manifests itself in the idolatrous worship of material things. Like a pygmy in the jungle worshipping the trees, the intellectual tends to reject the reality of anything he cannot see and feel. Wealth is believed to consist in things.

Particularly in this era, however, wealth consists not of things but of thoughts. An entrepreneur does not <u>find</u> value in a new product, or pool of oil, or a computer's design. He <u>brings</u> value to what was previously seen as worthless. And this value springs from his own <u>values</u> — his courage, ingenuity, diligence, and faith.

The Treasure Of Ideas And Spirit

The most valuable products of today largely consist in ideas of enormous complexity inscribed on silicon microchips. When scientists can inscribe whole new worlds on grains of sand, the value of particular territories and resources plummets.

More than ever before in history, wealth is metaphysical rather than material. The "limits to growth" that supposedly mandate population-controls are actually the new frontiers of progress.

From the awesome reaches of the universe to the microelectronic galaxies of inner space, from microbiology to laser photonics, the world opens its portals, sloughs off limits and boundaries, and overcomes the "closing circles" of ecological expertise with ever widening spirals of possibility.

Nonetheless, the experts are afraid. They know they are living in an era of unprecedented perils — of scarcity, pollution, famine, and plague. Their morbid anxieties about "nonrenewable" resources, "finite" reserves, the "limits of growth," and the "closing circles of nature" all bespeak the predicament of any mortal worshiper of matter and flesh. Matter is nonrenewable, flesh is finite and exhaustible, youth is fleeting and beset by natural laws and depletions of energy.

The contemporary intellectual, denying God, is in a trap, and he projects his entrapment onto the world in a kind of secular suicide. But the world is not entrapped; man is not finite; and the human mind is not bound in material brain.

Like most of the hype and hysterics of modern intellectuals (for instance, the population crisis, the energy crisis, or the pollution crisis), the crisis of the day is most deeply a religious disorder, a failure of faith. It can be overcome chiefly by worship: By a recognition that beyond the darkness and opacity of our material entrapment is a realm of redemptive spirit, reachable thru that interplay of faith and fact which some call science, others poetry, but which is most truly grasped as forms of prayer.

Beyond the long labyrinth of things and the multifarious carrels of fact, the inspired explorer can finally break out into the mansions of providential mind. He then sees the limits of the culture of thanatopsis, with its dismal mazes of sense and flesh, and vain hoards of sterile wealth. He can stand at last with wild surmise on the frontiers of matter where life and God again begin, and see a world renewed and shining with possibility.

Where your treasure is, your heart is also. It is Marxism and statism that are based on the materialist superstition, and believe in the treasure of things. It is capitalism that is based on the treasure of ideas and spirit.

The fable of Midas, the king who turned everything to gold until he had nothing to eat, is not the story of the perils and contradictions of capitalist wealth. It is the tale of the pitfalls of materialism itself. The real capitalists have the anti-Midas touch: They turn gold and liquidity, thru an alchemy of creative spirit, into productive capital and real wealth. The foundation of wealth is always giving, not taking. The deepest truth of capitalism is faith, hope, and love.

Christian intellectuals, in their understandable frustration at the prevalence of vice in *Vanity Fair,* often blame capitalism. But capitalism is not the problem. The problem is secular hedonism. And it is largely liberal culture that refuses to ban pornography, or effectively suppress vice, or uphold the moral values of family life.

To the extent capitalists — looking at liberal culture and sensing the short-term profit opportunities — produce depraved goods, they are destroying the moral conditions of capitalist progress, by undermining the families from which all true natural resources flow.

The value of a nation's goods stems from the values of its people. If the churches would more confidently and effectively evangelize for their own moral and religious values — rather than endorse socialist and materialist fantasies — depraved capitalists could not easily make money off the vices of others, and society would become more righteously prosperous. Profits from vice are spurious in a capitalist society because they undermining the faith and trust, the hope and charity, on which real growth and progress depend.

The central truths of Christianity are vital to capital. The crucial capital of the system is not the physical accumulation of natural resources and machines, but the metaphysical capital of human life. The most essential capitalist act — the essence of giving, "investing," without a predetermined outcome — is the bearing, raising and educating of children.

Above all, in advanced societies where child labor is rare, children entail a prolonged and precarious commitment of work and wealth, love and faith, with no assurance of future return. They require elaborate decades of expensive preparation before they can make their own contributions to the society, negative or positive; and all too often, at least in the view of the parents, they turn out wrong. (In fact, Ann Landers' famous poll suggested that 70% of mothers felt betrayed by their children and, given the choice, would not bear them again.)

Here emerge the most indispensable acts of "capital formation": The psychology of giving, saving and sacrifice, in behalf of an unknown future, embodied in a specific child — a balky bundle of possibilities, which will yield its social reward even further into time than the most foresighted business plan. Thus are parents the ultimate entrepreneurs — and, as with all entrepreneurs, the odds are against them. Yet all human progress — of businesses and families as well as societies — depends on such an entrepreneurial willingness to defy the odds. It is in the nuclear family that the most crucial process of capitalist defiance and faith is centered.

Owning, Giving, Understanding

Thus the Pope is completely consonant with capitalism when he denounces materialism. Materialism is the perennial enemy — and temptation — of capitalism.

The Pope is also right in supporting a broad ownership of the multinational means of production, and he is right to denounce the exploitation of the many by the few in a class society. But modern corporations, with their millions of free customers and shareholders (many of them workers with pension funds), diffuse the control and benefits of production more widely and concretely than could any bureaucracy of socialism or any United Nations commission.

Capitalist systems now assign some 85% of income to labor, and comprise millions of small businesses owned by their leading workers. It is small firms, in free economies, that have impelled the vast increase in human wealth and destroyed the class society, while class war persists virulently between bureaucrats and proletarians in every socialist state.

If the Church is truly concerned with the material problem of world hunger and poverty, it should temper its own efforts at distributing food and instead promote the moral and spiritual conditions of capitalist farming. Wherever entrepreneurship is extended to the production of food — from China to Bangladesh — people begin feeding themselves. Wherever government rules, famine and dependency spread.

Most of all, the Pope is correct in exalting equality. As

Tom Bethell, a brilliant Catholic writer in Washington, has pointed out, equality <u>before the law</u> is basic to capitalist prosperity. Without equality before the law, private property cannot be preserved from the powerful, and the free exchanges of capitalism cannot take place. In order to <u>give</u>, you first must be able to <u>own</u>. In a stratified society where the powerful control the law, the entrepreneurial challenge to established industries cannot take place.

Capitalism thrives because it defends equally the property rights of all. Thus it constantly benefits from the creative surprises of the poor.

In America today, many of the most creative and successful new companies emerge from the ideas and sacrifices of unlettered men. Very often, these men are penniless immigrants without personal charm or even mastery of English; they do not even have high-school diplomas to show. But they work 16 hours a day and eventually outdo all the credentialed powers and principalities of the world.

Because leading entrepreneurs are rarely elegant, tall, eloquent, or well-educated, they do not often impress academics or aristocrats and do not always spend their money in fashionable pursuits. But capitalism is the only economic system in which the last regularly become first — by serving others, in humble ways. The Pope's constant stress on the position of the poor is thus a source of replenishment for capitalism, not an attack on it.

If I may be so bold, I would suggest the Pope may see that the worldly society of his dreams must be entrepreneurial and capitalistic. Although many capitalists fail to fulfill the essential values of the system, the problem of free economies is — again — not the nature of their economics but their corruption by a secular hedonist and amoral culture.

Capitalism is suffering from the increasing betrayal of its moral, spiritual and religious foundation by churches and schools, by preachers and politicians who believe that the paramount natural laws of giving and faith are irrelevant to the great dramas of human creativity and production, science and art. The problem is a crisis of religion. Too many clerics have renounced the claims of the spirit in favor of inept ventures of materialism and social politics, thus depriving capitalism of its indispensable moral rules and roots and spreading famine and poverty in the name of social justice.

As the late Monsignor Escriva writes: "Don't forget that charity, more than in giving, consists in understanding." Understanding is hard. But it is the arduous first step in successful charity. Giving requires a hard-earned understanding of others. That is the chief insight that the experience of capitalism offers the Church.

Indeed it is the very genius of capitalism that it recognizes the difficulty of successful giving, and understands the hard work and sacrifice entailed by the mandate of Christian altruism.

To give without hurting is hard. Excessively "generous" welfare or foreign aid, for example, hurts its recipients, demoralizing them or reducing them to an addictive dependency that can ruin their lives. The anonymous private donation may be a good thing in itself. As an example for others, it may foster an outgoing and generous spirit in the community.

But, as a rule of society, it is best if the givers are "given unto" — if they seek some form of voluntary reciprocation. The spirit of giving will then spread, and wealth gravitate toward those who are most likely to give it back and are most capable of using it for the benefit of others — in short, toward those whose gifts evoke the greatest returns.

Capitalism transforms the gift impulse into a disciplined process of creative investment based on a continuing and inspired analysis of the needs of others. The investor cannot be fundamentally selfish. A truly self-centered capitalist will eschew the very initiatives — the risky but redemptive ventures of innovation — that, being untested and unproven, depend most on an imaginative understanding of the world beyond himself and a generous and purposeful commitment to it.

I quote from Monsignor Escriva's homily "In Joseph's Workshop," where our Lord chose to work for the first 30 years of his life: "As the motto of your work, I can give you this one: If you want to be useful, serve. For in the first place, in order to do things properly, you must know how to do them... It's not enough to want to do good; we must know how to do it."

This is the know-how that is the prime source of wealth in the modern economy. It is based on faith, hope, and charity. And it is tempered with spiritual discipline. It is the way, as Michael Novak has put it, we can respond to the mandate of our creator, who made us in his own image, to be creative.

The sanctification of work is a prime mission of the Church — I believe this is its paramount gift to this diurnal world. When work is sanctified, it becomes the work of God, and it obeys the laws of God. Serving others and serving God, in useful enterprise, is the secret of prosperity and freedom.

Science Reconciled With Religion

Let us return to the quantum revelation in its correspondence with scripture. Scientists no longer see the foundation of all matter as Newton did, as inert, blind, impenetrable, blank particles. Rather physicists now agree that matter derives from waves, fields, and probabilities. To comprehend nature, we have to stop thinking of the world as basically material and begin imagining it as a manifestation of divine consciousness, suffused with sparks of informative energy.

The fundamental entities in quantum theory are wave-particles, a profound paradox that was first launched in 1887 when Albert Michelson and E.W. Morley did their famous experiments that showed that there is no such thing in the universe as "ether." Until the experiments of Michelson and Morley, the fundamental belief was that the universe is filled with solid matter, which would be needed as the medium thru which light waves could propagate.

Earlier experiments had demonstrated conclusively that light is a wave; it was assumed, therefore, that there must be a material medium thru which the waves of light could travel. By dispelling the notion of ether as the luminiferous medium bearing light, Michelson and Morley effectively banished most of the matter from the universe.

In the quantum revelation of science, light emerged as an esoteric paradox of waves without substance traveling at a fixed speed in relation to a medium without substance. In

1905, in a Nobel Prize-winning paper, Albert Einstein declared that if there was no ether, light could not be a wave. It had nothing to wave thru!

Extending the insight of Max Planck, Einstein said that light consisted of quanta — packets of energy — that he called photons. Although said to be "particles," photons possess no mass and observe the equations of wave motion developed by James Clerk Maxwell in the 1860s. They seemed to be a cross between a wave and a particle.

In the beginning was the word, the idea. By crashing into the inner sanctums of the material world, into the microcosm, mankind overcame the regnant superstitions of matter and regained contact with the primal powers of mind and spirit. Those new powers have rendered obsolete all the materialist fantasies of the past — the notion that by comprehending things, one could understand thought, and that by controlling things, one could rule the world.

The quantum era is the epoch of free men and women, scaling the hierarchies of faith and truth, seeking the sources of light

In this unifying search is the secret of reconciliation of science with religion. The quantum vision finds at the very foundations of the firmament a cross of light. Combining a particle and a wave, it joins the definite to the infinite, a point of mass to an eternal radiance.

What else would a Christian expect to find at the foundations of the world? In this light, we can comprehend the paradox of the brain and the mind, the temporal and the divine, flesh and the word, freedom and fatality. By this light, we can even find the truth.

But we cannot see thru it. In science and technology, religion and economics, we can triumph only by understanding that truth is a paradoxical and redemptive cross at the heart of light and life, radiant in the microcosm and in the world. And all Satan's powers cannot prevail against it.

Glad Tidings

Artificial Intelligence

[C]omputer technology is still in its infancy. After all, the computer can still barely see or hear, let alone walk. Because of these handicaps, it is now fashionable to disparage Artificial Intelligence: "It's been going on for some 30 years, and apparently achieved little."

The computer industry is said to have thrived by doing well what human beings do badly. But AI seems to thrive by doing badly what people do well [laughter]. This charge is partly true.

But assume that you are a computer — essentially, a deaf, dumb and blind machine. If somebody allowed you to see and hear, even relatively inefficiently, wouldn't you hail them as the new Edison?

1986 BOSTON

Two human eyes do more image-processing than all the world's supercomputers put together.

1992 HILLIS

Marvin Minsky has said that a prime discovery of the AI Movement is that the bulk of human intelligence is acquired during the first year — all the perception and motor-skills and hearing, and all the perceptive mechanisms of the brain. By overthrowing the old von Nuemann agenda, AI will make the computer into a toddler, and change the world. And I think the result will be another 10-millionfold rise in the cost-effectiveness of computing. And this time it may not even take 30 years.

1986 BOSTON

Buchananism and Nostalgia

Pat Buchanan — who is correct about many things — has, I think, been somewhat twisted by this [presidential] aspiration to cut into the unionized lower-middle-class Democrats Perot is alleged to have attracted. It is chiefly a political appeal he's making; he's trying to expand the Republican Party — [but he has] stumbled on a bad one [by demanding] a moratorium on immigration. Not just a slight little error, but a truly deadly mistake.

It resonates, though, because [of this] nationalist fervor among people who believe their jobs and livelihoods are being taken away from them. I think they are largely union people who've grown up in unionized homes; that's been the culture that they've been familiar with, and that's what America always was to them, and now it's vanishing. Union membership is down below 15%. And those who still survive are having to "give back" wage gains and benefit gains. They think that anybody who wants to save their livelihood and their tradition is a great American, because that's what America was. "America was not the computer. It wasn't the microprocessor, the microchip, or Microsoft. It wasn't the Internet. America was steel. It was coal. It was the Teamsters and truck-drivers."

We had the Korean War. There were bodies coming back in bags, and three recessions, and people lived eight or nine years less [than they do now].

And you had to have a bomb-shelter in the back yard. You had to get civil-defense instructions, and to see that the drinking water changed every three weeks in case they nuked us.

And, in many of these same union families, their parents came here on a boat and struggled in some appalling jobs, by anybody's standards today. I mean, to celebrate coal miners' jobs! One of the great triumphs is to get beyond this kind of work, where people died years younger. It just is a false nostalgia. Here we had, during this early period toward which people are nostalgic, two World Wars, the Great Depression, the Korean War.

It's an economic nostalgia. They remember the days where, on a salary of $12,000 a year, you could buy a house [and] send your kid to college; and there were no credit cards, so you didn't go into debt. Now the average cost for a house is 10 times what anybody makes a year.

But the average house is 20% bigger than it was, and 79% of new houses have air-conditioning.

So you would agree with the premise that every day in America is a better day.

Yes, absolutely. And my grandchildren are going to live phenomenally, incomparably better than we do.

1996 LIMBAUGH

Career Drive

KARLGAARD: What is the most rewarding thing about your career?

It really is this process of learning and discovery. I think life is essentially a process of learning. When the learning is accelerated, it's more exciting; when you get in a rut, it is more discouraging. So far as the career is concerned, the most exciting facet is learning new things and seeing the promise of the coming era — seeing the upside. You can see the upside by focusing on the microcosm, on the frontiers. The people who don't function on the frontiers find the world very gloomy.

1990 UPSIDE

Excitement

All these dolorous predictions of our grandchildren living less well than we do are totally misconceived. This technology will generate wealth in extraordinary quantities and ways. It will also address, almost perfectly, most of the key problems our society faces — from family structure, to traffic and environment, even cultural decay from television.

Every individual with a computer workstation will command the kind of creative power that was held only by industrial tycoons in the previous era. And a single person at a workstation, or at a PC, will command the kind of <u>communications</u> power that only broadcast executives commanded in the past.

This is a technology of empowerment and democratization. It will change the world economy and lead us to an era of unexampled prosperity.

1993 DISCOVERY

When matter moves toward the speed of light, it bursts the invisible rainbows of the electromagnetic spectrum. Time and space collapse in new wavescapes of information. You experience the spatial collapse when you talk to a politician in Japan over a fiber-optic connection: Your voice reaches him before it reaches your assistant across the room. In the next decade, the assistant may move around the world with no impairment of services. The waves of light that bear your voice could carry your image just as well, and the image of any document or the code of any program that you need. Your computer could reach across the globe to run a printer, an automated machine tool, a schematic plotter, a giant screen, or even a microchip fabrication line making new computers of your design.

1992 DEM-GOV

It's the most exciting time to be in the phone business since Alexander Graham Bell.

1991 AMERITECH

Japan: Also Ran

I have predicted for years [that the U.S. will] remain the leader in the Information Age. The Japanese made a mistake by focusing all their efforts on manufacturing small consumer products and missed the tremendous development of computer networking and personal computers... When the home computer and television converge into a single box, a worldwide electronics market worth hundreds of billions of dollars a year will be at stake. It will dwarf the present home-entertainment market, which the Japanese control.

1993 DISCOVERY

Jobs: What Shortage?

Since the ascendancy of the microchip, beginning around 1970, the U.S. has outperformed all the other economies in the world, overwhelmingly, in job-creation. You just can't make the argument that we've been losing jobs to other countries. We've created some 35 million net new jobs in the past 30 years — while the Europeans, for example, have created almost no net new jobs outside of government consumption. The Japanese have created new employment, but substantially less than we have.

How can we be losing jobs to countries that are creating jobs radically more slowly than we are?

But the manufacturing sector is what many people look to and say, "Hey! You can't be a unionized worker anymore and afford a house. You used to be able to in America in the '50s. You can't do it anymore."

Anybody whose livelihood depends on examining union jobs and the performance of unions, or collecting statistics for unions, or mobilizing campaigns for unions, has a great incentive to disparage all this new employment and opportunity in America, because it does largely arise outside the unionized sectors. That is true. The unions have all flocked to the dinosaurs. They all attempt to preserve jobs in old industries that are declining.

The new employment has been emerging in semiconductors, software, computer-manufacturing, as well as services in software. Manufacturing has continued to grow. We're the dominant computer-manufacturer in the world. We also lead telecommunications and networks. And the Internet, which is entirely an American creation, is now the dominant force in the world economy.

1996 LIMBAUGH

The more computers in an economy, the more jobs created. For example, the United States has created more jobs in the last decade than any other country in the world — and we've deployed more computers. This new technology creates its own antidote to its own job-displacement, because wealth then can be invested to create more opportunities and jobs.

1994 USWEST

Learning Over Education

I send my daughters out to the side of the road in the winter. They wait for awhile in the snow for a bus that weaves thru 10 miles of countryside to get 'em to a schoolhouse three miles away, where I think we have a pretty good school.

But most people send their kids to schools where they get taught about condoms in the classroom and get mugged in the restroom — and end up knowing less than they did when they started. This system is just plain obsolete.

Imagine when you can summon to your living room the best professors in the world, or the best teachers, for your children — upholding the values that you cherish. It really becomes less and less inviting to go out and stand in the snow.

I expect a huge proliferation of home-schools, and microschools, and neighborhood schools, which will bring to secondary education the kind of improvements that have been achieved in the proliferation of American colleges. The multimedia personal computer is going to transform all sorts of industries and create enormous opportunities for the improvement of American education.

1990 HILLSDALE

The computer essentially replaces vertically organized institutions with horizontally organized institutions. It distributes intelligence and power rather than concentrates them; it endows teachers with authority and responsibility rather than reducing teachers to being instruments of some educational bureaucracy.

And the reason teachers don't care about anything but money (as far as their organizations are concerned) is that the bureaucrats have destroyed the experience of teaching and the gratification of teaching. This is why schools are such perverse institutions. As [*School's Out* author] Lew Perelman says, academia is a socialist bureaucracy as big as the Soviet government at its height, and it is going to fail just about as cataclysmically.

1994 EDUCOM

Today, I teach my kids at home, and it's really a good option; the computer tools work very well. But, in the next three or four years, it's going to be possible for anybody to teach their kids at home more efficiently and better than they get taught at school — that will be possible. It will be a technological change that cannot be resisted successfully, I think, by the NEA or anyone else.

The changes that are forthcoming offer huge promise for conservatives and [that's why] we should understand these technologies and explore them and pursue them — because they're not hostile territory. They are really ours. They're entirely the product of conservative culture.

1993 CON-SUM

Light: Spiritual Plus Real World

In the next decade, the appropriate message, for both education and industry, is "Let there be light." With its biblical roots and symbolic importance, "light" really does convey the kinds of changes that are sweeping thru the world economy. "Light" is a paradox. Quantum physics shows that light is a combination of an infinite wave and a definite particle — it's a cross between a wave and a particle. And this "light," which is at the root of the most powerful technologies of day, also bears a powerful symbolic message — of freedom, family and faith.

1990 HILLSDALE

Where once people saw a whole series of very strict dualities, you have the emergence of a luminous "unity," at the center of both technology and worship.

PARROT: What does this do to theology?

I think it makes theology a much more "practical" pursuit, and I wish the theologians would begin to understand a little better that their own investigations are central to everything that happens in the world. [Then they could stop] pretending that somehow there's this "practical" area of business — which is somehow amoral — while theology is somehow transcendent, with very little intercourse between the two domains.

The fact is that business can only succeed to the extent that it's moral, in any long period of time. To the extent that it's immoral, it erodes the very conditions of truth and faith that make possible interactions among human beings, and the creation of new worth.

1989 MONITOR

Medical Gains

All this [medical] equipment is coming on line...faster all the time. And, because it has to respond to the needs of human beings who are mobile, it often has to be wireless. You see the beginnings of it in hospitals, where you can walk around with wireless monitoring. Soon you'll see it in remote diagnosis and remote services.

The information economy is becoming dominant in medicine, in education, and in a wide range of other areas. And it really does address the key problems this society faces — such as medical-care costs, the environment, education. All of these are essentially information problems, and they can be solved by the combination of wireless and mobile communication services.

1993 KMB-VID

Net Prophet

I say that, by the turn of the century, a little over three years from now, virtually anyone in America who wants a broadband Internet connection will be able to get one. I define "broadband" as T-1 speeds (1.544 megabits per second) or higher, which offers, with compression, what is termed "VCR quality."

Full-motion video downstream at two to six megabits per second for MPEG-2 (like the DirecTV satellite images that give the best available picture in homes today) will be accessible almost everywhere from satellites, fiber and cable. These downstream pipes will complement upstream modems over telephone and coaxial lines or new microwave networks.

I focus on availability, not penetration. The key issue to me is when the top 20% of households — comprising some 50 million people with most of the intact marriages, online children, PCs, productivity, income and wealth — begin buying broadband Internet links in volume. Everyone else can get them a few years later at one-seventh the price.

1996 NEWSLETTER

Privacy

How do you think the change from one-way TV to two-way communication with target audiences will relate psychologically, with respect to people and privacy?

People constantly raise this question... I _want_ people out there constantly working to satisfy my needs — I really do. I think it's great to have all these corporations knowing enough about me so they can supply me precisely the products I want at low cost. I don't think this is a negative, I think it's a positive.

Now, in those few instances where you really want to be private, there is encryption [and] this market for private products of various sorts — I think those private needs can be satisfied. But it's fundamentally impossible to use the technology in ways that are less personal...

As it is today, anybody is embarrassed by the idea that they're watching television shows. With broadcast television getting more and more embarrassing to watch, it should escape that problem. So maybe there is a future for broadcast television after all [laughter].

1993 ACTUARIES

What is _really_ an invasion of privacy is a telemarketer who gets you out of bed or [out of] the shower. They don't have any idea who you are, no notion of what you want. That's what really offends you: <u>Ignorant</u> intrusions, not intrusions from companies that really do understand your needs and know when you like to be called and the kinds of things you buy and don't buy.

They might even be conscious, thru your entry into some bulletin board, of your intent to purchase a new car or house. They call you and try to solve your problem. That is much less of an "invasion" than an intrusion by a company that doesn't know anything about you.

So a lot of the so-called invasion of privacy will be a positive experience for most people. Computer communications can be sorted thru; you can keep what you want, and kill what you don't. Increasingly, as your communication is channeled thru computers, you will increase your control over it.

It's the dumb terminal — the phone — which is the model of the violation. It violates your time and your attention because it's dumb. If you have a really smart terminal that can sort thru the communications and identify them, you can reject anything you don't want.

1994 UPSIDE

Productivity

Forty years ago, a single transistor, with supporting circuitry, might cost $7; a worker in a wafer fab could make five per day. Today a transistor costs a few millionths of a cent. A single semiconductor fabrication line can process in a pipeline some 90 million transistors a year, 250 billion a day, and 50 billion a day — per worker. If you measure productivity by counting transistors per worker, it has risen five billionfold since 1956 [and] a millionfold since 1980.

1997 NEWSLETTER

Progress

[M]any people think America's standard of living has been declining. Yet the average span of life in the United States has been increased by five years over the past 40 years — which makes me somewhat skeptical about claims that the standard of living is not improving. I think it <u>is</u>

improving.

If one were to catalog the new kinds of products that people have in their homes, you would see that the "inflation deflators" that are used [by government agencies] to measure real incomes are very deceptive. I mean, what would you pay for 150 channels of high-resolution color video if you [had been confined to] three channels of black-and-white television or six channels of color TV? In that area alone, the advances are huge.

It is hard to put a price on many of the consumer surplus elements that have been rendered inexpensive by technologies and which are constantly dropping in cost.

1996 INT-ENG

[O]ver the past 25 years or so, the companies created by junk bonds and by corporate restructuring have been the most important contributors to the steadily expanding standard of living and life-expectancies and prospects of the American people...

Between 1976 and 1993, U.S. corporations did 42,621 merger-and-acquisition deals worth about $3.1 trillion. Telecom, tires, tobacco and technology were all heavily restructured, and the result was $899 billion in shareholder gains and the creation of whole new industries in cable television, fiber-optics, communications, cellular telephony, pharmaceuticals, computers, chips, software — the huge affluence of the American economy that certain economists [in this room] seem to have completely missed in their preoccupation with wage data, which happens to be the only series of data that is going down.

During the same time that all this new wealth was created, the stock market doubled in real terms and has now more than tripled in real terms. The median wealth of American households about doubled, from $24,000 to $48,000, in real terms. Per-capita income went up by almost a third, there were some 31 million net new jobs created, and the American economy is steadily rising in real incomes.

It was a phenomenal, amazing feat of job-creation that is the envy of the world.

People ended up living five years younger. They had two color TVs and a VCR in their home instead of one black-and-white television set. They had longer vacations than before, some 22 days of paid vacations a year, and an immense expansion of technological benefits.

Meanwhile these economists obsess over the one piece of data that misses all the major changes in the economy.

I think the assumption that the period between 1950 and 1973 was a golden age, and the subsequent period one of stagnation, is preposterous. There's just no evidence for it, except in this one lonely statistic that you people lovingly cultivate, which is wages...

ROBERT REICH: George, your enthusiasm is inspiring and, as usual, it knows no bounds.

1996 HARPERS

Women-Owned Enterprise

This is a tremendous period for women's entrepreneurship, and I predicted it in *Sexual Suicide,* talking about the new technology allowing a tremendous resurgence of "cottage industries" — the household [being] given a great opportunity for creating new companies and then expanding 'em beyond the household into the community. And this is happening all across the country.

As a matter of fact, perhaps a majority of the formers of unincorporated businesses or proprietorships are women.

1984 KING

Index

Discovery Institute
Mission Statement

Discovery Institute's mission is to make a positive vision of the future practical. The Institute discovers and promotes ideas in the common-sense tradition of representative government, the free market and individual liberty. Our mission is promoted through books, reports, legislative testimony, articles, public conferences and debates, plus media coverage and the Institute's own publications and award-winning Internet website (www.discovery.org).

Current projects explore the fields of technology, science and culture, reform of the law, national defense, the environment and the economy, the future of democratic institutions, transportation, religion and public life, foreign affairs and cooperation within the bi-national region of *Cascadia*. The efforts of Discovery fellows and staff, headquartered in Seattle, are crucially abetted by the Institute' members, board and sponsors.

How Discovery Institute Functions

Discovery Institute fellows submit their analyses and proposals for dialogue through seminars, conferences, and debates; they produce reports, articles, books, Congressional testimony, films and an interactive Internet website that helps spread the knowledge of the Institute's ideas. They also consult with elected and appointed officials, business people, academics, media and the general public to show how 21st-century humanity can benefit from the principles, policies, and practices advocated by the Institute.

The point of view Discovery brings to its work includes the principles of representative democracy and public service expounded by the American Founders; a belief in God-given reason and the permanency of human nature; free-market economics domestically and internationally; the social requirement to balance personal liberty with responsibility; the spirit of voluntarism crucial to civil society; the continuing validity of American international leadership; and the potential of science and technology to promote an improved future for individuals, families and communities. Fellows, members, board, advisors and staff of Discovery constitute a distributive public policy community, connected through cyberspace, with headquarters in Seattle and an office in Washington, D.C. Fellows are multi-disciplinary in background and approach. A research and advocacy project is selected when it is in harmony with Discovery's mission, when the Institute can make an original and significant contribution to the issue's development and when it is within the Institute's resources. Most issues selected are of national or international scope and fall in the fields of science, technology, environment and economy, international affairs, culture, defense, legal reform, religion and public life, transportation, and institutions of representative democracy, as well as bi-national cooperation in the international Cascadia region.

Financially, the Institute is a non-profit, educational foundation funded by philanthropic foundation grants, corporate and individual contributions and the dues of Institute members.

Help make a positive vision of the future practical

DISCOVERY INSTITUTE MEMBERSHIP FORM

As a non-profit organization, Discovery Institute is dependent upon your support. Discovery is a collaborative association of fellows, staff, interns, volunteers, and participating members, all of whom seek to discover policies that will shape the future in the common-sense tradition of representative government, the free market, and individual liberty. If you are not a member, please consider joining us as we look for tomorrow's solutions today. If you are already a member, we urge you to pass this form on to others who might be interested in our work.

• •

Subscriber Member ($50) - Receive Discovery Institute's *Journal, Views, & Inquiry* as well as advance invitations to Discovery events.

Associate Member ($100) - Receive all of the above, plus a 20% discount on Discovery events, and one free selection from our library of books by Discovery Fellows.

Sustaining Member ($1000) - Receive all of the above, plus complimentary attendance at select Discovery events, special invitations to private receptions and colloquia, and a free copy, upon request, of each book published by Discovery Fellows.

Your Interests (please circle)

Defense & Foreign Policy   Environmental Policy   International

Legal Reform   Regional Cooperation (Cascadia)   Religion

Science & Culture   Millennials/Generations   Technology

Enclosed is my check for $_____ made payable to **Discovery Institute**

NAME	TITLE	ORGANIZATION

ADDRESS

CITY	STATE/ZIP

E-MAIL	PHONE	FAX

MC OR VISA	CARD NUMBER	EXP. DATE

NAME AS IT APPEARS ON CREDIT CARD

**MAIL THIS FORM TO: DISCOVERY INSTITUTE, 1402 THIRD AVE. SUITE 400 SEATTLE, WA 98101, OR FAX TO: (206) 682-5320.
FOR MORE INFORMATION CALL (206) 292-0401 EXT. 106 OR VISIT THE DISCOVERY WEBSITE AT WWW.DISCOVERY.ORG AND SEND E-MAIL TO MEMBERS@DISCOVERY.ORG**